THE COLLAPSE OF POWER

THE COLLAPSE OF POWER

Mutiny in the High Seas Fleet

David Woodward

Arthur Barker Limited
London

First published in 1973 by Arthur Barker Ltd.,
11 St John's Hill, London SW11.

ISBN 0 213 16431 0

Printed in Great Britain by
Bristol Typesetting Co Ltd
Barton Manor St Philips Bristol

CONTENTS

ACKNOWLEDGEMENTS

In the first place I must express my gratitude to four great institutions – two in the United Kingdom and two in West Germany – and to the members of their staffs who, over the past five years have so generously replied to my requests for help: these are the Naval Library of the Ministry of Defence, and the library of the Imperial War Museum in London; the Militärgeschichtliches Forschungsamt, Freiburg-im-Breisgau and the Bibbliothek für Zeitgeschichte, Stuttgart. I am particularly glad to have this opportunity of thanking the directors of the two latter organizations, respectively Kapitän zur See Friedrich Forstmeier and Dr Jürgen Rohwer. I also wish to thank Mr J. D. Lawson of the Ministry of Defence and the Meteorological Office which provided information on the state of the weather in the North Sea during the critical days of October and November, 1918.

Acknowledgement is due to the copyright holders of the following books and periodicals for permission to quote or to adapt material from them:

E. S. Mittler & Sohn, Frankfurt am Main, *Der Krieg zur See, 1914-18*; Kommission für Geschichte des Parliamentarismus und der Politischen Parteien, Bonn-Bad Godesberg. *Der Regierung des Prinzen Max von Baden;* A. P. Watt, *The Life and Letters of David, Earl Beatty*, by Rear-Admiral W. S. Chalmers; HRH the Margrave of Baden and A. P. Watt for *The Memoirs of Prince Max von Baden*; Her Majesty's Stationery Office, *Official History of the War, Naval Operations*, Vol. V by Sir Henry Newbolt; Rutgers University Press, *War, Mutiny and Revolution in the German Navy* and *The German Naval Mutinies*, both by Daniel Horn; Koehler's Verlaggesellschaft, Herford, *Meuterei in der Kaiserlichen Marine*, Ernst

Legahn; Wm. Kimber, *Memoirs of Admiral Raeder*; Hutchinson Publishing Group, Ltd., *Memoirs of Ludendorff, Death of a Fleet* by Schubert and Gibson, and *Scapa Flow*, by Ludwig von Reuter; Verlag für Wehrwesen Bernard & Graefe, Frankfurt am Mains, *Der Admiralstab* by Walter Hubatsch. *Die Deutsche Seekriegsleitung* by Michael Salewski; Verlagsgruppe Bertelsmann, Gütersloh, *Deutsche Seekriegsgeschichte*, F. O. Busch; Oxford University Press, *From the* Dreadnought *to Scapa Flow* (Volume V), Arthur Marder. *History of the Peace Conference*, H. W. Temperley; Editions Payot, Paris, *les Mutineries de la marine allemande*, C. Vidil. *Un croiseur dans la révolution*, Peter Cornelissen. *Six ans de croisières sous-marines*, J. Spiess. *La tragédie de la flotte allemande*, Ludwig Freiwald; Weidenfeld and Nicolson, *Inside the Third Reich*, Albert Speer; articles by the present author in *History Today*, and *Journal of the Royal United Service Institution; Der Spiegel*, Hamburg, publishers of *November Revolution – die Rolle der SPD*, by Wolfgang Malanowski; Deutsche Verlags Anstalt, Stuttgart, *Die Ursachen des deutschen Zusammenbruches*; Gerhard Stalling AG, Oldenburg. *Scapa Flow 1919*, by Friedrich Rüge; Musterschmidt Verlag, Göttingen, *Regierte der Kaiser*? edited by Walter Görlitz.

ONE

In mid-October 1918, less than four weeks from the end of World War One, the German Naval High Command decided that its main force, the High Seas Fleet, which for months past had been held back to support the unrestricted submarine warfare campaign, should carry out an operation on the largest scale and of great daring. To interrupt the supplies of the Allied armies in France, the entire force of German battleships and battle-cruisers was to enter the mouth of the Thames to attack merchant shipping, while at the same time light cruisers and destroyers were to bombard the ports of Flanders and raid the Straits of Dover.

The Germans believed that these raids would bring down the British Grand Fleet from its bases in Scotland, tempted by the prospect of cutting off the Germans on their way home. The British fleet was greatly superior in strength, but the Germans planned to station U-boats and lay mines off the British ports so that, it was hoped, much damage would already have been done to the Grand Fleet before the two forces met for a decisive battle in the southern part of the North Sea, somewhere off the Dutch island of Terschelling.

The U-boats sailed for their patrol areas and the High Seas Fleet gathered in Schillig Roads outside Wilhelmshaven. It was at once clear to the crews that an important operation was planned. Spontaneous meetings were held on board several of the big ships and ratings denounced the planned move on the grounds that it was designed to cause the Allies to break off the negotiations for an Armistice which they were then conducting with the German Government. Moreover, the men in the big ships declared that the operation had no prospect of success; the sortie would be a suicidal venture. It might serve to save what the officers considered their honour, but it would cost the lives of thousands to no purpose.

Accordingly, the disaffected crews announced that they would not sail. Hipper, Commander-in-Chief of the High Seas Fleet, had no means of compelling them to do so, and the Fleet was dispersed to different North German ports. One battleship squadron went to Kiel, where its arrival at once caused an outbreak of rioting amongst the dockyard workers and the sailors at the base. The rioting spread all over Germany, with a hoisting of red flags and the setting up of soldiers', sailors' and workers' councils on the lines of the Soviets in Russia. The army and the home front were both near exhaustion and many rallied to a movement which seemed to promise an end to the war and the injustices of the Kaiser's government.

War-weariness and hunger had already provided plenty of incendiary material, but it was the naval mutinies which set fire to it and which seemed to bear the major share of the blame for the German revolution, so that these events became the centre of a series of violent propaganda battles which have now lasted for more than half-a-century. First was the dispute as to who was responsible for the mutinies themselves. Had discipline been too strictly imposed by the officers or had it been undermined by a left-wing conspiracy? Or were both statements true? Had the planned operation had any chance of success? If it had been successful would it have had any effect on the outcome of the war?

As for the revolution which followed, were the 'Red sailors' spreading over the Reich really responsible for it, and was that revolution responsible for Germany's defeat? Early in the debate, numbers of senior officers and conservative politicians decided that it had been. Led by Ludendorff, Chief-of-Staff of the German army with the title of Quartermaster-General, they proclaimed that 'Germany had been stabbed in the back', adopting a phrase which had been suggested by a British general. This theory was enthusiastically upheld in German

Conservative circles as it seemed to acquit them of blame for what had happened. Later, Hitler was to make great use of the phrase in his propaganda, while throughout the period of the Weimar Republic, that is, between the end of the World War One and the coming to power of Hitler, the debate went on between Right and Left as to who was responsible. As part of an enormously long parliamentary enquiry into the cause of the German collapse in 1918, two years were spent between 1926 and 1928 dealing with naval affairs, producing a vast amount of evidence and no real conclusions. Hitler's regime, on the other hand, imposed a complete censorship on events, coupled at about that time with the destruction of the logs of the ships involved, a step taken, it was said, because of the shameful nature of what had happened.

Since World War Two the controversy has been reopened, in the course of the immense amount of work done by German historians in excavating the facts of the history of the past one hundred years from thick deposits of propaganda. Much material has been produced on the political background of the last few weeks of World War One and of the mutinies, and at the same time there has been continuous controversy between West and East Germany, with East Germany claiming the mutinies to have been due to the revolutionary activities of the extreme left-wing parties. Neverthless there has been, in one respect, a certain measure of agreement; Max Reichpietsch, one of the two men executed for their part in an earlier mutiny in 1917, has been honoured on both sides of the Berlin wall. The Communists have named a fast rocket-carrying patrol-boat of their navy after him, and another after Albin Köbis, executed with Reichpietsch. The Socialist authorities of Herr Brandt's West Berlin have given the name Reichpietsch Ufer to a stretch of the embankment running along the Landwehr canal in the heart of the city; this particular part of the canal was formerly called the Tirpitz Ufer, after Grand Admiral von Tirpitz, who established the German Navy as a force of primary importance in world affairs.

The fiftieth anniversary of the German revolution in 1968

showed that strong feelings about the mutinies still persisted on both sides of the Berlin wall, and it is still remembered that in 1958 a meeting of West German officers, past and present, broke up in disarray because one speaker, now a General in the *Bundeswehr*, said that he preferred Reichpietsch and Köbis to the two Grand Admirals of Hitler's navy, Raeder and Dönitz, both convicted war criminals.

History is studied backwards. Of any completed episode we know the end probably better than the beginning, because it is closer to us and, in addition, it may have been more sensational. We are also perfectly supplied with hindsight. Thus, looking at the High Seas Fleet immediately following the mutinies at the end of World War One, we see great unkempt ships on rainy days in Kiel or Wilhelmshaven with red flags hanging listlessly while dishevelled gangs of seamen and dockyard workers prepared them, without any apparent emotion, for internment by the enemy.

But that was not how the Fleet had begun the war. On 31 July 1914 the 1st Scouting Group and the First Squadron had left Wilhelmshaven to meet the rest of the fleet which was on its way from the Baltic through the Kiel canal. It was a brilliant, blue, sunny day; the ships were cleared for action, with decks and superstructures stripped of railings, boats and other needless top hamper, with the crews manning the sides, cheering and singing, while ashore the watching crowds echoed and re-echoed the cheers and songs. What followed was complete anticlimax, for the combined fleet gathered in Jade Bay on 1 August and the battleships remained at anchor there for more than three months.

The morale of the men was then at its highest. Their principal complaint appears to have been, on that day, that it seemed unlikely they would have to fight Britain, and that the German Navy would be confronting only the much weaker French and Russian fleets; but when, five days later, Britain declared war the German seamen do not seem to have been in the slightest abashed.

If the morale of the German Navy was good in August 1914, this was not due to any tendency to underestimate the task before it, at least as far as the senior officers were concerned. Admiral Friedrich von Ingenohl, commanding the High Seas Fleet as *Flottenchef*, wrote before the fighting began:

> The proud old tradition of the English Navy, its seamanship, fostered by long service, thorough training of personnel, especially in gunnery, and the courageous and determined nature of the English people, known from long ago, and finally the skilful and energetic leadership of the enemy forbade any underestimation of his quality. Despite the highest evaluation of the performance of our own personnel no special superiority could be taken for granted at the beginning of the war, except perhaps for the more thorough exercising of the battle fleet in manoeuvre and in damage control, and the better training of our torpedo-boat crews.

Vice-Admiral Reinhold Scheer, who was to command the High Seas Fleet at Jutland, and in 1914 was commanding the Second Squadron of that Fleet, concurred with Ingenohl's judgment, writing:

> The English fleet had the advantage of looking back on a hundred years of proud tradition which must have given every man a sense of superiority based on the great deeds of the past. This could only be strengthened by the sight of their huge fleet, each unit of which in every class was supposed to represent the last word in the art of naval construction. The feeling was also supported by the British sailor's perfect familiarity with the sea and with conditions of life on board ship.

In the face of the challenge represented by the British Navy, the Germans followed a policy of caution, in the long run to ruin the German Navy as completely as if it had suffered a defeat as decisive as Trafalgar. The fact that the Fleet's inaction was responsible for the failure of morale was recognized by Scheer after the first mutinies in 1917, when he wrote that, 'The general situation made it necessary to hold the big ships in reserve and this deprived their crews of the constant vigorous activity which was needed to convince them that they must endure'.

More than ten years later the report of the Reichstag enquiry into the causes of the mutinies made the same point: 'Discontent was increased by the fact that the big ships were not in action,' adding 'It was not possible to obtain agreement as to why the fleet was employed as it was'. Now, of course, unlike the Reichstag commission, we can see why 'the fleet was employed as it was'.

It was, however, not simply this respect for their enemies that was to overawe the German admirals at the beginning of the war. There were two primary considerations which restrained them. The first was their numerical inferiority. In August 1914 Britain possessed twenty-nine dreadnought capital ships* while Germany had seventeen.

The second consideration which led the German admirals to hold back the fleet was their idea, shared by the German generals and politicians, as to how the war would develop. They envisaged events very similar to the wars which Germany or Prussia had waged against the Danes in 1864, against the Austrians in 1866 and against the French in 1870-1. In each

* The number of dreadnought capital ships was the yardstick by which naval strength was measured in World War One. These ships took their name from the British battleship *Dreadnought* which, when completed in 1906, had by its gunpower, speed and armour made all previous battleships obsolete. Nevertheless at the beginning of the war both the British and German main fleets included a few pre-dreadnoughts – i.e. ships built before the *Dreadnought*; but they were found to be too slow and too weakly armed for modern warfare and were assigned to subsidiary duties. Some of the British pre-dreadnoughts were for a time employed to steam in front of the modern ships of the Grand Fleet in the hope that they, and not the new ships following them, would strike any mines that were in their path. None did.

Capital ships were divided into two types, battleships carrying heavy guns and armour but having only moderate speed, and battle-cruisers in which high speed was a primary consideration. To obtain this the British sacrificed armour and the Germans gunpower. The loss of three battle-cruisers in one afternoon at Jutland and of *HMS Hood* in World War Two, compared with the very great powers of resistance shown by German battle-cruisers at the Dogger Bank and at Jutland, proved that the Germans had unquestionably devised the better formula.

Of the twenty-nine British dreadnought capital ships at the outbreak of war, four were in foreign waters and one was in dockyard hands. One of the seventeen German ships, the famous *Goeben*, was also in foreign waters.

case there had been one tough campaign on land, with two or three decisive German victories, and the enemy had then been ready to make peace, without the Prussian or German Navy becoming seriously involved.

In 1914 the Germans expected that the French Army would be defeated within a few weeks, and that France would then surrender, while the small British Expeditionary Force would be taken prisoner or driven into the sea and the German army would then turn against Russia. Britain, recognizing the impossibility of fighting alone, would agree to a peace settlement from which Germany would gain massively. The resemblance between this scenario and the events of 1940-1 is clear.

Meanwhile, planning in 1914 for the peace conference which was to close the war, the German Chancellor, Bethmann-Hollweg, had decided that the German position at the conference table would require support by great naval strength, and he laid down that it was: 'Absolutely essential that we should have a big fleet at the end of the war'.

In addition, Bethmann said that he did not believe that the British intended to wage war seriously, and that it would therefore be unwise to inflict upon them any grave reverse. In support of this contention the Chancellor adduced the successful escape of the two German warships, *Goeben* and *Breslau*, into the Dardanelles; if the British had been in earnest about fighting the war, he said, they would never have permitted this to happen.

The processes of thought which produced the theory that the function of a great navy in wartime was to preserve itself for peace may appear baffling, but it was a vital part of the German conception of the deterrent strategy for which their navy had been built. In the first place the fleet was intended to be so big that the British would be unwilling to challenge it; for that, it did not need to be as large as the British fleet, but only strong enough for the British to fear that, in battle with the Germans, they would suffer such damage even in a victorious action as to cost them their place as the strongest naval power in the world. The second part of the same theory was the idea that Germany, with a strong fleet as well as a great army, would seem so desirable an ally that Britain would henceforward willingly support German policy throughout the world.

However, the deterrent had failed to deter. What it had done, as Professor Marder has pointed out, was to make certain that Britain entered the war against Germany; for the possibility of a Germany victorious against France and in possession of Flanders and the Channel ports appeared a terrible threat to Britain.

While the Germans waited during the late summer and autumn of 1914 for their Army to bring them victory on the Continent, they hoped that the odds against them at sea would be reduced as losses were sustained by the British who, it was believed in Berlin, would mount a close blockade of the German North Sea ports with ships kept continuously patrolling in the Heligoland Bight. These would be targets for the German destroyers and submarines. When sufficient British ships had been sunk, the High Seas Fleet would then sortie and fight a decisive battle.

However, as far back as 1911, after Churchill had become First Lord of the Admiralty, the British had begun to change their plans precisely because they believed that the development of torpedo craft and mines would make a close blockade of the Bight too dangerous. Instead, it was decided that if war came the blockade maintained would be a distant one, on a line from Scotland to Norway, kept up by obsolete cruisers and armed liners, while the battleships of the Grand Fleet would be based on Scapa Flow in the Orkneys, whence they could emerge to support the blockading forces if needed.

As a result of this change in British policy, the eastern and central North Sea became a kind of no-man's-land and neither side knew the whereabouts of the enemy. Both accordingly sent submarines to find out. On the morning of 5 August the British submarines *E-6* and *E-8* sailed from Harwich on the first war patrols in the history of the British submarine service, and on the following day ten U-boats of the German First Flotilla left

Heligoland in a long line abreast, seeking the Grand Fleet in a north-westerly direction.

The two British submarines frightened away a large number of fishing craft and then returned home – two nights in enemy waters in those days was considered something of a feat. A few months later a patrol lasting four or five weeks by boats of the E-class was found perfectly possible, albeit extremely strenuous.

Meanwhile one of the U-boats searching for the Grand Fleet had in fact found it at sea, fired a torpedo at a battleship, missed and disappeared, having probably been sunk by an escorting British light cruiser. Another U-boat was also lost on this same patrol.

Any doubts about the British being in earnest about the waging of the war were cleared up by 23 August, when the British army began its first battle in western Europe since Waterloo. No effort had been made by the German Navy to hinder the transport of the British troops to France, the German Army taking the view that the easiest way of disposing of them would be to defeat them on the field of battle.

On 28 August the British Navy struck its first blow, both at the material and the morale of the German fleet. British light craft, supported by battle-cruisers commanded by Sir David Beatty, attacked the German patrols in the Bight. As six German light cruisers straggled into action one by one, in an area which stretched from Dutch to Danish territorial waters, the British sank three of them as well as a destroyer, and lost no ships themselves. The German battle-cruisers, then commanded by Rear-Admiral Hipper, and intended to support their light craft in just such an emergency, were trapped behind the Jade Bar off Wilhelmshaven at low tide and could reach the open sea only when it was too late. By then the British, not altogether conscious of the extent to which luck had been on their side, had begun to withdraw.

These events constituted the first battle of Heligoland. Their immediate result was the withdrawal of the German outer patrols from the Bight and their replacement by mines. At the same time there was much criticism of the faulty disposition of the big ships and the passive attitude of the High Seas Fleet, arguments which sowed the first seeds of defeatism in the big ships.

Hipper was blamed for having been trapped by the tide, not only by Grand Admiral Tirpitz, the Secretary of State for the Navy, but by the German ratings as well; and his career, which in fact by the end of the war left him with the reputation of being the most skilful admiral on either side, was very nearly brought to an end. Some of Tirpitz's criticism may have been intended to deflect the attacks which were made on him after the battle. Responsible for the design and construction of German warships since 1897, he was blamed when it was seen at Heligoland that the German light cruisers with their 4.1-inch guns (firing a 31-lb shell) were hopelessly outmatched by the 6-inch guns (firing a 100-lb shell) mounted in British ships of the same category. Tirpitz tried to justify himself by pleading that shortage of money had made it impossible for the Germans to build the two types of light cruisers which were really required – fast, comparatively lightly armed vessels for use as scouts, and bigger and better armed ships to act as commerce raiders on the high seas. As a result, he said, a compromise type had been built, too weakly armed to deal with the British light cruisers and too slow to act as a scout.

Whatever was made of this argument, Hipper succeeded in escaping the consequences of Tirpitz's wrath and was the first senior German naval officer to react officially against the policy of the High Command in holding back the Fleet. On 9 September, the day upon which the German Army began its retreat from the Marne, he urged Ingenohl, whose ships were still lying at anchor in Schillig Roads, that something should be done at once to dispel the gloom caused by the events off Heligoland. Accordingly he wished to take his three battle-cruisers northwards to strike at the British blockade line. Ingenohl agreed, but the chain of command at this time was organized in such a way that he had to obtain the approval of Admiral von Pohl, the Chief of the Naval Staff, who had in turn to obtain the approval of the Kaiser as 'Supreme War Lord'.

Meanwhile Pohl's deputy, Rear-Admiral Paul Behncke, had endorsed the plan, adding the proposal that the battle-cruisers should be joined by four of the latest battleships of the Kaiser class, and that the whole Fleet should be sent out in support of the battle-cruisers and the Kaisers to a position about one hundred miles from Heligoland, to cover the return of the raiders and, possibly, to cut off an advanced part of the British forces if they were in hot pursuit.

The operation was fixed for 22 September and was only cancelled at the last moment when large British forces were reported at sea.

Commenting on the cancellation, Behncke wrote to Pohl, who was at Imperial Headquarters at Charleville in France in attendance on the Kaiser:

> A modern fleet cannot be kept forever in port without suffering grave damage. Its strength disintegrates and its readiness for action is lost. Then, when it is faced with a great task, possibly one of decisive importance, there arises the danger of failure. This, to my mind, decisively overrules any political considerations . . . A fleet which has spent the war in port, and never fought, is a less important political factor than one which has shown of what it is capable.

This was the first warning of the disaster which did occur when the Fleet had been too long inactive.

By the time that Behncke had written this letter the whole course of the war had changed. After the battle of the Marne there was no prospect of the 'fresh, joyous war' that the Germans had planned. Instead, through the autumn mists and rains both sides on the Western Front began 'the race to the sea', a series of northerly moves in which each tried to outflank the other and thus take a firm grip on the Channel ports. These had assumed enormous importance now that the war might continue for years.

General von Falkenhayn, Chief of the German General Staff from 1914 to 1916, was explicit:

The conquest of the [Channel] coast was the sole means of frustrating the war of blockade which England was contemplating and of retaliating through our destroyers, submarines, aeroplanes and Zeppelins . . . If we succeeded in driving the enemy out of the Yser valley and pursuing him at the point of the sword, there was no doubt that we should be in a position to overthrow the Western Front.

The two German chiefs-of-staff, military and naval, were in agreement, a rare enough event at any time during the war. This was seen when one of the 'activist' captains of the High Seas Fleet, Magnus von Levetzow, then commanding the battle-cruiser *Moltke*, wrote to Ingenohl's predecessor as *Flottenchef*, Admiral Henning von Holtzendorff, then in retirement, complaining of the inactivity to which the Fleet was being condemned. Holtzendorff replied that the Navy would not have freedom of action until the Army was in possession of the Channel ports, but once the Germans had taken Calais and Boulogne they would be able to do so much damage to British shipping that the Grand Fleet would be compelled to challenge the High Seas Fleet to battle in the Heligoland Bight, where everything would be in the Germans' favour.

However, although the Germans, during the autumn campaign of 1914, took Antwerp, Ostend and Zeebrugge, they were, after fierce fighting, obliged to leave the Allies in possession of the Yser valley, Ypres, Dunkirk, Calais and Boulogne.

While this fighting was still going on, the German Naval Staff decided that the first two months of the war at sea had shown the need for agreement on future plans, and a meeting was arranged to be held on board Ingenohl's flagship, the *Friedrich der Grosse*, at Wilhelmshaven on 3 October.

To follow what happened at this meeting and afterwards it is necessary to understand the crazy system, or rather lack of it, by which the German Navy, and, indeed, the German Empire was governed.

The text may be taken from Lord Haldane who, when Lord Chancellor, visited Germany in 1911 to discuss the possibility of an Anglo-German limitation of naval armaments. He wrote: 'When you attain the top of this highly organized people you find not only confusion, but chaos'.

Nominal head of all the chaos was the Kaiser, a sort of Emperor of Misrule, known and feared for his wild strokes of policy, so that his own people gradually edged him away from power. He was, in name, the Supreme War Lord and was allowed to take command of one side in the annual great army manoeuvres, in which he always ended victorious after an enormous and quite useless cavalry charge. However, no Hohenzollern ruler since Frederick the Great had been allowed by the army to command it in wartime, and although emperors, kings, grand dukes and crown princes appeared high in the army lists and in the Orders of Battle, decisions were taken and orders given by those who held the posts of Chief of Staff to those princes.

However, so far as the Navy was concerned, the Kaiser claimed and tried from time to time to exercise personally all the authority that theoretically belonged to him and to act as if the grandiose title of Supreme War Lord really meant what it said. One of his most remarkable acts of folly, and one which remained in people's minds until the end of his reign, had been to give an interview to the *Daily Telegraph* in 1908 in which he declared his deep affection for Britain and detailed the real or imagined action which he had taken to help her, which had included, he said, giving advice on how the Boer war should be won. It was all fairly harmless except for the fact that this stroke of foreign policy had been made without the knowledge or approval of Bülow, the Chancellor, or of the German Foreign Office which, in theory, had the right and the duty to stop it if they considered that necessary.

Not for the first or last time the Kaiser was ill served by his advisers who, on this occasion, did nothing at all, leaving the All Highest to receive the full weight of criticism and scorn when it became known that he had, without consulting anyone, launched a new initiative in foreign affairs. The irresponsibility of his action was such that the possibility of his abdication was discussed, and, suffering from something like a nervous breakdown, he went off to shoot foxes at Donaueschingen. His recovery was interrupted by a gruesome and fantastic tragedy. The Chief of his Military Cabinet, General Count Hülsen-Haeseler, dressed himself in the frilly skirt of a ballerina and, while performing for the Kaiser's amusement, dropped dead.

The *Daily Telegraph* incident caused both the Army and the Foreign Office to redouble their efforts to keep the Kaiser as far as possible from any position of authority, and this they were largely able to do. The Navy, however, were less successful, although in December 1907 the Chief of the Naval Staff, Admiral Büchsel, had already issued an order that 'Secret papers must no longer be passed to His Majesty the Emperor'. Büchsel was relieved in the following year and there was a great difference right up to 1918 between the Kaiser's relations with his army and with his navy.

He spoke frequently of 'My army' and 'My will', but other people commanded 'His' army and determined 'His' will. In the case of the Navy, however, he endeavoured to stick meticulously to what he considered to be his Imperial prerogative. He defined this very clearly: 'I have made the Fleet a weapon and trained it. How, when and where I intend to use it is my business alone, as Supreme War Lord. Everyone else must keep silent and obey.' On another occasion it was simply: 'How I use my navy is my affair alone.'

When it became clear during the war that some centralized operational control of the Navy was necessary, and the setting up of a *Seekriegsleitung* (directorate of the naval war) was suggested, the Kaiser rejected the proposal, saying: 'I am the *Seekriegsleitung*'.

It was only a few weeks before the end of the war when he finally agreed that a genuine *Seekriegsleitung* should be set up, and appointed Scheer (then commanding the High Seas Fleet) as its head, at the same time that he became Chief of the Naval Staff. In addition to the Chief of the Naval Staff, the German Navy had at its head two other admirals, each with separate responsibilities and no over-riding authority.

The best known of all the German admirals and probably the best known man in Germany after the Kaiser was the formidable and famous Grand Admiral Alfred von Tirpitz, Secretary of State for the Navy and Head of the Admiralty. A striking figure, with a great bald domed head and a long forked white beard, he had been Secretary of State since 1897 and, with the Kaiser's support, had devised and carried out the plans of naval construction which had raised the German fleet from a small coast-defence force to become the second naval power in the world. Had he wished he could probably have become Chancellor of the Reich, and he certainly came within measurable distance of that post. He represented the Navy in the Reichstag and dealt with the design and construction of ships, and with their weapons and equipment. He had also been responsible for a nation-wide propaganda campaign in favour of the Navy, based upon the Navy League with its million members spread all over Germany, from Berlin to the smallest and most remote villages. In British eyes, the predominant role that he had played in the building of the German Navy made him appear an Anglophobe, a charge which he endeavoured to refute by pointing out that his wife and his daughter had both been educated at Cheltenham Ladies' College.

On the material side of naval development he had done well. He had laid down the plans for the expansion of the Fleet in a law which was almost unalterable, and this meant that he was spared the necessity for a yearly wrangle with the Reichstag over the estimates; but he, more than anyone else, had been responsible for the chaos of the Naval High Command.

Anxious to be left undisturbed at the Admiralty, he had hived that organization off from the rest of the Service and was then chagrined to find that, while in accordance with his wishes the Chief of the Naval Staff and other senior naval officers could not interfere with him, he, on the other hand, could not enforce their compliance with his own designs. To remedy this, he proposed on 30 July, three days before Germany declared war on Russia, that the posts of Secretary of State and Chief of the Naval Staff should be amalgamated and that he should hold both. This move failed, but he returned to the charge a fortnight later with the suggestion that he should take command of the High Seas Fleet, while remaining Secretary of State, and conducting the business of the Admiralty from Wilhelmshaven, rather than from Berlin. He admitted that he was sixty-five years old and that he had not served afloat for seventeen years but, he said, that was not important since, in the nature of things, he would not often go to sea.

On both occasions it was the third of the independent admirals, Georg von Müller, head of the Kaiser's naval cabinet, who had secured the rejection of Tirpitz's plans. He was the liaison officer between the Kaiser and the Navy and dealt, in particular, with personnel matters and the appointment of senior naval officers. His diaries impress disagreeably with the idea that he was very much of a courtier and, following recent research, their accuracy is now considered very doubtful. He was nicknamed 'Rasputin' in the closing stages of the war from his fondness for intrigue, and throughout his career he seems to have been considered something of a freak because he strove to persuade his brother officers to drink less.

The Chief of the Naval Staff was Hugo von Pohl, responsible for operations and plans. In peacetime he had built up a good reputation as a ship-handler and later as a squadron commander, but on shore he seems to have become a cross between a courtier and an official rather than a sea officer. He had spent too much time in close proximity to the Kaiser to have escaped the unreality and sycophancy of the Court and was, predictably, in agreement with the Kaiser on the need to keep the Fleet intact. In the chain of command Ingenohl, as *Flottenchef*, came under the orders of Pohl.

An additional complication in the German naval hierarchy was the position of the Kaiser's brother, Prince Heinrich of Prussia, who held the rank of *Grossadmiral* (Admiral of the Fleet) and was Commander-in-Chief of the Baltic Fleet. His rank made him senior to all the other serving officers of the German navy, a fact of which he constantly took advantage, although Ingenohl, Pohl and later Scheer and Hipper all held commands of much greater importance than his own. Before the war he had himself commanded the High Seas Fleet, when he had gained the reputation of a dull and limited man of conservative disposition.

Finally, to complete an extremely confusing picture, after the Germans had occupied the coast of Flanders, a new command independent of both the Army and the Navy was set up under Admiral Ludwig von Schröder. Under him came the coastal defences and Marine Corps which formed the garrison of the area.

With all these forces at play, and others as well, it is easy to understand how German officers could be tormented by situations like that in which the procurement of a trawler for patrol duties in the Baltic required the agreement of the Admiralty, the Naval Staff, the Commander of the Baltic Fleet, the Commander of the High Seas Fleet and the Flag Officer commanding the Baltic Station.

A further handicap for the Navy was the jealousy of the Army. From the point of view of prestige the situation of the latter changed drastically as the plans for the Navy grew. Thus, shortly after the beginning of his reign, the Kaiser had said: 'The only pillar upon which our Empire rested was the Army, and that is still so today'.

In January 1896 Hohenlohe, then Chancellor, had said: 'Germany will never be in a position to maintain a Navy which will be equal in rank to the Army'. But in April of the following year the Kaiser had telegraphed to his brother Heinrich, saying that he would not rest until he had brought his Navy to the same height as that of the Army at that time.

Inter-Service rivalry was increased by the growing share of the Navy in the defence budget. Thus, in 1896-7 the Army estimates totalled £27,190,545 and those for the Navy £4,372,069, while in 1913-14 the Army was spending £60,000,000 and the Navy £22,887,000. The Army's view at this time was that the Navy's sole contribution of value to the conduct of the war was its control of the Baltic which kept open the routes by which iron-ore came to Germany from

Sweden, and also prevented an enemy landing on the coast of Pomerania or Mecklenburg. From the very beginning of the war the Army began to complain of the Navy's attitude. Falkenhayn, successively Prussian Minister of War and Chief of the General Staff, was repeating loudly at Imperial Headquarters in Luxembourg that, since the Navy was remaining a bystander, it would be better that its ships should be paid off and the crews brought ashore to fight.

Later Tirpitz wrote: 'Falkenhayn is no friend of the Navy, on the contrary. He was already saying in Luxembourg it was all the fault of the Navy'.

This view persisted throughout the war. In 1919, when Groener was Quartermaster-General, Tirpitz reported: 'Groener energetically spreads the view that the Navy was to blame for everything'.

At the meeting of admirals on board the *Friedrich der Grosse* on 3 October 1914 there were present Pohl, Ingenohl, Rear-Admiral Eckermann, the latter's Chief-of-Staff, and Vice-Admiral von Lans and Vice-Admiral Scheer commanding respectively the First and Second squadrons, and the commander of the North Sea Station, Vice-Admiral von Krosigk. Behncke learned of the meeting too late to attend and afterwards suspected an attempt by Pohl deliberately to keep him away. In an effort to get from Berlin to Wilhelmshaven in time he travelled all night across Germany by car, something of a dashing proceeding in those days. When he reached Wilhelmshaven he found that Ingenohl, after debate, had been overruled by Pohl with the support of Eckermann and Lans. From subsequent study of Ingenohl's writings it seems that he would have obeyed orders to fight as wholeheartedly as he now obeyed orders not to do so, and probably more happily, but he did not consider it his duty to challenge his orders and, a little later, this was to cost Germany a very important success.

The central fact which faced the German admirals was that it was not possible to hope that the balance between the two fleets would be affected by British losses. Although four British armoured cruisers and two light cruisers had already been sunk by U-boats in the North Sea, the ships were of minor importance and their loss did not affect the strength of the Grand Fleet.

From the records of the meeting in the *Friedrich der Grosse* it is surprising to find that Scheer apparently supported Pohl's caution; for Scheer, with Hipper, was almost certainly one of the most skilful naval leaders on either side in World War One. After the war he explained that the paper which he approved had been watered down by Pohl after he had left the flagship, so that it no longer gave that degree of freedom of action to the *Flottenchef* which, according to Scheer, it had originally done.

The other squadron commander present, Wilhelm Ritter von Lans, then aged fifty-four, was one of the few German naval officers who had ever been in action. During the Boxer Rising he had commanded the gunboat *Iltis* and had been severely wounded in action against the Chinese shore-batteries. He walked with a bad limp, which gave rise to the belief on the lower deck that he had lost a leg.

He was a very popular officer and, years after the end of the war, when the Reichstag enquiry was investigating events in the Fleet, there were still men from the lower deck who, when asked whether there was anyone who would have been able to lead the High Seas Fleet to battle in October 1918, answered: 'Yes, Lans!'

But between the young commander of 1900 and the vice-admiral of 1914 there was a great gap. Now his counsel was of prudence; fighting would be too great a risk. He was tired, and was already complaining: 'For us old admirals, continuous life on board is very hard to bear'. Nevertheless, Lans survived until 1947. The German Official Historian, Captain Groos, hints at his disloyalty to Ingenohl, but others who knew him have described him as a man who always spoke his mind frankly with a consequent disturbance of relations between him and the *Flottenchef*.

The end product of the Wilhelmshaven meeting was a directive submitted to the Kaiser and then promulgated by him, which laid down:

> His Majesty orders that the Fleet hold itself back, and avoids action which might lead to heavy losses.
>
> This does not cancel orders issued by the All Highest that favourable opportunities must be exploited to harm the enemy.

Such opportunities were not to include operations outside the Bight (for example, in the Skagerrak) nor was the directive to be construed to cover an attack by the High Seas Fleet on the Grand Fleet if the British battleships were to enter the Bight. If that happened it would be the task of the U-boats to attack the enemy. The Kaiser, it was noted, reserved to himself the right to decide when the Fleet should be committed, and that time had not yet come.

Finally, preparations were to be made to exploit the fact that the Channel ports seemed likely to fall into German hands. Minelaying was to be continued and, in addition, operations by the battle-cruisers to harm the enemy received the Kaiser's express approval.

Contrasting these decisions with what Tirpitz, Behncke and other 'activists' proposed at this time when they urged that the High Seas Fleet should give battle to the British, it should be understood that the activists did not envisage a fight to a finish between the two fleets but operations in which detached parts of the Grand Fleet might be cut off and destroyed by superior German forces.

This, in fact, the Germans came near to achieving. The German Official History, written with sympathy for the 'activist' cause, lists eleven occasions between August 1914 and January 1915 when individual British battle squadrons, usually numbering six or eight ships, approached unsupported and sufficiently close to Heligoland to give the High Seas Fleet a good chance of cutting them off. On three occasions one of these British forces came within fifty miles of Heligoland; on three more occasions they came within one hundred miles and on five additional occasions within two hundred miles.

To take advantage of one of these situations and fall upon the detached British forces with his entire Fleet, Ingenohl needed to be able to take his ships to sea at once, without telegraphing the Kaiser or Pohl for permission to do so and then having to await a reply.

The first move in the extended minelaying campaign was made by the Germans on 17 October when four destroyers sailed from Borkum to lay mines in the Downs.

The sequel was another of those German reverses at the hands of a more powerful opponent which contributed to the sense of inferiority in the High Seas Fleet, which ended by becoming so intense that the Fleet finally refused to fight.

The destroyers selected for the raid were obsolete and outgunned by the faster British ships, twice their size, which intercepted them and sank them all. The weakness of the Germans' armament (four-pounder guns, compared with the thirty-one pounder British) and the higher speed of the British due to their use of oil fuel, were both laid at the door of Tirpitz. Why these old destroyers were sent on this mission instead of more modern, stronger and faster ships has never been made clear, but it is worth noting that the morale of the German crews concerned was of the highest. They appreciated clearly the risk of the operation, and all were offered a chance to withdraw from it. This they refused to do. It is hard to think of a justification for the waste of those lives.

On the same day another German minelaying effort failed, although without any loss. The minelayer *Nautilus* and the light cruiser *Kolberg* sailed to lay mines off the Firth of Forth. However, off the Dogger Bank they learned that British ships were nearby and accordingly they returned home. The Germans decided that, in future, minelaying operations would have to be supported by the heavy ships. This idea, plus the permission already given for the use of the battle-cruisers 'to harm the enemy', led, within a fortnight, to the first sortie by German capital ships across the North Sea, an operation which temporarily altered the whole face of the naval war.

But before the combined operations by the battle-cruisers

and the minelayers took place, the Germans secured the first great success of their mine war. On 19 October the former *Norddeutscher* Lloyd passenger liner *Berlin*, fitted as a minelayer, sailed with two hundred mines on board. She laid her first field off the north-west coast of Ireland; and, passing through the Denmark Strait between Iceland and Greenland, altered course towards the North Cape to lay another field in the approaches to the north Russian ports, by brilliant moonlight and under a great display of the aurora borealis. She had reached a point off Vardö when she was ordered to return home; but with the British blockading cruisers closing in and her engines in poor repair, she was forced to take refuge in the neutral port of Trondheim on 17 November, where she was interned.

However, on 27 October the *Berlin*'s minefield laid off the Irish coast had sunk the new British battleship *Audacious*, the only British dreadnought battleship to be destroyed by enemy action throughout the entire war.

TWO

The sinking of the *Audacious* brought to a head the first great crisis of the naval war and with it a situation which offered the Germans the most favourable opportunity of defeating the British they were ever to have in the course of the war on the surface of the sea.

Not only had the *Audacious* been sunk, but no fewer than seven other capital ships of the Grand Fleet were out of action owing to damage which they had sustained, mostly as a result of the strains of being at sea for long periods in the autumn weather of northern latitudes. The absence of these eight ships brought the total British strength in home waters down to twenty-two dreadnought capital ships. In comparison, the Germans at full strength had a total of nineteen similar ships. Commenting on the relative strength of the two fleets at this time, the German Official History says: 'There could be no question of any English superiority worth speaking of'.

The British Admiralty had tried in vain to prevent the loss of the *Audacious* becoming known. They were, however, able to conceal from the enemy the absence from the Fleet of ships under refit.

Ever since the beginning of the war Admiral Sir John Jellicoe, Commander-in-Chief of the Grand Fleet, had been worried about the threat of mines and torpedoes. Now, after the loss of the *Audacious*, his fears grew and on 30 October he told the Admiralty that the danger was so great that he did not propose to engage the enemy in the southern part of the North Sea, where they would be close to their bases and the British far from theirs. This, Jellicoe explained, would mean that the Germans could go into action with their fuel supplies almost intact, while the British cruisers and destroyers, having come down from the north of Scotland, might already be running short of fuel.

Jellicoe also said that he was afraid that, under certain circumstances, half his fleet might be disabled before the main battle began. This, he believed, could happen if the German fleet, withdrawing before him, succeeded in luring him over U-boats lying in wait or minefields already prepared. Accordingly, he said, under those circumstances he would not follow the enemy directly, despite the fact that this might be construed as a refusal to give battle. He asked the Board of Admiralty, at the head of which Churchill then was, whether they approved these ideas and the Board replied that they did.

On the day that Jellicoe wrote, Churchill had appointed a new First Sea Lord, Admiral of the Fleet Lord Fisher, who replaced Prince Louis of Battenberg, and at once began to plug a great gap which had developed in the vast British schemes for controlling the seas of the world. Slowly, during the past three months, the German Far Eastern Squadron under Graf Spee had been making its way homeward across the Pacific, hunted by ships of the British, Australian, French and Japanese navies.

As Spee neared the coast of South America, he had the option of turning north and passing through the newly opened Panama Canal or turning south and reaching the Atlantic via the Straits of Magellan. He chose the southern route and, off Coronel on the coast of Chile, met head-on one of the British hunting groups, commanded by Sir Christopher Cradock. This force was a great deal weaker than that of Spee, and Cradock's two most important ships were sunk; it was a great success, without loss to the Germans, of which they did not fail to make the most; and at this moment they decided on the first of their battle-cruiser raids on the English coast, accompanied by minelaying in the southern part of the North Sea.

The target of the German bombardment was to be the town of Gorleston, next to Great Yarmouth, which was to be shelled by three battle-cruisers, *Seydlitz, Moltke* and *Von der Tann*, and the armoured cruiser *Blücher*. While Hipper was thus engaged, the main body of the High Seas Fleet under Ingenohl was to support him, in theory, by taking up a position fifty miles west of Terschelling, further than which the High Seas Fleet was not to go. This restriction meant that they would have no chance of cutting off any part of the British fleet, while with a measure of luck the British might be able to cut off Hipper.

In fact very little happened; some German shells fell on the foreshore at Gorleston, which had historic interest since they were the first missiles from an enemy fleet to fall on English soil since the Dutch wars. British light craft engaged the German ships, which made off. In these operations each side lost one ship, the British a submarine which struck a mine, and the Germans the armoured cruiser *Yorck*, which, on her return to Jade Bay, lost her way in a fog, went the wrong side of a buoy marking the edge of a minefield and, when trying to extricate herself, drifted broadside on to two mines which exploded. She quickly turned over and sank bottom up. More than fifty years later salvage work was begun on the wreck.

Meanwhile, the German victory at Coronel was having its repercussions in London and at Imperial Headquarters. Tirpitz was anxiously awaiting Spee's homecoming, for he intended to get him appointed to command the High Seas Fleet. Fisher, to destroy Spee and his squadron, was preparing to send no fewer than three of his battle-cruisers across the Atlantic; two, *Invincible* and *Inflexible*, to the South Atlantic to intercept the Germans near Cape Horn if they chose to return that way, and one, *Princess Royal*, to the West Indies in case the Germans came through the Panama Canal. A fourth battle-cruiser, H.M.A.S. *Australia* had been in the Pacific since before the war.

The two ships which went to the South Atlantic destroyed Spee off the Falkland Islands, but the news of this action revealed that the Grand Fleet battle-cruisers had been seriously reduced in strength, and the Germans decided to take advantage of this to make another raid on the English coast.

This took place on 17 December, an extraordinary 'Day of Dupes', in which first the British and then the Germans seemed to be on the very point of cutting off a detachment of the enemy's capital ships and destroying them. In both cases the detachments were so large that their destruction would have changed the whole balance of the war at sea. First the British, learning from the cryptographers in the famous Room 40 OB that the raid was afoot, sent south Beatty's four battle-cruisers and a squadron of six battleships under Vice-Admiral Warrender. Jellicoe had wished to take the whole Grand Fleet to sea, but the Admiralty, not knowing that the Germans were out in full force, considered six battleships would be sufficient. In rough and thick weather Beatty and Warrender missed Hipper's battle-cruisers after they had shelled Scarborough, Whitby and Hartlepool and failed to cut them off. On the other hand, Ingenohl turned back prematurely, thus losing the chance to cut off Beatty and Warrender and confront them with overwhelmingly stronger forces (Germans 14 dreadnought battleships, eight pre-dreadnoughts and four battle-cruisers against six British dreadnought battleships and four battle-cruisers).

Both sides were disappointed deeply by their own failures, and Tirpitz wrote that he boiled with emotion when he thought of Ingenohl's lost chance. The time was near when Ingenohl would be removed from his post and replaced by an admiral even more cautious and unenterprising.

Pohl's senior assistant as Chief of the Naval Staff at Supreme Headquarters was Captain Zenker who, at the end of 1914, set himself to write a paper for his master on the future conduct of the war at sea and, in particular, on the employment of the High Seas Fleet. Like Behncke before him, he urged that the Fleet should go to sea for training purposes and to maintain and improve the morale of the crews. He wrote:

I am entirely convinced that after five months spent almost without interruption lying in river estuaries or in harbour the tactical training of units is no longer at its former level. . . .

The spirit of the crews and their desire to come to grips with the enemy are certainly as excellent as they ever were and will prove themselves fully when it comes to action. But the degree to which they are used to being at sea, with its great influence on gunnery, cannot remain at the same height, so that, with the best will in the world, military performance must in the end decline . . . the dangers which the fleet has to run at sea are less than those which it faces in the river mouths where, although they are protected, their striking power and their readiness for action is always decreasing.

After urging again that the Fleet should obtain as much time at sea as possible, Zenker ended by proposing that the Fleet should exercise as often as it could with long-range U-boats and with Zeppelin airships. Ingenohl, commenting, said that the danger of the Fleet growing 'rusty' was not as great as Zenker believed. The estuaries gave sufficient opportunities for target practice and most exercises. Moreover, ships and squadrons could go to the Baltic for torpedo practice and night firing.

After the war was over Admiral Sir Percy Scott, who had been the outstanding force in the campaign to improve the gunnery of the British Navy in the first years of the twentieth century, wrote: 'The German sailors were made in Kiel harbour. This harbour is like the Serpentine, and that is what was the matter with the German Navy.'

Another proposal for offensive operations, put forward by Zenker and afterwards by other senior German naval officers, was to send commerce raiders to sea to replace those which had been sunk – the ships of Spee's squadron, *Emden*, *Karlsrühe* and others. In the first instance Zenker proposed that the light cruiser *Regensburg* and the 20,000-ton liner *Cap Polonio*, armed with 5.9-inch guns, should be used; but he admitted that the ships would be lost sooner or later, and neither Ingenohl nor Pohl thought that the sacrifice would be justified.

However, it was decided that Hipper should make another sortie into the North Sea. This time he was to go only as far as the Dogger Bank, to sink some of the large numbers of British trawlers fishing there and any British patrols which might be encountered.

For his main striking force Hipper had three of his full-fledged battle-cruisers, *Seydlitz* (his flagship), *Derfflinger* and *Moltke*, and *Blücher*, the latter described as a 'pseudo-battle-cruiser', being weaker, smaller and slower than the battle-cruisers. *Blücher* was taken to sea on this occasion because the fourth regular member of Hipper's battle-cruiser force, *Von der Tann*, was refitting.

Warned by Room 40 OB Beatty, with five battle-cruisers, came up with Hipper on the morning of 24 January. Hipper at once headed back to port at full speed. The Germans, to their horror, saw that the guns of the big British ships had a longer range than their own, and the shells began to fall among the German ships before the latter had any chance of being able to reply. The three leading British battle-cruisers mounted 13.5-inch guns which had a range of 20,000 yards, while the 12-inch guns of the most powerful German ship, *Derfflinger*, had a range of 19,000 yards, and the other two big German ships, *Seydlitz* and *Moltke*, had a range of 18,500 yards.

The Germans were caught by surprise, so thoroughly that the first ship to meet the British, the light cruiser *Kolberg*, had her watch below at breakfast; and the stokers' watch which had just been relieved were in their bathrooms. The *Blücher* was last in the line, behind *Seydlitz*, *Derfflinger* and *Moltke*, and she was soon hit and dropped astern. Shot to pieces and finally sunk, her behaviour and that of her crew earned this praise from Sir Julian Corbett in his Official History: 'For three hours, during which she had been the focus of an overwhelming concentration of fire, she had never ceased to reply. Twice our light cruisers had approached to complete her destruction and twice she had forced them to draw off. As an example of discipline, courage and fighting spirit her last hours have seldom been surpassed.'

The *Seydlitz*, Hipper's flagship, was terribly damaged, and a ship and a crew less stout would surely have perished. Both her after magazines were set on fire, cremating alive the crews of both turrets, so that out of a total of 165 men only two escaped. Flames and dense clouds of smoke rose higher than her masts, and all the time she continued firing with her remaining guns at a rate of six rounds per minute each, as compared with one round every forty-five seconds which was their normal rate of fire.

Meanwhile the huge fire aft was threatening at any moment to blow up the magazine. Petty Officer Wilhelm Heidkamp made his way through the smoke-filled alleyway, the walls of which were now red hot, reached the flooding valves for the magazine and, despite the fact that they were red hot, succeeded in turning both with his bare hands and thus saved the ship.

The *Lion*, with Beatty on board, had been disabled and fallen astern. Through a misunderstanding and a badly worded signal the British admiral second-in-command abandoned the pursuit of the fleeing Germans, who reached harbour safely.

To many in the German fleet the loss of the *Blücher* appeared to have been avoidable. They did not understand why a ship so weakly protected and armed should have been taken to sea in the first place nor why she had been given the most exposed place in the line.

These disconcerting events weighed heavily on morale. Nobody knew of the weaknesses which had been shown up in the British forces and, under the impact of the reverse at the Dogger Bank, it seemed that the High Seas Fleet had been written off as an offensive weapon. Tirpitz, of course, urged that the Fleet should act, but Ingenohl and his chief-of-staff Eckermann were removed from their posts.

Commenting on these changes, Captain Groos, the German Official Historian, suggests that Ingenohl may have lacked the complete loyalty of his admirals and especially that of Lans.

Pohl became Commander-in-Chief of the High Seas Fleet, being succeeded as Chief of the Naval Staff by Admiral Bachmann. Between these two men a dispute at once broke out.

When Pohl had been Chief of the Naval Staff he had successfully insisted that the *Flottenchef* should be subordinate to him. When, however, he became Commander-in-Chief himself he insisted that his relative status and that of Bachmann should be reversed, and he thus remained in control of the Fleet under the Kaiser.

However, surface operations of moment were not likely and, after the excitement of the beginning of the war, the Fleet was left to brood on its idleness and boredom began to gnaw at morale. Boredom faced the Grand Fleet too, but there the crews could sustain themselves with the knowledge that the British Navy controlled the surface of the sea, from which had been driven German warships and merchant shipping alike. Scapa Flow, after some months, became a base which was proof against U-boats. The Grand Fleet no longer had to keep on the move to make the ships more difficult targets, but Scapa offered nothing in the way of recreation. It was therefore necessary to provide amenities and this was done. Playing fields, tennis courts, golf courses, and huts to serve as canteens, concert halls and cinemas were built, while later an old freighter was fitted up as a theatre-ship with an auditorium and stage in the hold for amateur theatricals, the ever-present standby of bored Britons. The German authorities, however, did not think that arrangements of this kind were necessary, and crews had to make do with the traditional amusements of Kiel and Wilhelmshaven which were expensive and which grew scarce as the war continued.

Henceforward the British and German battle fleets spent most of the war in port. But there was a big difference between their respective positions. The Grand Fleet, by its mere existence and its ability to sortie when it seemed necessary, was able to support effectively the line of armed merchant cruisers from Scotland to Norway which cut Germany and her Allies from the supplies of the outside world. On the other hand, the High Seas Fleet was unable to interfere with the trade of Britain and her Allies, with the supply of their armed forces or with their movements around the globe.

Within the first few weeks of the war a number of German naval officers proposed that a counter blockade of Allied ports should be instituted by submarines. Blockade, or commerce raiding, by surface ships had meant that if a merchant ship, enemy or neutral, was stopped, a prize crew could be put on board and the ship sent into a friendly port, or else sunk after those on board had been taken off. Submarines could not operate like this but would depend for their success on being able to sink ships without warning, since a submarine on the surface is extremely vulnerable to any ship carrying even a single gun.

The idea of a U-boat blockade was submitted to Pohl and was rejected, partly because if such a blockade was to be successful it would entail sinking of neutral as well as Allied merchant ships (the sinking without warning of any merchant ship, Allied or neutral, was in fact contrary to international law); while an additional argument against the adoption of the policy was the very small number of U-boats in service at that time. This was a deficiency for which Tirpitz was blamed, but submarine development was still primitive in the first months of the war. Although the German navy possessed twenty-eight U-boats, four (*U-1* to *U-4*) were already obsolete and fit only for training purposes; fourteen more (*U-5 to U-18*) had petrol engines, the exhausts of which formed pillars of smoke by day and pillars of fire by night, while in bad weather when the boats were on the surface these exhausts admitted so much water that the engine-room personnel had to wear oilskins when on duty. Only the most recent ten boats (*U-19* to *U-28*) were really satisfactory, and at the outbreak of war there were only fifty-two spare torpedoes available for all the U-boats. Between August 1914 and the end of January 1915, eleven new boats were completed and eight had been lost; but Tirpitz considered that their boats were far too few for the planned operations. He proposed as a compromise that the blockade should be imposed only round the mouth of the Thames. However, after the Dogger Bank action it was decided that unrestricted submarine warfare should begin at once.

A comparison has been made between the opening of the

submarine campaign with only a handful of boats and the introduction of the tank during the battle of the Somme when only six machines were able to cross the British front line; in both cases the enemy was warned of the introduction of a new weapon under circumstances which did away with the advantage which surprise would have given had a large number of the new weapons been used.

At this time a shortage of officers, which was to have a fateful effect within two years on the High Seas Fleet, began to show itself; and seven battleships of the Fifth Squadron (five ships of the *Kaiser Wilhelm II* class, built 1895-1901, and two of the *Brandenburg* class, built 1890-94), were paid off because junior officers were needed for the new U-boats, destroyers and minesweepers about to come into service.

With the Naval High Command resolved not to risk the High Seas Fleet in a fight to a finish, and with the U-boats employed almost exclusively against Allied and neutral merchant shipping, mine warfare remained the only other method by which the Allied navies and merchant shipping could be harmed. German minelaying expeditions into the southern and central parts of the North Sea were made, to the great concern of Pohl, who feared lest the minelayers be caught by the enemy. Already, he pointed out in a memorandum, morale had been affected by the losses sustained by the German Navy since the beginning of the war, instancing notably the sinking on the first day of war of the auxiliary minelayer *Königin Luise*, of the light cruisers at Heligoland, the destroyer losses in the North Sea and the sinking of the *Blücher*.

Nevertheless Pohl agreed that the Fleet should make a number of short sorties to help cover minelaying operations. These sorties, numbering seven in all during 1915, were of very limited range and utility. The Fleet sailed in the morning, steamed on a course that was generally west-northwest for about 120 miles and then returned, to be back again off Wilhelmshaven by the evening of the second day. Trotha, captain of the *Kaiser* and a noted 'activist', was extremely critical of this proceeding for, he pointed out, the Fleet stood no chance of meeting any of the detached units of the Grand Fleet whose destruction might justify the risks that the High Seas Fleet was running from British mines or submarines. In an effort to reduce the pressure which his 'activist' officers were exercising upon him, Pohl had recourse to the Imperial family.

At that time one of the Kaiser's sons, Prince Adalbert, was serving as navigating officer of the battleship *Kaiser*, and Pohl approved the idea that the Prince be given special leave to visit his father at GHQ and explain to him how important it was that Pohl's policy should be upheld and that the Fleet should not be risked. In the course of one of these visits – made, it was discovered afterwards, without permission – the Prince told his father that in fact Pohl was risking the Fleet in sorties for which he should have asked the Kaiser's permission. Müller intervened and begged that the Prince should not bother his father with such matters. A piquant feature of this episode was the fact that at the time the Prince's captain was Trotha.

While these arguments were in progress the Army, on 1 August 1915, sent an SOS to the Navy asking for the help of the High Seas Fleet in the Baltic operations against the northern flank of the Russian army, in front of Riga.

The appeal was answered with bad grace by Pohl, and by protests and grumbles by less senior officers, led by Trotha who, though only a four-ring *Kapitän zur See*, wrote directly to Müller, Chief of the Kaiser's Naval Cabinet and a full admiral, under whom he had previously served.

There had been complaints before from the officers about the handling of the High Seas Fleet, but this letter of Trotha's dated 9 July was the first serious indication of what was happening and what the officers of the Fleet were thinking. Trotha began by saying that the Navy had entered the war with complete self-confidence, based on the fact that it was the favourite creation of the German people and was that part of Germany's armed forces which most clearly represented the expression of Germany's attainment of world power status. The Navy had been certain that it would justify the hopes placed in it.

> Today [went on Trotha] there can be no doubt that these bold ideas have faded. The backbone of the Navy and its strongest part, the High Seas Fleet, has not been employed. Doubt is growing more and more whether it ever will be. The more thoughtful men among the crews ask whether they had not been wrong to have cheerfully borne the strenuous work of the years of preparation for war. Had all this work not been in vain? . . . Why is it that the weapon which stood at the centre of policy at home and abroad during the last generation has not been employed in Germany's struggle for existence?
>
> It is admitted that the government must itself decide when to commit the Fleet.* Waiting for that time could easily be borne if there was confidence in a firm leadership. . . . More and more the feeling has spread that the decisive will of strong leadership is missing. As a result the crews of the Fleet feel that, on the occasions when the enemy has been met, a strong leadership has been lacking and that, when the whole Fleet went to sea, it avoided the enemy. And now comes the grave moment in which everyone feels his own honour endangered as is the honour of the Service. This danger can only be overcome by the personal influence of the leader and the selfless devotion of even the most junior officers to their superiors.

Above all leadership was needed, and that leadership, in the opinion of the vast majority of the officers of the Fleet, said Trotha, could only be provided by Tirpitz. Müller replied that he thought that Pohl was the best man available but that he could wish there were a better.

Captain Michaelis, Pohl's Chief-of-Staff, wrote at this time to Captain Zenker, Chief-of-Staff to Admiral Bachmann, who himself was Chief of the Naval Staff, also saying that the appointment of Tirpitz as Commander-in-Chief was highly to be desired. With Tirpitz commanding both the High Seas Fleet and the fleet in the Baltic, Scheer should be *Flottenchef* of the High Seas Fleet. As for the prospects of a fleet action, Michaelis said Pohl would obey orders but he should have a

* This view of Trotha's contrasts with the line which he took, together with Scheer, Hipper and Levetzow in October 1918, when the four men agreed to commit the Fleet in an all-out battle without any reference to the government.

chief-of-staff who put the chances of the High Seas Fleet higher than ten to one against. (This was Michaelis himself.) Such a chief-of-staff, he suggested, might be Trotha or possibly Behncke.

Summing up his views Michaelis, after a series of arguments with Pohl, said that he himself was full of 'bitterness and hopelessness'. Either the war was to be conducted with big ships, in which case the Germans would have to fight soon no matter where or against what odds; or, if they did not wish to fight with big ships, they should put as many men as possible into other branches of the Service, pay off the Second and Fourth Squadrons, abandon the prospect of using the High Seas Fleet against England and restrict it to maintaining command of the Baltic. Only in this way, said Michaelis on 15 July, would it be possible to defeat England. 'If it is not desired to wage war against England with big ships, a strong personality must be appointed as commander and everything devoted to the prosecution of the war in the air and under the sea'. Unfortunately for Michaelis's ideas, the submarine war was rapidly coming to a standstill at this time owing to American diplomatic pressure, and hope for a strong unified command of the German navy grew dim.

The dispute between the United States and Germany, following the sinking of the *Lusitania* without warning, had been temporarily settled by the Germans in reply to American protests, with a promise not to sink any more passenger ships. On 19 August, however, the White Star liner *Arabic* was torpedoed and sunk by *U-24* and two Americans were drowned. The demand by the United States government that the Germans cease to put American lives at risk by attacks on passenger ships was accepted by the Germans, who once again promised not to sink passenger ships and, to avoid a repetition of previous incidents, agreed to call off unrestricted submarine warfare on 18 September except for the laying of mines and for operations in the Mediterranean, where it was not expected there would be any Americans. For protesting against this decision, Bachmann was relieved of his post as Chief of the

Naval Staff and returned to Kiel as admiral commanding the Baltic naval station; while Tirpitz, whose offer of resignation was rejected, was told that in future it would not be his duty to advise the Kaiser on matters of foreign affairs.

Bachmann's successor was Admiral von Holtzendorff, who had been *Flottenchef* until 1913 and had then retired. Holtzendorff was an officer who liked very much to live as a *grand seigneur* and behaved accordingly, but without great gifts. He was remembered in the Navy for the delight which he took while on the Far Eastern station teaching young girls to swim in shallow water. During his period of command he had been involved in an unsuccessful attempt to secure the dismissal of Tirpitz. Tirpitz had then been strong enough to beat off the attack, but in the closing months of 1915 his power was ebbing fast and he had to appeal to Müller to intercede on his behalf with the Kaiser, an appeal which did not produce satisfactory results.

Now Holtzendorff was recalled because it was believed that he could bridge the gaps between the Kaiser, the Navy and the civil government, the first and last seeing as their over-riding priority the need to keep the United States from joining the war on the side of the Allies. In the autumn of 1915 this became of particular importance as the Germans were hoping to persuade Bulgaria to declare war on the Allies. This would revolutionize the situation in the Balkans, for Serbia would be overrun and a direct overland supply route between Germany and the Turkish fronts would be feasible. For the time being the Bulgarians hung back, unwilling to commit themselves for fear of being confronted by the United States.

The changes in the autumn of 1915 meant that the hopes of the 'activists' for a strong unified command of the Navy grew dim, but there was one important by-product of the suspension of unrestricted submarine warfare. There was to be a fundamental change in the policy governing the employment of the High Seas Fleet and this made it necessary that Pohl should be replaced and a new *Flottenchef* appointed, for he was now under fire from two directions; on the one hand the 'activists' were complaining because he had cut short the last sortie of the Fleet for no good reason and, on the other, he was criticized because he had taken the Fleet to sea at all. He had, it was said, only done so out of 'vanity'.

The Kaiser at this time was cultivating his theory that the war then in progress was the first of a series of Punic Wars between Germany and England. This first war would end in something like a draw but, after peace had been concluded, Germany would expand her navy and then throw down a second and final challenge in a later war.

Pohl rejected this idea firmly in a letter to the Kaiser on 28 December. On 7 January 1916 he received on board the *Friedrich der Grosse* Captain Magnus von Levetzow, appointed through the intermediary of Michaelis as the head of the Operations Division of the staff of the *Flottenchef*. Levetzow and Pohl talked together for two hours, Levetzow stressing the very great disappointment of the officers of the Navy at the passive handling of the Fleet. It should and would be possible, he said, to act offensively. The difference in the relative strengths of the two fleets should not be allowed to lead to complete passivity. There was no longer confidence in the leadership of the Fleet.

The interview between Pohl and Levetzow throws much light on the low level to which the morale of the officers of the High Seas Fleet had sunk, on occasion, almost to the level of insubordination. It will be seen that, after the mutiny of 1918, left-wing critics of the senior German naval officers were to refer to it as having been caused by what they termed 'The Admirals' Rebellion'. Whether such a 'rebellion' actually took place is something which can be examined later, but certainly the state of mind of the officers of the Fleet, characterized by Michaelis as 'bitterness and hopelessness', was providing raw material for it.

But there were now to follow events which put off for months any bold initiative by the Naval High Command acting independently of the German government; and, at the same time, the morale of the lower deck, which does not seem to have been affected by anything worse than boredom, was also to receive a great stimulus. Not for another eighteen months did the first symptoms of collapse show themselves, after the hardships of the Turnip Winter of 1916-7, the discouragement of Verdun and the Somme and the fact that the Fleet had once more been relegated to a policy of inactivity, as the leading part in the naval war was assumed by the U-boat arm.

For some time the unhappy Pohl had been suffering from cancer, a fact which he had tried to conceal, but he collapsed on 9 January, two days after his meeting with Levetzow. He was removed to a hospital ship and died six weeks later.

In the meantime a new team had taken over in the Fleet. Vice-Admiral Reinhold Scheer, commanding the Third Squadron, had temporarily succeeded Pohl when the latter became ill and was confirmed as *Flottenchef* on 24 January, with his flag in the *Friedrich der Grosse*. Trotha was Chief of Staff, and Levetzow remained in his new position as chief of the Operations Division of the Fleet Staff.

The three men began to plan future operations. There was no intention of challenging the Grand Fleet to a decisive battle. The moment for that had passed, thanks to the newly completed British battleships.

Notwithstanding this over-riding limitation on their action, Scheer and his staff believed that there was much that could be done to harry the Grand Fleet and damage it, from the point of view of material and of morale. In the first place Scheer still believed that, by a series of raids on English coast towns, it would be possible to lure to sea comparatively small British detachments which could then be cut off and attacked by superior German forces. The Kaiser approved Scheer's plans and the High Seas Fleet was thus no longer subject to the same crippling restrictions as it had been under Ingenohl and Pohl. For the time being there was a real break with the past. Another change followed on 12 March when Tirpitz finally resigned, despairing of being able to persuade the Kaiser and the Chancellor not to agree to American demands for what amounted to the suspension of the U-boat campaign against

Allied and neutral merchant shipping. Piqued by not having been invited to an important meeting which decided that the U-boat campaign was not to be restarted for the time being, Tirpitz wrote to the Kaiser saying that his health would no longer permit him to continue his work as Secretary of State. He at once received from the Kaiser the acceptance of his resignation and was succeeded by Admiral Capelle, like Holtzendorff a retired admiral brought back to the active list. Previous to this retirement Capelle had worked closely with Tirpitz at the Admiralty, but lacked the imaginative determination of his former master.

Meanwhile, Scheer, tentatively at first and then with increasing assurance, was opening his campaign. He had begun with an attack in the Hoofden, the German name for that part of the North Sea south of a line from Terschelling to the Wash. This was always an area in which the Germans hoped that they would be well rewarded by sudden raids. It was easy of access either from their own bases in Germany or from those in occupied Flanders. At the same time, it was a long way away from the bases of the Grand Fleet. Thus it was always possible for the Germans to make a dash against the merchant ships taking food from Holland to Britain, while if they pressed their attack the transport routes across the Straits of Dover, upon which the British Army depended, would also be exposed.

On the night of 10-11 February a force of twenty-five destroyers, disposed in a line of eight divisions abreast, each of three or four ships, steamed across the North Sea to the Dogger Bank, where they came upon a British minesweeping flotilla, one unit of which, the sloop *Arabis*, they sank. This was not a serious loss, but the *Arethusa*, one of the latest British light cruisers, struck a mine off Harwich, part of a field which had just been laid by one of the Flanders U-boats and was lost. Thus the Germans could be reasonably pleased with the outcome of the first of the new operations, despite torpedo failures; only three or four exploded out of nineteen fired at close range. To increase pressure on the Straits of Dover at this time a division of three German destroyers was based on Zeebrugge.

The prospect of further 'activism' by Scheer increased the fears which the British had had since the beginning of the war for the safety of shipping in the Thames Estuary and in the Dover Straits, for they had long thought it possible for the Germans to operate in the Flanders Bight and the Straits of Dover. Under cover of a sortie by the High Seas Fleet a force might be detached to raid Yarmouth or Lowestoft, or even the Thames Estuary. Despite mines in the Straits it would also be possible for a strong force to attack our cross-Channel communications.

Sir Julian Corbett wrote in the British Official History:

Another attainable objective was the mass of shipping which accumulated every night in the Downs, for a squadron of battleships which had penetrated into the Straits for a few hours would have been presented with a target of a hundred defenceless merchantmen. The havoc that a well-supported raid in the Dover Straits would have brought about in our supply of food and materials was, therefore, beyond calculation. Nor was this all; blocking operations might also be attempted against the vital French ports through which the army was drawing its supplies, and finally we had to be on our guard against an endeavour to turn the Allied sea flank by landing a force at La Panne between Nieuport and Dunkirk.

These were the prospects, glittering for the Germans and appalling for the British, which were held out by Scheer's next sortie. But in fact it had a very different objective. Ever since the beginning of the war, Irish extremists of the Sinn Fein had been trying to persuade the Germans to help them against the British. Sir Roger Casement, a former member of the British Consular Service, afterwards hanged for treason, had been in Germany trying to recruit an Irish Legion amongst the British prisoners-of-war, and eventually the Germans agreed to help. Twenty thousand rifles captured from the Russians and ten German machine-guns were to be sent to Ireland in a disguised merchant ship and landed at Tralee in the south-west of the country. Casement himself was to arrive in a U-boat and the rising would begin in Dublin over the Easter holidays.

Casement was arrested almost as soon as he landed but the rising began on Easter Monday, 24 April, facilitated by the fact that the local situation seemed so quiet that a large proportion of the British officers had gone to a race meeting. On the same day the High Seas Fleet left the Jade. The five battle-cruisers of the First Scouting Group were temporarily under command of Rear-Admiral Boedicker, Hipper being ashore ill. They were to shell Lowestoft and Yarmouth, while the battleships of the Fleet would remain in support about seventy miles off the British coast, to the west of Terschelling. A result of the operation would be the diversion of attention from events in Ireland.

On the way through the minefields in the Heligoland Bight Boedicker's flagship, the *Seydlitz*, struck a mine and had to return to port. Boedicker shifted his flag to the *Lützow*, and with the rest of the Scouting Force went on his way. Lowestoft was shelled on the morning of 25 April beginning at 04.10. The Harwich Force, under Commodore Tyrwhitt, arrived and tried to lure the Germans away. None of the British ships was larger than a light cruiser, and Boedicker failed to take an excellent opportunity to fall upon them with his four battle-cruisers and destroy them. Scheer, although only fifty miles away, made no attempt to exploit the situation because his Zeppelins were unable to provide adequate reconnaissance, and he and Boedicker both turned for home. Beatty led the British forces down the North Sea in heavy weather, missing the enemy by about forty-five miles.

The British and Germans were both disappointed by the outcome of the Lowestoft raid and began to plan further operations, Scheer intending another raid on the English coast while Jellicoe devized a scheme which might lure Scheer into a trap.

Both sides based their plans on the idea of sending forward a detached part of their fleet to act as bait for the enemy while keeping their main bodies out of sight, but within a distance from which it would be possible to intervene if the bait were taken.

Scheer's bait was to be his battle-cruisers of the First Scouting

Group, which were to bombard Sunderland. This, it was calculated, would bring the Grand Fleet southward through waters carefully prepared with U-boats released from their war on merchant shipping and by freshly sown minefields. Jellicoe's plan, on the other hand, was to send two squadrons of light cruisers through the Skagerrak and deep into the Kattegat, while holding the Grand Fleet to support them if attacked.

Scheer was obliged to postpone his operation day after day because the weather would not permit Zeppelin reconnaissance, until the submarines in waiting off the English coast were beginning to run out of fuel. He then decided that he would have to abandon his plan for an attack on Sunderland as he was still without the co-operation of his airships, and do something less sensational and content himself with taking the Fleet up the coast of Jutland as far as the entrance to the Skagerrak, believing that the presence of his Fleet at sea would soon become known to the British.

The operation by the Grand Fleet was fixed for 2 June, but before that date 40 OB began to pick up clues indicating that the High Seas Fleet was coming out, and the Grand Fleet left its bases to meet it.

The strength and the losses of both sides in the battle of Jutland which followed can be seen from the following tables.

Strengths of the Rival Fleets

British	*German*
28 dreadnought battleships	16 dreadnought battleships
9 battle-cruisers	5 battle-cruisers
	6 pre-dreadnought battleships
8 armoured cruisers	
26 light cruisers	11 light cruisers
79 destroyers	61 destroyers
1 seaplane carrier	

Losses

3 battle-cruisers	1 battle-cruiser
3 armoured cruisers	1 pre-dreadnought battleship
8 destroyers	4 light cruisers
	5 destroyers

The battle-cruisers of Beatty and Hipper, with their attendant light cruisers and destroyers, met very nearly head-on in the early afternoon of 31 May. Hipper, with the weaker force (five battle-cruisers to six) steamed at full speed back southwards to Scheer and the main body of the High Seas Fleet. The British followed in hot pursuit and lost two of their big ships, but, though it was now they who were the weaker, they continued the chase until they reached Scheer, when they turned round and headed back northward, followed by the Germans.

When Beatty and his pursuers came in sight of Jellicoe and the Grand Fleet, about three hours after the battle had begun, Jellicoe deployed his fleet between the Germans and their bases.

Three times in mist, in failing light and in darkness, the Germans tried to force their way through the long line of British ships, and at the third attempt they were successful in cutting through the tail of the British line, but the communications within the Grand Fleet were so poor that Jellicoe, far away to the south, did not learn what was going on; and, when it was clear that the Germans had escaped, turned despondently for home, conscious that the Grand Fleet had failed to take advantage of its opportunity to destroy the enemy.

It took some hours after Scheer had returned to Wilhelmshaven for him to appreciate that he had got his fleet safely home with the loss of but one major unit, and that he had succeeded in inflicting much heavier casualties on the enemy than they had inflicted on him. During the action he had remarked, according to his Flag Lieutenant, Ernst von Weizsäcker: 'If I'm chucked out of the Navy because of this, I don't care.'

The next morning, as they headed home, Scheer recalled that he had invited a general to dine on board, and decided that he had better cancel the invitation as no one would be feeling festive; but later in the morning when details of losses on both sides became known he decided that the invitation to the general could stand and he ordered champagne to be served on the bridge.

Officers and ratings alike were pleased and proud of their

battle. Months afterwards, in the dark days of 1917-8, a German sailor remarked: 'If only we could have had a battle like that every couple of months everything would have been all right.'

But by that time the German lower deck began to realize how easily the battle might have had a different ending. M. Charles Vidil, in his book *Les Mutineries de la Marine Allemande*, summarized what he considered to be the dominant impression in the minds of the German crews after the battle:

> The sailors had kept the memory of interminable lines of British ships, seen between banks of fog, and formed the impression, not altogether inaccurate, of having had a fortunate escape. Without needing to leave Scapa Flow the British battleships contributed to victory. Their grey shapes once seen never ceased to haunt the minds of the German sailors.

The two points of view were not mutually contradictory. It was natural that, after successfully escaping from the superior force of their enemy upon whom they had inflicted much greater damage than they themselves had received, they should be pleased, excited and ready again for the fray. But it was equally natural that a reaction should occur and that they should realize that another battle, however well they fought, would not bring them final victory.

Scheer certainly saw this immediately upon his return to harbour, and reported to the Kaiser on 4 July 1916: 'There can be no doubt that even the most successful outcome of a fleet action in this war will not force the English to make peace.'

Accordingly he recommended the resumption of unrestricted submarine warfare.

It seems strange now to think that the factor which, up to the winter of 1916-7, delayed the German decision to resume unrestricted submarine warfare was not the prospect of American intervention, backed by the whole weight of American industry and a huge fresh army being thrown into the struggle, but the threat of the tiny armies of Holland and Denmark. The intervention of those two countries, it was feared, would follow the sinking without warning of their merchant ships; and in the late summer of 1916 the German army was so very hard pressed that it seemed to the German General Staff that the entry into the war of fresh enemies might prove fatal, for the great German offensive at Verdun and the Franco-British offensive on the Somme had cost the Germans terrible casualties. In addition, the Russian offensive in Galicia and Romania's declaration of war against the Central Powers further worsened the position of the latter, which appeared to be on a knife edge. Accordingly, it was decided on 14 August that for the time being there could be no question of risking the reactions of the neutrals to unrestricted U-boat war.

While the German Government and the High Command were discussing these problems, Scheer decided to take the High Seas Fleet to sea again. According to the German Official History the purpose of this was 'to force the English Fleet to come out and show the world the unbroken strength of the German Fleet'. However, Professor Marder remarks, 'the sortie was partly intended to restore the morale of the Fleet after its recent shattering experience'.

Another attempt was to be made to bombard Sunderland. U-boats would again be posted to intercept the Grand Fleet when it emerged from its bases, and on this occasion aerial reconnaissance would be provided by Zeppelins. Room 40 OB was at the top of its form; so quick off the mark in its appreciation that the enemy was putting to sea on 18 August that the Grand Fleet was already on its way to intercept him before he himself had sailed.

The total strength of the High Seas Fleet was now down to nineteen battleships and two battle-cruisers, against twenty-two battleships and five battle-cruisers at Jutland, owing to losses and damage sustained there and also to Scheer's decision to leave behind the pre-dreadnought battleships of the Second Squadron.

Early in the morning of 19 August the British submarine *E-23* torpedoed the battleship *Westfalen*, the last ship of the long German line, which was obliged to return home, signalling its plight despite strict orders to maintain wireless silence.

The Germans steamed on a westerly course towards the English coast, while the British were steaming south to intercept. Just before 06.00, however, the light cruiser *Nottingham*, scouting ahead of the fleet, was torpedoed twice by *U-52* and half-an-hour later was again torpedoed, and sank. It was not clear whether the explosions had been due to mines or torpedoes, and as there was a possibility that the sunken ship had been caught in a minefield into which the Grand Fleet would be steaming, Jellicoe turned back while the possible existence of the minefield was investigated. After two hours it was clear that a U-boat had been responsible and the Grand Fleet resumed its course to the south.

Meanwhile Scheer had also been diverted from his objective. The Zeppelin *L-13*, scouting to the southward of the High Seas Fleet, spotted the Harwich Force coming northward and reported it. The airship's captain was the peacetime head of the Magdeburg Fire Brigade and inexperienced in ship recognition, so that he reported the British light cruisers as capital ships. If this signal were correct it meant that part of the Grand Fleet was separated from the main body and Scheer had only to turn south to be able to achieve a great success.

Scheer did turn south but, ignorant of his presence, the Harwich Force turned south as well, and it soon became clear to Scheer that he would not be able to overtake it. Accordingly, as it was too late to attack Sunderland, he decided to return home, and there was nothing for Jellicoe and Beatty to do but follow his example.

On their way back north the Grand Fleet ran into the U-boat patrol line off Flamborough Head. The light cruiser *Falmouth* was hit four times by *U-66* and *U-63* and finally sank while being towed home forty-eight hours after she had been first hit. Scheer planned another sortie for the month of September but had to give up the idea because of bad weather.

In October the High Seas Fleet did make a brief sortie, the last for eighteen months, when on 18 October it swept as far as the Dogger Bank without incident, save for the fact that one of its scouting light cruisers, the *München*, was twice torpedoed by the submarine *E-38*. As usual the British torpedoes failed to do enough damage to sink the ship that they had hit, and the *München* was towed home.

The Grand Fleet did not put to sea, as there seemed no chance of being able to catch the enemy, while there was a strong possibility of more submarine ambushes having been laid, and Jellicoe did not consider that he had sufficent destroyers to provide an anti-submarine screen for the cruisers and capital ships of the Grand Fleet in the southern waters of the North Sea, that is, those closest to the German bases. In fact Scheer had no U-boats with him; for the Naval Staff had decided, against Scheer's advice, that they be used against merchant ships in accordance with international law. This meant that an attacking U-boat was obliged to surface to stop a merchant ship and then wait until its crew had taken to the boats before sinking her. Scheer held that this exposed the U-boat unnecessarily to the attack of enemy anti-submarine craft. For the time being, however, political considerations, urged by the Chancellor, persuaded the Kaiser that challenging the neutrals by sinking their ships without warning was too risky a policy at a critical moment of the war.

Scheer was now unwilling to go to sea without the U-boats of which he had been deprived, while Jellicoe was unwilling to enter waters near the enemy coast because he feared those same U-boats which had, without his knowledge, been withdrawn to take part in the war against merchant shipping.

However, despite the fact that the Grand Fleet was limited in its freedom of action, it was still able to protect the movements of Allied shipping all over the world, from its bases in Scotland. The transport of troops, war materials, foodstuffs and the like still went on across the surface of the sea, of which the Navy's command was so very nearly as absolute as could be imagined. Nor did it appear to the Germans that this command could be shaken save by underwater attack. Their one hope at sea was the U-boat, and for the rest of the war the U-boat was the German capital ship. The value attached by Scheer to individual units of the U-boat fleet was shown in an incident which occurred at the beginning of November, when *U-30* and *U-20* were returning from patrol. The diesels of the former broke down and her calls for help were heard by *U-20* with Lieutenant Schwieger in command (this was the boat and the man which had sunk the *Lusitania*), who came to her aid. Running repairs were carried out and the two boats made their way cautiously down the coasts of Norway and Denmark towards home. Driven off course by a strong current, they both ran aground in a fog off Bovbierg in Jutland. By altering their trim and running their engines full astern, both boats got off after about two hours, whereupon *U-20* ran aground again, and this time it proved impossible to free her. Next morning she was sighted by the British submarine *J-1* (Commander Noel Laurence) while on patrol. Laurence decided not to take immediate advantage of the German's plight. Instead he settled down to watch her through his periscope and explained to his crew what he was doing.

'They'll not leave her like that. They'll send up tugs to get her off and destroyers to protect the tugs, and light cruisers and maybe a couple of battleships as well to protect the destroyers . . .'

J-1 spent the night waiting, and in the morning there came out of the mist from southward, as Laurence had foretold, tugs, destroyers and no fewer than eleven battleships. The sea was rough with a heavy swell, which not only made it difficult for Laurence to aim his torpedoes but suddenly forced him to the surface in full view of the enemy. He dived again, but this time the sea forced him down below periscope depth, so that he was blind. Gingerly J-1 was brought upwards until Laurence had a momentary glimpse of what he took to be the leading battleship of the German line, right in front of his sights, at ideal range. He pressed the button, the torpedo ran true and the battleship was hit, just as the seas forced *J-1* down again. She went so deep that he could no longer see the next battleship and had to fire blind. Once again he was rewarded by hearing an explosion. The two battleships hit were the *Grosser Kurfürst* and *Kronprinz*. Both were damaged and, in addition, *U-20* was lost as it was impossible to tow her off, and she was blown up where she lay. Laurence had already torpedoed the battle-cruiser *Moltke* during operations in the Gulf of Riga the previous year, and is the only submarine commander in history to have torpedoed three capital ships.

When news of Laurence's successful double attack reached Imperial Headquarters at Pless, Scheer was summoned by the Kaiser, who criticized him for having risked his big ships for the sake of a couple of submarines.

Scheer replied by saying: 'Every U-boat is of such importance that it is worth risking the whole available fleet to afford it assistance and support.'

With this the Kaiser seems to have been satisfied, and Scheer went on to urge again the re-introduction of unrestricted U-boat warfare.

THREE

The winter of 1916-7 proved to be the turning point of the war. Although it was to continue for two more terrible years, at vast cost of life, its course, once the U-boat menace had been countered, was to run straight to victory for the Western Allies.

Two important events in the last month of 1916 had been the prelude to the year of decision. First, on 12 December had come a German offer of peace negotiations. This had been rejected by the Allies because, they said, there was no indication given of what terms the Germans had in mind. Lloyd George, who had just become Prime Minister, declared that there could be no settlement which did not provide for 'restitution, reparation, guarantee against repetition'. And of the Germans being ready for that, there was no sign.

Second, on 15 December the year's fighting at Verdun ended with a sudden and successful French counter-attack which so shocked Ludendorff that he stated that only unrestricted submarine warfare could save Germany. This was at last decided upon and the campaign began on 1 February. Doubts as to the wisdom of this step were temporarily removed by the victory of the combined Austrian, German and Bulgarian forces, which drove the Romanians out of the war. 1 February was chosen to coincide with the first shipments of the Argentine grain harvest to Europe. All Europe was suffering from a very severe winter, known in Germany as the 'turnip winter', which had much intensified the effects of the Allied blockade on the food supplies of the Central Powers.

On land the German strategy was to stand on the defensive

in the West during the year. In preparation for this and, in particular, to deal with the feared reaction of Denmark and Holland to the U-boat war, which meant moving troops to cover the Danish and Dutch frontiers, the Germans on the Western Front carried out a notable withdrawal to shorten their lines, taking up new and well-prepared positions behind a twenty-mile belt of scorched earth, known to them as the Siegfried Line and to the Allies as the Hindenburg Line.

Holland and Denmark did not move; the United States entered the war and during the next few months everything turned upon the U-boats preventing troops from America and supplies from all over the world reaching Europe. The Germans were optimistic. Before the resources of the United States could be mobilized, Britain would be starved out of the war. In January 1917 Holtzendorff said: 'I do not hesitate to declare that under existing circumstances we can force England to make peace, thanks to unrestricted U-boat warfare'.

Similarly, Capelle, Tirpitz's successor, forecast in April 1917 that six months would be sufficient to bring victory to Germany. Despite these forecasts Admiral Spindler, the official German historian of the U-boat, says that the German Navy at no time claimed that it would be able to operate with decisive results against the transports bringing American troops to Europe.

As the United States came into the war Russia went out and, in between the two revolutions in March and November, the huge Russian Army, having suffered vast casualties, crumbled away. Amidst these tremendous happenings it is perhaps not surprising that the German Naval High Command failed to appreciate the fact that the first tares were appearing in the discipline of the High Seas Fleet.

From the evidence which was presented to the post-war enquiry by the Reichstag on the causes of Germany's defeat, it appears that the first evidence of indiscipline going as far as sabotage was provided in the battleship *Helgoland* during the first part of the month of September 1916, when someone interfered with the firing mechanism of one of the guns. As a result, sentries were placed on all guns in the ship, but it is significant that the sabotage was believed on board to have been committed as a protest against poor food, and that the crew considered that the food had improved considerably afterwards.

Just at this time the Germans were forced once again to take steps to deal with the shortage of junior officers needed for the new U-boats, destroyers and minesweepers which were being completed. The war was becoming a little ships' war or a 'lieutenant-commanders' and lieutenants' war', and to supply officers for these ships it was necessary to draft from the big ships of the High Seas Fleet many officers of middle rank, the watch-keepers and the divisional officers who were those in closest touch with the ratings, charged with their discipline and with listening to their complaints.

In the first stage of the process of finding more officers the pre-dreadnoughts of the Second Squadron were paid off. Later it was necessary to take officers from the more modern battleships and battle-cruisers remaining in commission. These were replaced by young midshipmen and sub-lieutenants who had just completed their training. Many of them, it will be seen, were too inexperienced to carry out their duties.

Another result of the resumption of the unrestricted submarine warfare was a change of priorities in shipbuilding, the most important of which was that work was stopped on all but one of the ten German capital ships building or on order. This, however, did not prevent the Kaiser plaguing the overworked construction department of the Admiralty with demands for the design and construction of new capital ships of 45,000 tons, and the production of gigantic 50-centimetre (19.75-inch) guns.

Meanwhile Capelle had to draw up a U-boat building programme for the immediate future. He was in an embarrassing position, for if he really believed his own prophecy that the war would be victoriously ended by October 1917 there was no point in laying down any further craft, since at that time the types of submarines on order were taking between eighteen months and two years to build. In fact, however, he did order fifty-one boats in February 1917 and ninety-five more in the following June, only to be reproached in the Reichstag for not having ordered more.

His reply was remarkable; at the end of the war, he said, there would be so many U-boats that it would be necessary to set aside a whole port in which to lay them up. Moreover, it would be a bad thing for the officers' career structure of the future navy if there were too many U-boats, as there would not be sufficient big ships as commands for more senior officers.

The savage gale of the submarine war blew up on 1 February, and gathered intensity day after day. In January 180 ships had been sunk, totalling 285,000 tons, British, Allied and neutral; in February these figures were 260 ships of 469,000 tons, in March 338 ships of 524,000 tons and in April, the most dreadful month of the war, 430 ships of 852,000 tons. 19 April, the worst day of the worst month, saw eleven British merchantmen and eight fishing vessels destroyed, and one out of every four ships leaving a British port did not return.

We know the dramatic way in which that most undramatic person, Jellicoe, now British First Sea Lord, broke the news of the frightful crisis to Rear-Admiral W. S. Sims, United States Navy, who, on the declaration of war by the United States, had been sent to Britain to arrange co-operation between the two navies, and who was himself to command the United States naval forces in Europe. Jellicoe set out the stark facts.

Sims commented: 'It looks as though the Germans are winning the war'.

'They will win unless we can stop the losses, and stop them soon', said Jellicoe.

'Is there no solution for the problem?' asked Sims.

'Absolutely none that we can see now.'

These are Jellicoe's words as quoted by Sims in his book *The Victory at Sea*, published in 1920. Afterwards Jellicoe claimed that, to the best of his memory, what he actually said was: 'None, at present, as the measures devised cannot be immediately successful'.

There followed, within the confines of the Admiralty and No. 10 Downing Street, the greatest of all convoy battles. This was not one in which submarines opposed escort vessels, merchant ships and aircraft, and in which torpedoes were matched against depth-charges and bombs, but one in which the brash determination of Lloyd George clashed with Jellicoe's dreary pessimism. The Prime Minister was resolved that something must be done to save the sea communications of Britain and her Allies, and he believed that it could only be the introduction of the convoy system. This meant organization of the threatened merchantmen into groups around which the anti-submarine craft could be concentrated for their defence. Hitherto, for the most part, the merchant ships had sailed individually and the anti-submarine craft had simply patrolled given areas of the sea, so that it was almost by chance alone that they encountered a U-boat. Now, however, the enemy, if he wished to attack a merchantman, could only do so by seeking out a convoy and challenging its escort.

However, when faced with the proposed general use of the convoy, Jellicoe maintained the same attitude of hopelessness which he had adopted when discussing the U-boat problem with Sims. After convoys had been introduced during the summer of 1917 and had proved a success, there was a great shifting of ground by the First Sea Lord and his supporters, who tried to excuse their opposition on the grounds that, until the United States entered the war, there were not sufficient warships available. But, as the tides of controversy swirl away over the past half-century, it would seem that, in fact, Jellicoe made some vast miscalculations which had nothing to do with the number of his escort vessels. Typical of his negative attitude was his contention that merchant service officers would be unable to sail their ships in convoy, partly because of inexperience and partly from lack of various special fittings needed in the engine-room and on the bridge for accurate station-keeping. Further, Jellicoe declared that the convoy system would also be unworkable because all the most capable officers of the merchant service had entered the navy through the Royal Navy Reserve. The tactlessness of this statement, made at a time when ever more difficult and more dangerous work was being demanded of the merchant service, was matched only by its inaccuracy and was particularly surprising because Jellicoe's own father had been a merchant service captain.

Meanwhile, after April the merchant shipping losses had begun to fall; to 551,000 tons in May, rose again to 663,000 tons in June and then a gradual if intermittent decline to 260,000 tons in November and 353,000 tons in December. At the same time sinkings of U-boats rose from two boats in April to ten in September. The surface ships, with rapidly expanding use of aircraft, especially small non-rigid airships nicknamed 'blimps', had the upper hand and held it to the end of the war, although the U-boats continued to do great damage and never gave up the struggle until they were ordered to do so by their own government in October 1918.

It had not taken long for some Germans to realize that, despite their great successes in the first weeks of the U-boat campaign, they were not going to win the war within the wildly optimistic time-limits set by Holtzendorff and Capelle. As early as 10 June, Matthias Erzberger, a leading Catholic member of the Reichstag who had not opposed the U-boat war but who had been very doubtful about its success, discovered from Colonel Bauer, the General Staff's representative in Berlin, that the Supreme Command was making preparations for a campaign during the winter of 1917-8, although the official story had been that the war would be over by then. Moreover, on 19 June Hindenburg revealed his doubts when he wrote to the Chancellor warning him to check excessive optimism in the press as to the results of the U-boat campaign and, in particular, against papers spreading the belief that the war would be over by the autumn.

During the first months of the U-boats' ferocious onslaught, the High Seas Fleet had remained confined in its little area of the Heligoland Bight or had gone, squadron by squadron, into the Baltic for exercises. The submarines were now the teeth of German sea-power and the rest of the navy took up a supporting role. Accordingly Scheer issued an order explaining that the Fleet would now be obliged to take second place in the waging of the war at sea; but, he said, when the U-boats had achieved victory, that would signify the rebirth of the High Seas Fleet. This, of course, was a reappearance of the idea that the principal role of the High Seas Fleet was to make an impressive show of Germany's strength in peacetime.

But Scheer himself was not satisfied with such a performance by the High Seas Fleet. The war was to be won by the sinking of Allied and neutral merchant shipping and he believed that the Fleet should be allowed to take part. Accordingly he proposed an operation against British and Dutch shipping which, running between the Dutch ports and the Thames, was a most important source for the British of fats and dairy produce. The plans for this operation are interesting because they foreshadowed those adopted more than two years later for the first phase of what was to have been the final decisive battle between the British and German battle fleets.

Hipper, with his battle-cruisers and light cruisers, was to seek out the enemy shipping and attack while the High Seas Fleet would be in close support on a line between Schouwen Bank and the Galloper Shoal. After the raid was over the Germans would then carry out a bombardment of the English coast between Lowestoft and Orfordness.

When the plan was put before the Kaiser he approved it on condition that air reconnaissance by Zeppelins was available; Scheer, remembering his misfortune with the head of the Magdeburg Fire Brigade during the sortie of the previous August, was by now disenchanted with air reconnaissance and claimed that it was not indispensable. The Kaiser disagreed, firmly, and the planned operation was abandoned.

But if the Kaiser would not permit the big ships of the High Seas Fleet to be risked there was still the possibility of attacking cross-Channel traffic on a smaller scale, using destroyers; and during the winter of 1916-7 five such raids were made, described by the British Official History as 'A brilliant episode in German naval operations'.

The first attack took place on the pitch dark night of 26/27 October 1916, when two German flotillas totalling twenty-four destroyers raided from Zeebrugge as far west as Folkestone. The destroyers had two targets. One flotilla was to attack the line of small patrol vessels, drifters, trawlers, motor launches, etc., whose lights and flares were supposed to constitute a barrier against the passage of U-boats through the Straits by forcing them to dive into the deep minefields already laid to avoid detection.

The second flotilla, pushing further westward, was to attack any cross-Channel transports to be found. A total of fifty-seven of these transports were due to cross on the night of the raid; the Germans missed all of them save one, which they sank, but they also sank one British destroyer (*Flirt*) and six drifters as well as damaged another destroyer (*Nubian*)* and withdrew without loss. A smaller raid followed on 23 November, when thirteen destroyers appeared at the north end of the Downs, briefly shelled Margate, damaged a drifter and made off unscathed.

Dissatisfaction in London with the failure to deal with these raids was one of the reasons why the First Lord of the Admiralty, Arthur Balfour, and the First Sea Lord, Sir Henry Jackson, were replaced by Sir Edward Carson and Jellicoe respectively.

On 23 February 1917 the German destroyers were back again in three detachments. One group attacked patrol craft and merchant shipping in the Downs and fired a few rounds against Margate. The second group attacked the drifters of the Dover barrage, but was driven off after ten hot minutes' exchange of fire, while the third group searched in vain for ships on the routes between England and Holland.

These weeks saw the height of the Straits raiding season, coinciding with the opening of the unrestricted submarine war-

* *Nubian* had her bow blown off by a torpedo; her undamaged stern was afterwards joined to the bows of another destroyer, *Zulu*, which had lost her stern on a mine. The combined ship was named *Zubian*. When *Nubian* was hit, one of her boilers fell through the hole made by the exploding torpedo and for more than fifty years afterwards could still be seen on the foreshore under the cliffs of Dover.

fare campaign; and on the night of 17/18 March raiders reappeared, shelling the English coast, sinking one destroyer (*Paragon*), damaging another (*Llewellyn*), and once again making off without loss. However, on the night of 20/21 April the Germans were intercepted for the only time in the whole series of raids, and one of the most famous naval actions of the war took place.

Twelve German destroyers, in two divisions of six, were to attack Dover and Calais respectively and do what damage they could to the small craft of the barrage. Two British flotilla leaders, large destroyers, *Swift* and *Broke*, came upon the Dover group of the enemy and attacked them at a range of 600 yards. The *Swift* steered for the leading German to ram her and opened fire, whereupon her captain was temporarily blinded by the flash of his own six-inch gun, a huge weapon for a destroyer. As a result the *Swift* missed the enemy which she was attempting to ram, and was nearly rammed in her turn by a German. The *Broke* torpedoed one German destroyer and then rammed another. The two ships were jammed together and the Germans, feeling their own vessel sinking beneath them, began to scramble up on the deck of the *Broke*. The order, dating from long before the days of Nelson, 'Away boarders' was piped and the Germans were attacked with pistols, cutlasses and cups of hot cocoa, which were thrown at them. In a few minutes it was all over, the *Broke* forcing the German down by riding over her until she sank.

The captain of the *Broke* was Commander E. R. G. R. Evans, who had already distinguished himself as a South Polar explorer.

After this, as the nights grew shorter, the Germans abandoned the Channel raids for nearly a year.

Meanwhile monotony, discomfort and poor food spread their discouraging influence over the big ships of the Fleet and over the whole land. There were strikes in Berlin factories during the winter in protest against food shortages, and similar demonstrations in Kiel.

In the ships there had been no more trouble since the incident in the *Helgoland* in the previous September, except in January 1917 when anti-war slogans were set up conspicuously, first on board the *Oldenburg* and then in the *Posen*. The perpetrators were sent to prison, two men from the *Oldenburg* being given nine months each and one from the *Posen* twenty-five months.

Ashore, the early spring brought the first Russian revolution, and extreme excitement in Germany, for it coincided with the first cracks in what had seemed the monolith of German political unity. This had been created at the beginning of the war and its principal manifestation had been, at first, support by all parties of the government's request for the voting of the credits needed for the war effort.

Now, however, a split developed within the Social Democratic Party (SPD) whose left-wing members broke away in April and formed the Independent Social Democratic Party (USPD) which voted against further credits for the war and set up an agitation for 'Peace without annexations or indemnities', propaganda for which was sympathetically heard by some of the men in the big ships, for two-and-a-half years of war had not been sufficient to break the ties which existed between Socialist politics and the crews of the Fleet, two-thirds of whom were conscripts and many, especially the engine-room personnel, came from the big industrial towns. Most of these men had gone straight from school into factories where they had been members of the well-organized German trades union movement, and had been exposed to the political propaganda of the SPD. In peacetime, after three years' service they were released into the reserve, went back to their jobs in industry and were once more involved in politics and the trades union movement. It was natural that they should seek enlightenment from the political sources with which they had been in touch during peacetime. It was natural, too, that the extremist USPD should attract many who had grievances; and to the USPD headquarters in the Schiffbauerdamm, near the Reichstag, men began to make their way during the critical month of June 1917. This was, apparently, the first direct contact between men of the High Seas Fleet and the USPD. Max Reichpietsch, a seaman from the *Friedrich der Grosse* on leave in Berlin, went to the party headquarters and presented them with a list of grievances which he and some of his messmates had drawn up. Details of what happened did not transpire until much later.

The political consciousness of the lower decks was heightened at this time by an order from Admiral Bachmann, at Kiel, forbidding the circulation of left-wing papers on board. This caused a particular amount of ill-feeling because at this time right-wing leaders, including Tirpitz himself and Wolfgang Kapp, who was to give his name to the unsuccessful right-wing *Putsch* in Berlin in 1920, formed a group of their own called the Fatherland party, which engaged in propaganda of a kind described as 'patriotic', calling for German conquests, annexations and indemnities. When officers began to make propaganda for this group there were protests that the political truce was being broken, to which the leaders of the right replied that their propaganda was 'patriotic' and, as such, above the domestic political battle.

It was also in June that Capelle ordered the creation of messing committees in the big ships in an attempt to reduce discontent about the food situation. These were in part made up of men elected from the lower deck and were usually headed by the ship's executive officer, with the paymaster and a warrant officer or petty officer from the ship's catering department. Naturally these bodies soon found themselves faced with grievances which had nothing at all to do with the food situation.

At this stage, individual action was taken by a seaman who felt his responsibilities in the situation, and it was taken in a somewhat remarkable way, to improve morale and discipline.

Conrad Lotter, then serving in the cruiser-minelayer *Bremse*, a very religious and hyper-conscientious young man, became so worried by the tone in the Fleet that he decided to go to Hipper, who was his admiral, and tell him of his concern.

This happened more than fifty years ago; the Western countries and their fighting services have grown much more democratic since then but, even today, it requires a considerable amount of imagination to contemplate the possibility of a British rating or an American enlisted man calling on his admiral as Lotter did. Even in the Federal German navy of today, with its armed forces ombudsman, this step of Lotter's would seem startling, while in the Kaiser's navy it seemed quite impossible, so very great was the gulf between the two men, the admiral and the seaman. It is not surprising that Lotter was filled with apprehension as to the outcome of the step which he planned to take. Nevertheless, he took it; he went to Hipper's private residence in Wilhelmshaven and asked to see him.

He was admitted, faced the admiral and said: '*Es stinkt in der Flotte, Excellenz*. It would be a good thing to let in some fresh air'.

Hipper cross-examined him, but he added nothing more and, after a while, left. Hipper then sent for Lotter's captain, Bülow, and asked him about his visitor. Was he mentally unbalanced, or did he just wish to draw attention to himself? Bülow answered that, on the contrary, Lotter was one of his best hands, and the admiral and the captain parted, puzzled by what had happened.

Back on board, Lotter wrote to his father in Bavaria, describing what he had done, giving reasons for his concern about the state of the Fleet and adding that he was willing to take all the consequences of his action:

'And if I were to have bad luck, and the *Lieber Gott* in his mysterious wisdom should deal heavily with my action, if for now, or for all eternity, I will accept it, believing that it is better that a man should die rather than a whole nation decay.'

Lotter senior was understandably very troubled by his son's letter and showed it to his parish priest, who shared his concern and passed the letter on to the Dean of Cologne Cathedral, who, in turn, sent it to Dr Pfleger, the naval expert of the Catholic (Centrum) party in the Reichstag, who forwarded it to Capelle, without disclosing whence he had obtained his information. Pfleger wrote:

From sources in the High Seas Fleet I continue to receive news which, in the interests of our national defence, I cannot disregard, especially as I have reason to believe that Social Democrat members of the Reichstag have already been informed by lower deck sources.

I have been informed that on board the *Friedrich der Grosse, Prinzregent Luitpold* and *Pillau* there have taken place full-scale mutinies and insubordination; on board the *Thüringen* a short while ago water was poured on officers sitting in the wardroom, without it being possible to identify the culprits. The causes of these highly unpleasant events are said to be:

(1) The bad example of the officers
(2) Shortage of food
(3) Treatment of ratings by officers, contrary to regulations
(4) Broken promises regarding leave.

Pfleger asked that an immediate investigation be made into the state of affairs within the Navy, especially as the Socialist opposition might be expected to raise the matter when the Reichstag next met.

This letter was dated 28 July, and a somewhat ineffectual enquiry was set on foot by Capelle. It was carried out by Rear-Admiral Hebbinghaus, head of the General Department of the Admiralty, who apparently did not speak to any ratings during his enquiry. In any case the enquiry came far too late to be of any value.

Throughout the troubled summer of 1917, in the High Seas Fleet two battleships led the way in setting a bad example; the *Prinzregent Luitpold* and the *Friedrich der Grosse*, which, until a few weeks earlier, had been the fleet flagship.

In the *Prinzregent Luitpold* hands, ordered to coal ship, had sabotaged the coaling gear, cutting the lines and throwing the blocks overboard. A little later, when the ship was on her way from Kiel to Wilhelmshaven, through the Kiel Canal, there had been more trouble. The engines were stopped and the ship, losing way, drifted slowly for a time, blocking the canal.

Then, on 6 June, a flurry of protests and insubordination started to run round the big ships of the Fleet, prompted by the shortage of rations and their poor quality. On that day the stokers' messes of the *Prinzregent Luitpold* suddenly announced that they would not eat the dried vegetables, unappetisingly nicknamed 'barbed wire', with which they were being served. At about the same time thirty seamen from the *Helgoland* refused to unload a consignment of flour which had gone bad and which, they said, was not worth unloading as no one would eat it.

Friedrich der Grosse joined in on 4 July. Uproar had started on board the ship after a night-firing exercise. When the exercise had ended some of the men had eaten bread which was part of the next day's ration. When the next day came they were refused any more and, in consequence, announced that they would not do any work. The executive officer of the ship, after some time, persuaded them to return to their duty, having arranged for them to be issued with porridge instead of bread.

On 11 July there was more trouble in the *Friedrich der Grosse*, and although order was restored without any serious consequences, the news spread through the Fleet and the idea of similar manifestations quickly developed. Not until later was it possible to discover the details of the semi-coherent organization which lay behind the events which followed.

There was trouble again in the *Prinzregent Luitpold* on 19 July. Soup served was described as being full of worms, the men refused to eat it and another hunger strike followed. An *ersatz* soup was then prepared and, as the original soup was itself *ersatz*, the quality of the *ersatz ersatz* soup may be imagined, and it is not surprising that this, too, was refused. Finally the men succeeded in securing the issue of slices of bread three centimetres thick, together with sausages.

At this time, too, the stokers of the *Posen* complained about the turnips which they were given to eat, but on 20 July there came a more serious manifestation when 137 men from the light cruiser *Pillau* walked off their ship when she was lying alongside at Wilhelmshaven complaining that their leave had been stopped without any explanation. They went into a café, made speeches, had a few drinks and, after a couple of hours, came back on board and, without orders, got on with the work which they should have been doing when they were demonstrating, and, to show their good will, worked on through a stand-easy period. The captain and officers of the *Pillau* did not take this event seriously, for they considered their crew to be a good one, and all that happened was that the men concerned were given three hours' punishment drill.

On 25 July in the evening, Captain Thorbecke of the battleship *König Albert* fell into the water while going on board his ship and was drowned. Thorbecke had a reputation in the Fleet for great severity, and it was known that only a few days before he had punished a seaman because he had canvassed for subscriptions to the Socialist daily newspaper *Vorwärts*. Now, because of the general state of mind in the High Seas Fleet, rumours spread around Wilhelmshaven that he had been attacked and thrown overboard by his own crew. From that day to this there has been no proof of the story, but it was exactly the kind of story which men, in their thousands, wanted to believe at that time.

The mildness of the punishment inflicted on the crew of the *Pillau* may have been an encouragement to the ringleaders in some of the other ships and, in particular, to those in the *Prinzregent Luitpold*, who proceeded, on 1 and 2 August, to stage the biggest demonstration of all. Drill ashore had originally been planned for the morning of 1 August. Then, owing to the prospect of bad weather, the drill was cancelled and a cinema performance, something of a novelty at that time, was organized on board instead. The weather cleared up and plans were once more changed, the cinema being cancelled and the men ordered to parade for a route march. In protest, a group of forty-nine stokers went ashore without permission and held a meeting in a railway waggon, agreeing to make a further protest on the next day. When the forty-nine men returned to the ship, eleven of them, presumed to be ringleaders, were arrested and placed in the cells.

There now emerged from the confusion of protests, speeches

and demonstrations, the personality of Albin Köbis, a stoker in the *Prinzregent Luitpold*, who threatened another demonstration if the arrested men were not immediately released. They were not released, and on the next day, Köbis, with a party of about four hundred men, left the ship, forced their way past the sentries at the dockyard gates and marched up the dyke to Rustersiel, where they entered the *Weisser Schwan* and made speeches, in one of which it would seem that arguments for the first time took a political turn, as Köbis made a speech in favour of the USPD. In the middle of the meeting there arrived a sergeant of the Marine Artillery and several of his men. He ordered the demonstrators back to their ship. They refused to go. He spoke to them again, pointed out that he himself would be in the greatest trouble if it were found out that this meeting had taken place and that he had been unable to stop it. Would they please, he asked, go back to their ship?

After a while they agreed, and set off in the pouring rain, escorted intermittently by the sergeant and his men. From time to time the sailors shouted that they would not go back under escort and halted until the Marines withdrew. They then resumed their march and, a little while later, the Marines closed in again. These cat-and-mouse proceedings were repeated several times until a figure riding a bicycle and wearing a streaming wet, black waterproof cape was sighted, coming up the dyke from Wilhelmshaven. This was one of the officers of the *Prinzregent Luitpold*, Lieutenant-Commander von Wiehe who, still on his bicycle, led the protesting men back to their ship.

The authorities judged that the first thing to be done with the *Prinzregent Luitpold* was to get her away from Wilhelmshaven, where she could far too easily infect the rest of the Fleet. Accordingly she was sent to Schillig Roads, where a number of men were arrested and taken ashore under armed guard.

The *Friedrich der Grosse* felt bound to compete with the *Prinzregent Luitpold* in demonstrations, and refused duty. There was also trouble in the *Kaiserin*, where men refused soup from the galley and would not relieve the duty watch. A good deal of argument followed and that night the officers posted sentries on the alleyways and companionways leading to their quarters. However, no threats of violence were made to any officers at this time. The authorities, learning that the Wilhelmshaven Socialists were planning a demonstration in favour of the mutineers on the evening of 5 August, decided to send the *Friedrich der Grosse* away at once.

On the morning of the fifth the *Kaiserin, König Albert* and *Kaiser* were also sent to Schillig Roads and then to Brunsbüttel, where attempts were made to get the crews in hand and to provide them with better food, more leave and organized amusements for those obliged to remain on board.

The last flickers of this series of troubles began on 16 August, in the *Rheinland* and the *Westfalen.* In the former a protest was made, unsuccessfully, against a stoppage of leave. In the *Westfalen* thirty or forty men refused to obey orders and went ashore because they had not received a supplementary ration which they believed due to them for coaling. A number of the crew were arrested and a deputation from the remainder protested to their captain, threatening to use force if he did not explain within twenty-four hours why the arrests had been made and to say how long it was proposed that the arrested men would be held. No answer was given by the *Westfalen*'s captain, no action was taken by the men, and those under arrest were eventually placed on trial.

In October a rating from the *Moltke* was arrested for shouting insults and peace slogans. There was then calm in the Fleet for the next twelve months; in the same month of October 1917, the Third and Fourth Squadrons of the High Seas Fleet, including the *Friedrich der Grosse, Prinzregent Luitpold, König Albert* and *Kaiserin,* sailed to cover the successful landings on the Russian islands of Dagö and Ösel (now called Khiuma and Sarema) at the entrance to the Gulf of Riga, an important, large-scale operation which was carried out successfully in the face of a surprising amount of resistance from the Russians, although they were then on the verge of the November revolution and an armistice with the Central Powers.

It is now more than fifty years after all these events but it is still impossible to find out exactly what happened in these mutinies, because of the destruction of relevant documents. Volume Seven of the German *Official Naval History of the War in the North Sea*, published in 1965 and covering the years 1917-18, describes the events in the *Friedrich der Grosse*, *Prinzregent Luitpold*, *Westfalen* and *Pillau* and says that apart from these there were no noteworthy breaches of discipline. Other incidents, says the *History*, were 'normal irregularities that arose when food was limited and routine dull.'

Herr Walter Görlitz, in a footnote to the diaries of Admiral von Müller, which he edited, says: 'In the period between 6 July and 16 August 1917 there took place on board the battleships *Friedrich der Grosse*, *Prinzregent Luitpold* and *Westfalen*, and the light cruiser *Pillau* acts of insubordination, mass desertion, hunger strikes and acts of sabotage in which some five thousand men were involved'.

The British official naval historian of the post-Jutland period of World War One, Sir Henry Newbolt, lists, in addition to the four ships mentioned by the German official account, the *Kaiserin* and *Rheinland*; while one of the chief mutineers, Leading Stoker Sachse, a boastful man, says that mutinies also took place in the *König Albert*, *Grosser Kurfürst*, *Helgoland*, *Ostfriesland*, *Posen*, *Schwaben*, *Zieten* and *Kaiser* as well as in the ships named by Sir Henry Newbolt and Herr Görlitz.

The extremely superficial report by Hebbinghaus which had been ordered by Capelle was completed on 7 August; its author, in his conclusions, said he could not discover that the men had any legitimate grievances at all.

Summing up, he said: 'No sensible man would take seriously the grouses and arguments. A mosquito becomes an elephant by repetition and exaggeration'.

Hebbinghaus does not seem to have considered that grouses are the very things to which attention should be paid, if only to prevent the mosquitoes becoming elephants. Besides, a mosquito can do quite enough harm on its own.

By now members of the Reichstag had learned of the events

in Wilhelmshaven. One of them who refused to become excited was Gustav Stresemann, then leader of the National Liberal party and later Chancellor and Foreign Minister of the German Republic. He wrote later of the days of 1917: 'We knew what had happened at Wilhelmshaven, and we also knew that it was comparatively unimportant'.

Under these circumstances it is not surprising that some of the men arrested for their part in the mutinies and disorders were hardly worried about what the future held for them.

Thus Willy Weber, a leading stoker from the *Friedrich der Grosse,* who was to be sentenced to death for his share in these events, but whose sentence was commuted to fifteen years imprisonment, said: 'Nobody wanted a revolution, we just wanted to be treated more like human beings; we realized that we were committing an offence, but not one so grave that it would be punishable by death'.

Later, he added: 'Nineteen-seventeen was no revolution, but a military strike and nothing more'.

That a 'military strike' was virtually a mutiny and might be treated as such does not seem to have occurred to the lower deck at all. A sailor from the *Nassau,* echoing Weber, said: 'We didn't want a revolution, we only wanted our human rights.'

Typical of this somewhat naïve outlook were the words of Haase from the *Westfalen* who said, when charged: 'I never thought that this could be dangerous to the ship or the State'. *Nassau,* incidentally, was the one big ship in the Fleet at this time in which there were no complaints; and Beckers, one of the leading agitators in the *Prinzregent Luitpold* at this time, said afterwards that he had found it impossible to interest the greater part of the ship's company of the *Nassau* in any demonstrations at all.

In their defence, in the courts martial which followed, the accused men always emphasized that, when they left their ships to take part in a demonstration, they always returned on board before their ships could possibly have sailed. In port, ships were left as a rule at three to six hours' notice for sea.

Accordingly, if the men were ashore for a lesser period they would probably be punished for leave-breaking or a similar irregularity, but they did not run the risk of being charged with desertion, which might have been the case had their ship sailed without them.

However, although the Admiralty, the Reichstag and the lower deck of the Fleet may be said to have taken the mutinies fairly lightly, Scheer did not do so. He began with the crew of the *Prinzregent Luitpold*; two hundred men were arrested and put in the cells to await further examination and one hundred and fifty more were disrated, out of a total ship's company of about one thousand. A series of courts martial were held, at the outcome of which seventy-seven men were found guilty, nine of whom were sentenced to death, a sentence which was, however, carried out in only two cases; the other seven men had their death sentences commuted to terms of imprisonment. The two men shot were Albin Köbis from the *Prinzregent Luitpold* and Max Reichpietsch from the *Friedrich der Grosse*.

Eight men were condemned to between ten and fifteen years' penal servitude; eleven received sentences of penal servitude ranging from five to ten years; four were imprisoned for more than five to ten years; seven were imprisoned for more than two to five years; twenty-one were imprisoned for more than one to two years; twenty-four were imprisoned for more than one year. The imprisoned men were released with the coming of the revolution, just over a year after they had been sentenced.

It is worth noting that Admiral Gladisch, in the *Official History*, says that events in all the ships, apart from the *Friedrich der Grosse, Prinzregent Luitpold, Pillau* and *Westfalen*, were 'normal irregularities'. However, the sentences passed on some of those guilty of these 'normal irregularities' give an idea of the seriousness with which they were regarded. Linke, in the *Helgoland*, was sentenced to ten years' penal servitude, Petty Officer Telegraphist Franz Schlegel in the patrol vessel *Zieten*, and Bieber in the *Helgoland*, each received ten year sentences, reduced on appeal to six years, and Bräuner in the *Kaiserin* was sentenced to twelve years, reduced to ten on appeal.

The political views of the convicted men spanned a very broad spectrum of middle-of-the-road and left-wing opinion, although it would appear that, at the beginning, few were politically minded at all, but simply very discontented. However, Rebe, a stoker from the *Moltke*, was certainly a full-blown left extremist before the Communist party existed, and survived to become editor of the Communist newspaper *Rote Fahne*; while Linke, whose crime was having been elected by his shipmates to their messing committee, after the war joined the right-wing Navy League. The messing committees of the Fleet had chosen from amongst themselves a central committee of five: Sachse, Reichpietsch and Weber from the *Friedrich der Grosse*, with Köbis and Beckers from the *Prinzregent Luitpold*. Of these Weber was SPD, Reichpietsch said to be inclined to the USPD, Beckers and Köbis were thought to be anarchists, while Sachse was a radical of the Left.

When the trials and executions were over, Scheer drew up a long report on the whole affair, in which he described what he believed had gone wrong and laid down a series of measures to prevent a recurrence of the trouble. The principal points which he made were:

On board all ships under the command of the High Seas Fleet as well as within the German Empire and in the Army at the Front, food supplies were short during the summer of 1917.

Home leave and letters from home gave a discouraging picture of the difficulties in obtaining food, and the worry of having relatives leading a miserable existence destroyed the pride and joy which the crews had in being able to carry on under the monotonous conditions of life on board.

The requirements of submarine warfare had brought about continual changes among the officers, and particularly among those who had proved their quality and had been in the closest touch with the men, and the latter no longer felt themselves guided and supervised in the ways to which they had been used.

To conserve the men's energies they were given more leisure

time, some of which they spent in political discussion and the reading of propaganda material.

It was in this way that some of them, with a higher degree of intelligence than their shipmates, welcomed certain ideas, in particular those of the Russian revolution. This was especially the case among the older men, already used to political debate.

These men sought and found sympathizers and, from their desire to spread their ideas, there evolved an organization which worked in accordance with well-tried political methods.

At the head of this work was Stoker Sachse of the *Friedrich der Grosse,* in which was established the central committee for the whole Fleet.

The movement became dangerous when a liaison was established with the chiefs of the USPD in the Reichstag. These people, taking care to protect themselves, engaged in a predetermined policy, in accordance with which the Fleet was to collect as many signatures as possible to take to the International Socialist Conference at Stockholm. This was done so that the USPD could claim the support of the Fleet in its programme of peace without annexations or indemnities.

To force the government to agree, according to Scheer, a general strike was planned on a pre-arranged day, in all ammunition factories, together with a refusal of obedience by the armed forces. There seems, in fact, to have been no such plan made, although such a scheme may have been discussed.

'It was represented to the men,' Scheer went on, 'that a similar movement was in preparation among the enemy, and that they themselves were committing no act of treason since they were planning no violence. In some cases pressure was brought to bear on men, other than by simple persuasion, in order to obtain signatures.' At this stage, by what Scheer termed 'a very unfortunate coincidence', the messing committees were introduced into the Fleet. This, he added, only made general a system which had already existed for some time in many ships, and for a long time previously in the army. At meetings of these committees, according to Scheer, discussion soon turned to the question of propaganda on behalf of the USPD, and he commented: 'It was natural that the agitation thus caused should show itself soon. Crews refused on several occasions to touch their food, and it was seen that duties were carried out with less enthusiasm'. Signs of this were not ignored by the Fleet command but, Scheer said, it was attributed by them to 'poor food and war weariness'.

The report describes events in the *Pillau* on 20 July and in the *Prinzregent Luitpold* on subsequent dates. It was the investigation of the demonstration by members of the latter's crew at Rustersiel which led to the discovery of the movement and of the entire organization. While this investigation was in progress a number of men in the *Westfalen* refused to take part in the work of coaling ship, but were later persuaded by their officers to do so. In the *Rheinland* there were cases of indiscipline and a large number of men, when fallen in, surged forward demanding leave.

Scheer claimed that the enquiry showed that the 'revolutionary movement' had also spread to the First Squadron and that 'although the leaders had been immediately arrested, their plan was carried out with almost fanatical tenacity by their followers. Despite vigilance they managed to hold another meeting which ended in the arrest of the representative of the USPD in Kiel and of the delegates of various ships.'

Scheer's investigation had penetrated the rudimentary organization of Reichpietsch and the others, but had produced somewhat dubious results. A seaman named Adams from the *Westfalen*, who had been used as a counter-intelligence operator, began his investigations by confessing to a murder which he said that he had committed in South America just before the war. Immediately after this he wrote anonymous letters to himself, denouncing himself as one of the leaders of the conspiracy which he was supposed to be investigating. It was, therefore, not surprising that the authorities decided that it would be unwise to call him as a witness at any of the courts martial. In addition, there was evidence suggesting that Adams had been acting as an *agent provocateur*.

Much more valuable information for the prosecution was provided by a young engine-room artificer in the *Pillau*, who complained in a letter to his father that he was being bullied by a stoker in his ship, named Fischer, to take part in the distribution of messages which seemed to him to be of a kind contrary to discipline. The engine-room artificer's father used almost exactly the same procedure as had the father of Conrad Lotter earlier in the summer, reporting the matter to his parish priest, who passed it on to a member of the Catholic party in the Reichstag who got in touch with the Admiralty which, in turn, informed the captain of the *Pillau*. Fischer promptly disappeared. His chest on board was found to contain seditious literature and the police were asked to search for him. It was discovered that he had fled to Switzerland but, shortly afterwards, he returned to visit his wife at Lörrach, on the German side of the Swiss border near Basle, where he was arrested, taken to Freiburg-im-Breisgau and charged. After a court martial he was given a sentence of fifteen years, later reduced to ten.

In many ways the most interesting of the 1917 mutineers was Willi Sachse who paid for his beliefs with his life, after a career which took him up many a winding stair. He was twenty-one when the mutiny occurred, and afterwards was very much of an exhibitionist, greatly exaggerating the entire scale of events in the Fleet and his own share in them. After the war he wrote widely, and somewhat boastfully, obviously aggrieved to find that Reichpietsch and Köbis were regarded by the Left in Germany as heroes of the mutiny. An ingrained sense of contrariness led him to espouse causes of the extreme Right, including National Socialism; but having boxed the compass of political belief, from extreme Left to extreme Right, he reversed the process and became a member of the Communist Uhrig group and, as such, was executed by the Nazis in 1944.

A very preposterous story was provided during the investigations by Paul Calmus, a seaman from the *Rheinland*. He told the authorities that he had visited the USPD headquarters, having been sent there by his shipmates, who were distrustful of the very optimistic statements made by Reichpietsch about the help which they might expect from that source. On the steps of the party offices, he said, he had met Dittmann, who took him to a meeting with various officers, some of them obviously foreign, who gave him a pistol and made him swear on a dagger that he would reveal nothing of what transpired. A major in German uniform showed him a bag containing 5,000 marks, which he offered him in exchange for lists of USPD members, and then asked him to assassinate the Kaiser by means of an infernal machine which would be supplied. Calmus said that he then became frightened and, covering the people in the room with the pistol which he had been given, backed out and returned to Wilhelmshaven after one more escape, this time from a young woman named Sissy, who tried to detain him.

Parts of all this nonsense seem to have been believed, and Dittmann was fortunate in being able to prove that he was, in fact, attending the Stockholm Conference when he was supposed to have been enlisting Calmus for the conspiracy.

Scheer stated that the various measures which he had taken and, in particular, the severe punishments imposed had brought the crews to order. The next task, he said, would be to prevent further trouble. He gave a list of the measures needed and began by saying that there were many complaints of the much higher standard of living enjoyed by officers. In future, he insisted, there should be no important difference in messing between officers and men, and shortly after this progressive adjustments were made in ration scales until they were almost identical for all ranks.*

Scheer insisted that in the daily life of the ship there should be as much variety as was consistent with the requirements of the service and wartime shortages. Everyone should be encouraged to play games, not only those who were particularly talented, and officers should take an active part. The older men, he said, had intellectual interests which needed care, and all

* In the autumn of 1917 the allowance per day was about 3.55 marks for officers and 1.77 marks per man, but by the end of the war the allowance per man had been raised to within 25 pfennigs of that for officers.

hands should be kept informed, as far as possible, of the development of the war on land and sea. Books and magazines of a higher intellectual level than those generally available should be supplied. To counter pacifist propaganda the plans of Germany's enemies for her downfall should be stressed, but care should be taken in dealing with internal affairs not to get involved in political controversy. This was a warning to the officers to avoid blatant right-wing propaganda which could easily exasperate the men since most of the politically conscious ratings supported left-wing or liberal parties. If men approached their officers about their family problems the officers should be as sympathetic, discreet and helpful as possible, Scheer insisted, adding that investigation had shown that 'grave faults' had been committed in handling welfare questions. The fact that many complaints had been forwarded, not through service channels but through members of the Reichstag, or relatives, or sent to the Army GHQ, the Admiralty, or to Scheer himself, showed, he declared, the lack of confidence the men had in their immediate superiors.

In conclusion, Scheer's report described various means of identification used by the mutineers, saying that a number of men were undoubtedly convinced supporters of revolution, and that it was vital that their activities be investigated and exposed. For fear of such investigation, Scheer went on, members of the USPD in the Fleet were protecting themselves against infiltration by various signs and passwords. Three were specifically mentioned:

1. On even days of the month keeping the left hand in the pocket, on odd days the right.
2. Metal discs with the radio call-sign of the men's ships and a membership number or card.
3. Passwords, such as 'Can we play cards here?'

In addition, it was believed that wearing a length of red cotton in a rating's uniform collar was also a secret sign, and an order was issued banning it. There seems never to have been any service reason why red cotton was thus used. One group of seamen, asked why they were wearing red thread, replied that they had nothing else to do with it. It is surprising that, in the general air of tautened discipline, nothing seems to have happened to them.

Summing up, Scheer wrote: 'The general situation made it necessary to hold the big ships in reserve, and this deprived their crews of the constant vigorous activity which was needed to convince them that they must endure.'

Even today Scheer's report stands up well as a reasonably accurate account of what happened, a reasonably accurate diagnosis of the causes of the troubles and an intelligent programme of reform. Only in his account of the USPD involvement does he seem to have been wildly astray, while his theory that there was a USPD conspiracy is matched by the claim of the Communists that there was such a conspiracy, not by the USPD but by a party still further to the Left, the Spartacists, who were the forerunners of the Communists in Germany. No evidence exists that either conspiracy ever existed; it is true that on the side of the German authorities there was a wholesale destruction of documents dealing with these matters and that the records of operations of the Communists and their allies have never been open for inspection. It would, however, have been in the best interests of both sides to publish any evidence which they possessed that supported the claims they made. For the Communists such evidence would serve to show the extent of their power, while, for the Navy, proof of the fact that there was a conspiracy would go far to acquitting them of blame for permitting the collapse of the morale of the High Seas Fleet; but if there was no USPD active conspiracy, except for the circulation of clandestine literature, there was very little, if any, justification for the swingeing sentences passed upon the mutineers.

Contact between the Fleet and the USPD began in June 1917 with Reichpietsch's visit to party headquarters in search of political propaganda; he was an embarrassing visitor, for the party was anxious not to lay itself open to the charge of tampering with the discipline of the armed forces since that could be construed as treason. On this first visit Dittmann showed reluctance in his dealings with Reichpietsch, but the latter was then seen by Frau Luise Zietz, a short, vehement woman who did not possess Dittmann's feeling of the need for caution. Later, at the Reichstag enquiry, Dittmann was to wax sentimental about how Frau Zietz's 'motherly love' was stirred by Reichpietsch, whom Dittmann described as a 'handsome, fair-haired blue-eyed young sailor', and who, from now on, was moving rapidly to a final court martial and a firing squad.

At this time Reichpietsch was twenty-three years old and had volunteered in 1912 to serve for four years. According to the evidence given at his court martial he seems to have made a good beginning in the Service, but soon acquired entries on his conduct sheet, starting off with comparatively minor delinquencies such as being late on watch and relieving himself on the deck. Later, however, he was convicted of theft, when acting as steward to a Lieutenant Jordan. To begin with, in order to impress the young ladies of Wilhelmshaven, he borrowed a suit of Jordan's plain clothes, a pair of silk socks and a pair of brown boots, and had then gone ashore. Unfortunately, as soon as he landed he ran into Jordan and came back to the ship on a charge. A little later, an officer missed a purse which he had left in the pocket of his greatcoat hanging outside the wardroom. After a search the empty purse was found in Reichpietsch's possession and there were plenty of signs that he had recently been spending a good deal of money. He eventually admitted the theft and was sent to prison, but later declared that he was innocent and that he had taken the blame to protect a shipmate with whom he was dealing in black-market cigarettes. Although he had been sent to prison and had, in addition, been punished for fourteen other offences it would seem that what he minded most was the fact that he had been disrated to Seaman, Second Class, and thus lost the right to wear on his cap-ribbon the red, white and black roundel which was the mark of a Seaman, First Class. It was perhaps characteristic of the unthinking drafting habits of the

German navy at this time that he was sent back to his old ship when he had served his sentence.

After World War Two the Communists of East Germany claimed him as one of their own, saying that he had been 'A member of the Spartacist Group, organized under the influence of the Russian revolution of February 1917, which had prepared the sailors' risings of the summer of 1917'. Dittmann, on the other hand, said of Reichpeitsch at this time: 'He gave the impression of an alert young man, but one completely untrained and inexperienced politically'. Similar praise of Köbis has also been given in East Germany, but there is no evidence that the claims made by the Communists for either man are true.

Afterwards, Reichpietsch said that he was encouraged by Frau Zietz and by Dittmann, and this they both denied. In any event, he began his career as a Socialist agitator by collecting signatures of USPD supporters and canvassing for subscribers to the SPD *Vorwärts* in Berlin and the USPD *Leipziger Volkszeitung* among his shipmates.

The drive for the collection of signatures ended when the authorities swooped on the collectors. By then Reichpietsch and others working with him had gathered some four thousand names, about seven per cent of all the crews of the Fleet.

When Dittmann heard of the collection of signatures he became alarmed, for it seemed that possession of these lists might be terribly dangerous to the Party, to himself, to Reichpietsch and to every man whose name was on them. Reichpietsch explained that he thought it would be of value for Dittmann to take the lists with him to the international Socialist conference which was about to meet in Stockholm, and thus show something of the strength possessed by the USPD.

At this Stockholm meeting the intention was that the representatives of all Socialist parties, from belligerents and neutrals alike, should meet in September 1917 to discuss the possibilities of a negotiated peace. After three years of war the German Socialists of both parties were depressed and nearly hopeless, so that this conference appeared to many as the last chance to achieve a peace based on the principles which they had espoused of 'no annexations nor indemnities'. However, the Socialist parties of the Western allies refused to take part and their governments refused to grant exit permits to any of their free-lance pacifists, so that the conference came to nothing.

In October 1917 Dittman was able to bring down Chancellor Michaelis by raising a matter connected with the affairs of the navy, when he gave notice of his intention to bring forward an interpellation in the Reichstag of Michaelis, on the subject of the ultra-nationalist, or pan-German propaganda campaign which was being carried on within the navy by its own officers. Michaelis had gathered against him all the elements in Parliament and nearly everybody of importance, including Hindenburg and Ludendorff and the Kaiser himself, outside it.

Earlier, on an occasion when Bethmann-Hollweg, as Chancellor, had been outvoted in the Reichstag he had gone to the Kaiser and said that he supposed he ought to resign, whereupon the Kaiser had told him not to mind, as the more the Reichstag disliked the Chancellor the more the Kaiser himself would like him. But now Michaelis was obliged to go, leaving the powers that were with the task of finding a new Chancellor, and the name of Prince Max of Baden was introduced into discussions of the vacant Chancellorship.

Prince Max was a man of known liberal beliefs, heir to the Grand Ducal throne of Baden. Unlike most of the German kings and grand dukes, dukes, princes and princelings, he had not gone through the war in a magnificent uniform of high rank with no real responsibilities or duties to perform, but had devoted himself to the care of prisoners-of-war and had sought every chance to further a compromise peace. With his noble lineage, his civilized bearing and his devotion to the cause of peace and justice, he recalls an English nobleman of this period and of the inter-war years, Viscount Cecil of Chelwood.

But the hour of the Prince had not yet struck, and it was not to strike until it was too late, for in October 1917 the Kaiser was unwilling to take advice from a contemporary, while the Prince's father, the reigning Grand Duke, did not like the idea of his heir mixing directly in politics. Finally the Prince thought that it would be unseemly were he to seek power for himself.

Accordingly the Chancellorship was vested in Count Hertling, the Bavarian prime minister, with the approval of the army who considered him as a kind of civil affairs officer who would look after the home front while the army waged war.

In January 1918 Dittmann was sent to prison, accused of having fomented the great Berlin munitions strike of that month, and he was not released until Prince Max issued an amnesty in the following October on being appointed Reich Chancellor. Once the war was over Dittmann busied himself protesting his innocence in connection with the events of 1917-18 in the Fleet, using two arguments which still seem mutually conflicting. On the one hand, he said that he would never have bothered to cause trouble in the Fleet for he had never taken it as an important factor in the war, while on the other hand, he was in favour of a compromise peace, which would require a balance of forces between the Allies and the Central Powers, and that would be impossible to achieve if the German Navy were put out of action.

FOUR

Despite the mutinies during the summer of 1917 the High Seas Fleet continued to play its limited part in the conduct of the naval war, which, as Scheer had told the Kaiser in November 1916, was to afford 'assistance and support' to the U-boat campaign.

This 'assistance and support' was provided in two ways. First, the big ships of the Fleet were used to protect the minesweepers which kept open the swept channels through the British minefields by which the U-boats entered and left port; and second, by light surface craft themselves carrying out attacks on Allied and neutral merchant shipping.

The value of the British minelaying effort in the Bight has tended to be minimized, but the German Official History makes it clear that, from the beginning, British mines were reckoned a great danger. The scale of their overall effectiveness is shown by the fact that, during 1917-18, the Germans lost twenty-eight destroyers and torpedo-boats, about seventy minesweepers and armed trawlers, and at least four U-boats during the Bight minesweeping operations.

At the height of the British minelaying campaign, between September 1917, when the new and efficient H2 mines came into service, and August 1918, hardly a night passed without an expedition either by destroyers or submarines and, from time to time, German minesweepers and British minelayers or their escorting destroyers met, usually at the outer end of the 'Yellow' swept channel, which ran from the Ems north-west past Terschelling. It was during the summer of 1918 that the British laid the first magnetic mines ever used.

As a consequence of British minelaying, the Germans began routing U-boats in and out of the North Sea via the Kattegat instead of the shorter passage from Wilhelmshaven, and this added another 250 miles on each journey to their patrol areas, with a consequent waste of time and fuel. By the end of the year no U-boat was allowed in or out of port without its individual minesweeping escort, save in exceptional circumstances.

In order to disturb enemy minelaying and to make sure that his swept channels were clear, Scheer in November ordered what was called by the Germans a *Stichfahrt*, an expression translated by the British Official History as 'thrust voyage'.

The German force for this operation was made up of the 2nd Scouting Group (four light cruisers under Rear-Admiral Reuter in the *Königsberg*), eight destroyers and fourteen minesweepers, together with *Sperrbrechers*, the whole supported by the battleships *Kaiserin* and *Kaiser*, in accordance with the German practice of using a pair of capital ships or a light cruiser squadron to back up the most important mine clearance operations.

On the morning of 17 November there was a slight sea and patches of mist which almost entirely prevented air reconnaissance. The British forces, well informed by submarine patrol and intercepted German signals, had put to sea the day before. They knew where and when to find the enemy and did so.

The Germans first saw them as smudgy outlines, some obviously of heavy ships, at a distance of about five miles at 08.35 Central European Time. Reuter's first thought was for his minesweepers, and in the *Königsberg* he set off to cover their withdrawal, but the sweepers and their escorting destroyers made smoke so enthusiastically in the fog that it was impossible for Reuter to make head or tail of what was going on. Friend and foe alike disappeared from sight, and the minesweepers slipped their sweeps and started for home while the *Königsberg* was still looking for them. Meanwhile the other three German light cruisers, *Frankfurt*, *Pillau* and *Nürnberg*, soon rejoined by the *Königsberg*, were steaming at full speed towards the east-south-east down the swept channel, trying to draw the British after them towards the heavy guns of the battleships.

Creaming along in pursuit, easily identifiable to the Germans by their high, heavy bow waves, were the large light cruisers *Glorious* and *Courageous* (each with four 15-inch guns, as compared with the 5.9-inch guns of the German light cruisers), together with the First and Sixth Light Cruiser Squadrons, while the battle-cruiser *Repulse* was coming up in support. Further astern, out of sight of the Germans, were four more battle-cruisers and, fifty miles further astern still, were the six battleships of the First Battle Squadron.

The crisis of the action came after a chase lasting two hours. The German light cruisers, which had been in great peril at the hands of the British 15-inch guns, were almost safe, while the pursuing British light cruisers, coming through the smoke, mist and shell splashes, now found themselves in mortal danger. The British big ships supporting them had turned away, either for fear of minefields which were actually not there or because they had come prematurely to the conclusion that contact with the enemy had been lost in the smoke and mist. The British light craft had accordingly to withdraw as the 12-inch shells from the *Kaiserin* and *Kaiser* began to fall close by, and the British pursuit had been brought to naught by discrepancies in the charts which they possessed and which differed in the locations they showed of the British and German minefields.

Later, of course, there was a big inquest in the Grand Fleet, directed unsuccessfully at finding out why things had gone so wrong; but if the British were disappointed in the events of the day, the Germans were also far from satisfied.

In the first place, they had narrowly avoided losing three or four light cruisers because the supporting battleships had been stationed too close to their base and therefore too far away from the first scene of the action, while much confusion had been caused during the action by inexperienced communications personnel who were replacing, in the surface ships, the trained ratings who had gone to the U-boats. Between the British and the Germans the luck had run both ways. The British had missed a chance to sink the German light cruisers, but the fate of the big British ships, almost without armour as they were, at the hands of the well-protected and well-armed pair of German battleships might have been the same as that of the three British battle-cruisers at Jutland. Following the enquiry into this action made on the German side, Scheer ordered that *Stichfahrten* in future should take place in day-light and only when air reconnaissance was available, while ships should not pass the line Terschelling-Horns Reef without special precautions.

One fact of importance had, however, been learned by the British during the battle, and that was the position of the German 'middle channel' through the minefields, down which they had chased the Germans for two hours. Accordingly, a few days later, the British submarine *E-34* was sent to lay mines in this fairway. These mines were never found, and as the Germans continued to use the channel without incident the inference is that, in the bad weather then prevailing, *E-34* made a mistake in her position and laid her mines in the wrong place.

Altogether the British laid 60,000 mines in the Bight and it was not until the end of July 1918 that the Germans were able to devise a counter. This consisted of laying mines in an area where it was appreciated that further British minelaying would take place. On the night of 1/2 August 1918 two British mine-laying destroyers, first the *Ariel* and then the *Vehement*, struck German mines. The *Ariel*'s bow was blown off and she sank within an hour. The *Vehement* caught fire after the explosion and the flames could be seen for miles over the sea in the fine summer night. After a vain effort by the *Abdiel* to tow her home she sank early in the morning of 2 August. These sink-ings were the only successes obtained by German mines in the Bight.

The effect on British minelaying was immediate and drastic. In the three months from 1 May to 31 July 1918 there had been fifty-eight minelaying expeditions; from 1 August to 31 October, the date of the last expedition of the war, there were ten.

There had been no regular German surface warships on the high seas since the spring of 1915, and surface operations against Allied merchant shipping had been left to the armed merchant raiders, of which the *Möwe* and *Wolf* were the best known and most successful. However, once it had been decided that merchant tonnage should have priority as the target for naval attack, the possibility of sending heavy raiding warships into the Atlantic to reinforce the U-boats was discussed. The battle-cruisers were considered too valuable to risk and, in addition, the difficulties of refuelling a large coal-burning ship at sea seemed very great. They did not, however, appear insuperable to the Allies; the danger of a German battle-cruiser breaking out into the Atlantic was in their minds until the end of the war, and to meet the threat three American battleships were stationed at Berehaven in September 1918.

When the Germans abandoned the idea of employing a battle-cruiser in the Atlantic they considered sending the two fast minelaying light cruisers *Bremse* and *Brummer*, together with an oiler, to the neighbourhood of the Azores. This would have enabled the two light cruisers to spend three days at a cruising speed of twenty knots in an area in which convoys, being outside the usual area of U-boat operations, were generally weakly escorted. This plan, too, was given up, apparently because replenishment at sea seemed too difficult, even for oil-burning ships. An additional handicap from which the *Bremse* and the *Brummer* suffered was that at speeds of twenty-two knots and over they steamed, at night, through clouds of red sparks whirling from their funnels.

On 21 September most of the High Seas Fleet, together with large minesweeping forces, were sent into the Baltic for 'Operation Albion'. The object of this was to finish off the naval war against the Russians by landings on the islands of Dago and Ösel at the entrance to the Gulf of Riga. The Third and Fourth Squadrons sailed for the eastern Baltic under Vice Admiral Ehrhard Schmidt with his flag in the *Moltke*, while Scheer in the *Baden* and the remainder of the battle-cruisers and battleships of the High Seas Fleet passed through the Kiel Canal, but remained at Kiel to cover the rear of the 'Albion' force against a possible British attempt to break into the Baltic.

The German historian Professor Walther Hubatsch, in his introduction to the third volume of the German Official History of the war in the Baltic, remarks that 'Albion' was of special interest in the first place because it showed that the High Seas Fleet had recovered from the effects of the troubles of the summer, the importance of which, he adds, should not be exaggerated. In addition, he claims that a study of the Baltic operations would have been of much greater value to the future German Navy than its continued preoccupation with Jutland. By 1917 the Baltic had seen the beginning for the Germans of tri-phibious co-operation between the Army, the Navy and aircraft, the organization of escort flotillas and hunter-killer groups, operating against Russian and British submarines, the creation of minesweeping units, the use of motor-torpedo-boats and explosive motor-boats operated by remote control, and torpedo-carrying and minelaying aircraft.

As for the Russians, Professor Hubatsch points out that 'the idea still current that the Russians in World War One had operated in the Baltic in a passive and unskilful manner' is not borne out by the German Official History, even though by October 1917 the Russians had been weakened by the March revolution. Altogether it would seem 'Operation Albion' was an excellent means of 'letting some fresh air' into the big ships of the High Seas Fleet.

By 15 October, it was clear that there would be no British interference with 'Albion', and the *Baden* returned to Wilhelmshaven. On the following day the *Bremse* and *Brummer* sailed to attack an east-bound Lerwick-Bergen convoy escorted by the British destroyers *Mary Rose* and *Strongbow*. The move was part of a plan to use terror as a weapon against the neutral Scandinavian seamen and frighten them from sailing out of British ports. On this occasion the convoy attacked consisted entirely of neutral ships, five Norwegian, two Swedish and two Danish. All these ships were sunk, as well as the two destroyers. It had originally been intended that the *Bremse* should break out further to the west and look for Allied convoys, but by the end of this action she was already beginning to run short of fuel.

In December this success was repeated, when German destroyers attacked another convoy on the same route, sinking the British destroyer *Partridge* and six merchantmen, while three more neutral merchantmen were sunk off the Northumbrian coast by other German destroyers.

These two raids on the Scandinavian convoys caused Sir David Beatty, who had succeeded Jellicoe as Commander-in-Chief of the Grand Fleet in December 1916, to decide that one squadron of battleships from the Grand Fleet should regularly be attached to the covering forces of the Scandinavian convoys. These covering forces also required some thirty destroyers as escorts, which likewise had to be taken from the Grand Fleet. This meant another reduction in battleship strength, as it was not always possible to take all the Grand Fleet battleships to sea owing to a lack of escorting destroyers. Accordingly some of the older battleships of the Fourth Battle Squadron were, on occasion, left behind in harbour. At this time, according to Newbolt, although there were in theory 120 destroyers with the Grand Fleet, such were the demands on them for other than Grand Fleet work that the position was considered fairly satisfactory if seventy or eighty were available, and sometimes this figure fell as low as forty.

The reduction in strength of the Grand Fleet passed virtually unnoticed by the Germans, and it was ironic that this should have been the case. Since they had started the naval construction race with Britain they had always believed that, in time of war, they would be able to whittle away British strength by mines or torpedoes or by setting a trap into which part of the British fleet could be lured and destroyed by a superior German force. Now, at the beginning of 1918, the British battle fleet was divided and its strength reduced to an extent of which the most sanguine of Germans had hardly dared dream, but the Germans entirely failed to take advantage of the situation.

Admiral Gladisch atrributes this to the fact that Scheer did not appreciate the importance of the raids by his surface ships, while it never occurred to him that the British would consider his five battle-cruisers greatly superior to the nine British, as in fact they did. Moreover, Scheer considered that the direct help of all the High Seas Fleet was required to aid the U-boat campaign which at the end of 1917 was still, according to Gladisch, thought to be assured of success, although sinkings had been falling off ever since August. Totals of tonnage sunk had been:

July, 555,500 tons
August, 473,000 tons
September, 353,500 tons
October, 466,500 tons
November, 302,500 tons
December, 411,500 tons

The decrease in sinkings, says Gladisch, had caused concern in political circles, as had the fact that no political moves in the direction of peace had been made by the Allies; but this concern was not shared by the German Navy, whose confidence rested on exaggerated claims of success. The Kaiser also shared this confidence as late as February 1918.

It was at this time that Beatty told the new First Sea Lord, Sir Rosslyn Wemyss, that he considered that 'it was in our interest to adopt measures which would postpone a fleet action'.

He went on: 'The correct strategy of the Grand Fleet is no longer to endeavour to bring the enemy to action at any cost, but rather to contain him in his bases until the general situation becomes more favourable to us'.

On St Valentine's Day 1918 the German destroyers returned to the Straits of Dover, carrying out the biggest and most successful raid of the whole war. Their Second Torpedo-Boat Flotilla, twelve boats under command of Captain Heinecke, left Wilhelmshaven in a thick fog. Mines were suspected in the swept channel and the destroyers felt their way through the sandbanks of the Frisian coast, sounding as they went. The fog dissipated in patches during the next day. By the time the Straits had been reached the moon had set but, although the night was dark, there were plenty of stars. The weather was very cold. Spread between the British and French coasts were a British monitor, a light cruiser and a patrol line of more than fifty drifters and trawlers, guarding the anti-submarine nets and minefields and burning lights. In addition, at irregular intervals, very powerful magnesium flares cast a fierce light on the black waters, and searchlight beams brushed to and fro across their shiny surface. These obstacles to the passage of the U-boats through the Straits were the primary objective of the German attack, rather than the cross-Channel traffic in the Straits.

Half-an-hour after midnight, without warning, the paddle minesweeper *Newbury* was suddenly overwhelmed by two German destroyers steering a parallel course. Hit at once, she was covered in scalding steam from a burst steam pipe, almost everyone on deck or on the bridge being killed or wounded. Out of control, the ship, still on fire, drifted through a minefield without coming to further harm and then was brought to anchor.

The Germans, having broken through the patrol line, turned to port and then to port again, thus taking the rest of the line in the rear, firing as they came, heading into a panorama of searchlight beams, shell bursts, starshells, and signal rockets. The Germans then went back again through the British line. In all they sank seven drifters, a trawler and a minesweeper. The Germans had no casualties, the British lost eighty-nine officers and men killed or missing.

Heinecke now steered for home. For a few minutes his ships were in great peril, as they were spotted by a British destroyer which, however, failed to report them, a circumstance that led to her captain being blamed by a court martial. There were plenty of other British mistakes made that night; although gun flashes and flames and flares could be seen up and down the Straits, no one on the Allied side was able to make up his mind whether the cause of it all was German aircraft, U-boats on the surface, gunfire on the Western Front, enemy destroyers or the British firing on each other by mistake.

On board the *Newbury* the signal rockets could not be found because the ship had just finished a refit in the London Docks and no one knew where they had been stowed. One skipper threw his cyphers overboard when the Germans burst upon him, opening very heavy fire, and then strictly obeyed the order against signalling in plain language. Other skippers saw distress and alarm signals around them but did not think that it was their duty to relay them, being sure that they would be seen by someone else. Throughout there was a general failure to tell Dover what was going on. Sir Henry Newbolt wrote: 'It was indeed truly remarkable that the real facts should have been so long unreported, for many vessels in the Straits were... aware of what had happened. The Straits were actually lit up and beaconed by blazing trawlers, and several ships were moving to assist them. Nothwithstanding all this, the Germans succeeded in passing the forces which lay along their track on the north-eastern end of the Straits'. Professor Marder summed it all up by saying: 'The denouement is almost incredible, even if one allows for the fact that patrol maintained for months on end without encounter tends to be less alert than it should be'.

Only at the very end of the operation did luck, for a moment, desert the Germans. Off Zeebrugge the destroyer *G-102* struck a mine but, steaming stern first to take the strain off her damaged bow, she was able to reach Zeebrugge safely.

Leaving aside German good luck and skill and British bad luck and mistakes, the attacking force in these raids always had a very great advantage, for they knew that every ship they saw was an enemy which they could attack at once; while the other side, if they saw a strange ship, had to challenge and await a reply before they could be sure that the vessel was an enemy.

Another German destroyer attack in these waters took place

very early in the morning of 21 March, coinciding with the great German attack launched on the British Fifth Army in front of St Quentin. To support the land offensive the German destroyers and torpedo-boats carried out a most intensive bombardment of Dunkirk which, with the surrounding countryside, was packed with dumps of stores and ammunition. Seven German destroyers and eight torpedo-boats opened fire as the flat coast of Flanders began to loom in the first light. Within eight minutes the attackers fired some 1,520 rounds, mostly 4.1- and 3.4-inch, which did considerable damage in the town, although they missed one of the most important targets, the coastwise railway which linked the Allied positions round Nieuport with the rear areas.

Two British and two French destroyers were lying off Dunkirk in readiness for such an emergency, and when star-shells from the British monitor *Terror* lit up three or four German destroyers, they slipped out into the Zuidcoote channel to cut off the enemy. However, the big Germans got away, but two small torpedo-boats which had been used as mark boats for the bombardment were intercepted. The leading Allied vessel, the British flotilla leader *Botha,* rammed the first enemy and cut her in half; proceedings were now enveloped in dense smoke and steam. The *Botha* was hit in No. 2 boiler room, and at the same time her fighting lights, used as an identification signal, were put out. Meanwhile, the French destroyers *Capitaine Mehl* and *Bouclier* and the British *Morris* were chasing the other German torpedo-boat. The *Capitaine Mehl,* coming out of the smoke screen, saw the *Botha* without lights and, taking her for a German, fired a torpedo which struck her in the after boiler room. The French destroyers then sank the remaining German vessel and the *Botha* was towed home by the *Morris*.

The results of these Straits raids encouraged Scheer in his belief that an attack on the Straits by his heavy ships would give valuable results. Accordingly, in the following months as the crisis of the war on the Western Front continued, Scheer once more proposed a big raid, backed by the High Seas Fleet, on the Straits. Once again the Kaiser vetoed the proposal. Instead it was decided to commit all five German battle-cruisers against the convoys running between Britain and Scandinavia; if the Germans were fortunate, they might meet not only a convoy but also a detached squadron of British heavy ships which they could overwhelm. In support of Hipper's battle-cruisers would be the whole of the High Seas Fleet which, on this operation, went further from its base than on any other occasion during the war.

The raid was fixed for 22/23 April to coincide with the beginning of the second great German land offensive in 1918, during which the Germans recaptured Passchendaele. Newbolt points out that the moral effect of the success of this operation at this time, in waters remote from German bases, would have been very great, especially upon the Scandinavian seamen. He says:

> To take the High Seas Fleet to the coast of Norway, to sink another convoy and its escorting cruisers under the eyes of the neutral skippers; to overwhelm a battle squadron almost within sight of the Norwegian coastguard stations and lighthouse keepers, and to do all this while the British armies in Flanders were reeling under the German onslaught, would be a success of the first order.

The greatest pains were taken to prevent news of the sailing of the High Seas Fleet from reaching the enemy; it was, however, sighted by a British submarine. But her captain had been warned that his own heavy ships might be in his patrol area, and it was for these that he mistook the Germans.

Next day it was the turn of the British to have the luck. A serious accident took place in the engine-room of the *Moltke*, and she was obliged to turn back in tow of the battleship *Ostfriesland*. Hipper, with the other battle-cruisers, persevered as far north as the latitude of Bergen before he, too, turned back, apparently because of the particularly high coal consumption of the *Von der Tann*. German radio traffic arising out of the accident to the *Moltke* alerted the Admiralty, and the Grand Fleet was sent to sea from its new base at Rosyth, but found nothing. On the way back to Wilhelmshaven the *Moltke* was torpedoed by the British submarine *E-42*, but once again the British torpedoes proved not powerful enough to do fatal damage to a big German ship.

After his return to port Scheer discovered that, had he been a day earlier or a day later with his operation, he would almost certainly have met an important convoy. Newbolt points out that details about the sailing of convoys to and from Norwegian ports were completely accessible to the German consulates in the area, but the Naval Staff never thought to ask its own Foreign Office for the information, and the Foreign Office never told the Naval Staff.

While the German effort at sea was losing its grip, on land in France and Flanders the German armies were struggling desperately for the decisive and final victory before the Americans arrived in strength. They moved the weight of their attacks from the Somme to Ypres and from Ypres to the Marne. Finally, in July, the German military machine ran down, the last of the offensives petered out after only four days and a counter-attack by the French produced surprisingly encouraging results. It was clearly no longer the same German Army; casualties and exhaustion had seen to that.

A great series of Allied attacks were mounted, the first of these in front of Amiens by the British, French, Australian and Canadian troops of the British Fourth Army. The Germans, too weary to dig themselves in, were lying in the ripening corn when the attack began. Its spearhead, to use an expression fashionable in a later war, was five hundred British tanks, with one hundred more following, carrying fuel, ammunition and stores. This force broke through the German line in a way which had never before been possible in four years of war on the Western Front. Ludendorff, chief-of-staff to Hindenburg, the *de facto* commander-in-chief of the German Army, wrote in a famous passage of his memoirs: 'This was the black day of the German Army's history of this war'.

Nevertheless, between the German defeat at Amiens on 8 August and the breakthrough in Macedonia five weeks later, the Germans passed through a period of euphoria during which they almost persuaded themselves that, although there was no longer any hope of winning the war outright, they could escape with a negotiated peace; and any peace short of a complete German collapse would have meant German control of Eastern Europe. The new states had not yet been formed, the writ of Russia and Austria-Hungary was on the verge of ceasing to run, and there was nobody on the spot possessing troops and power but Germany.

The process of reconciliation to a peace on these terms began immediately after 8 August, when the Kaiser said: 'We must draw only one conclusion; we are at the limit of our capabilities', and, on 11 August: 'It can't go on endlessly like this. We must look for a way to finish it'. We can see now that there might have been months available for such a process if the Balkan Front had held and a slow fighting retreat been possible in the West.

Also on 11 August there took place the first air versus sea battle in history, an action generally overlooked at the time and one whose lessons remained unlearned until World War Two was well under way. The action was brought about by the British in their constant efforts to harass the German minesweepers.

Early in the morning of this bright summer day, four German two-seater biplanes from the seaplane base at Borkum sighted light cruisers and destroyers of the Harwich Force about twenty-five miles north-west of the island of Vlieland. Detached from this force they also spotted six British coastal motor-boats heading parallel to the coast in the direction of Emden, clearly looking for enemy minesweepers. The boats, in pairs, showed up perfectly on the blue silken sea, with their glistening bow waves and broad white tumbling wakes in bow and quarter line.

Shortly after 07.00, when the boats were abeam of the island of Terschelling and within sight of the spectators on the dunes ashore, the German aircraft, now reinforced and numbering nine, began their attack at high speed from astern, machine-gunning as they came; then, as soon as they passed over the boats, climbing almost vertically, turning through 360 degrees, and attacking once again.

The coastal motor-boats were handicapped because their Lewis guns, which with their torpedoes were the only weapons they carried, were not designed for high angle fire, but they continued on their eastward course for about half-an-hour. Then, with the lighthouse on the western end of the island of Ameland abeam, five more German aircraft arrived and the boats were soon in grave danger. The enemy machine-gun bullets were zipping through their hulls which were leaking badly, and their ammunition was running low. Accordingly they turned back to the westward, hoping to reach the Harwich Force. But now, with the boats on a westerly course, the German planes were able to come out of the sun; they dropped bombs which broke up the tight British formation and it was clear that the British had very little left with which to fight. One German plane, anxious to press home its advantage, came down in a dive to within fifteen feet of the water, machine-gunning as it came, and was promptly shot down by one of the British boats. That was the end of the battle, for the coastal motor-boats were now within Dutch territorial waters, and a Dutch torpedo-boat arrived just as three of the coastal motor-boats sank within a few minutes of each other; the other three were taken in tow by the Dutch, but one of these also sank on the way to safety. None of the six boats returned home, the two survivors being interned.

Air cover from seaplanes of the Harwich Force had been planned for the coastal motor-boats, but the sea was so calm that it was impossible for them to take off. Then other aircraft took off from Yarmouth but, owing to a failure in W/T communications, they were unable to find the British ships. It had been a bad morning for the British, but later on that same day they received some consolation when a fighter aircraft, flown off a lighter towed by a Harwich Force destroyer, brought down the Zeppelin *L-35*.

These weeks formed the climax of the war, and 11 August

was also marked by a most important change in the naval high command, for on that day Scheer was appointed Chief of the Naval Staff, and was succeeded as *Flottenchef* by Hipper, while Reuter from the 2nd Scouting Group took over command of the battle-cruisers. Scheer, in his new post, was specifically charged with the control of the *Seekriegsleitung* – the direction of the naval war.

His first concern now was the intensification, on a long-term basis, of the U-boat war, since, as he was to say a little later, the U-boats were Germany's last offensive weapon. Ever since the failure of the German army at the second battle of the Marne in June it had been clear that there could never be another German offensive on land. There could be no longer any question of knocking the French out of the war and driving the British into the sea. The only hope for Germany now was that the U-boats might hinder the Americans from coming in sufficient force for them to mount a final offensive; while the British might, at the same time, be deprived of the supplies which they needed to support their own war effort and that of the Allies. In this way it might be possible for the Germans to secure a peace of mutual exhaustion.

It would all depend on the completion of a vast U-boat building programme. There were 300 boats building or on order, but to complete this programme by the spring of 1920 Scheer would need some 40,000 more men in addition to those already at work in the yards. This additional allocation of man-power was approved by the Kaiser on 22 September, during discussions in which no one pointed out that, in January 1917, the Navy had been confident that the U-boats would win the war within five months. Now, in September 1918, plans were being made for a U-boat force which could not begin to operate at full strength until the spring of 1920.

It is not surprising, therefore, that this 'Scheer programme', as the U-boat building plans were termed, has been dismissed by recent German historians as a mere propaganda measure, designed to compete for public attention with the vast Hindenburg programme of munitions for the Army.

In any case, the new programme and the reorganization of the Naval command following the appointment of Scheer as head of the *Seekriegsleitung* made necessary big changes amongst the officers of the Fleet. These very largely affected the captains and commanders of the big ships, who were drafted to new appointments while their places were taken by officers who were strangers to their crews just at a time when the best possible team work in each ship would be most required.

Hipper, too, was concerned with the effect on the Fleet of the over-all priority demanded by U-boat warfare. On 24 September he wrote: 'Keeping open the entry and exit channels for U-boats and the protection of the bases in the North Sea and the Baltic is henceforth the only task of the Fleet'. But by 24 September long-term planning of the sort represented by the Scheer programme and by Hipper's outline of the Fleet's routine was already a thing of the past.

On 15 September the Allied forces in Macedonia, French, British, Greek, Serbian and Italian, had broken through the Bulgarian front and swept northwards and eastwards. The British army marched on Constantinople, thus realizing the dreams of the Dardanelles campaign three years too late; French cavalry advanced to the Danube, for a blow at the rear of the Austro-Hungarian empire, within the boundaries of which Yugoslavs, Czechoslovaks, Poles, Italians, Romanians, Austrians and Hungarians were preparing for the end of Hapsburg rule.

On the next day, at the other end of Europe, Scheer had his first intimation of collapse; on a tour of inspection of the naval establishments in Flanders, he was warned by Admiral von Schröder, commanding the Marine Corps and the coast defences, that the next Allied attack could take the German position in the rear and it might be necessary to evacuate the whole of the Belgian coast. This coast and its fortification was the great strongpoint by which the whole German line on the Western Front was secured. Once it was lost no one knew where, or indeed whether, the front could be re-established. At the same time the U-boat and destroyer base at Bruges and Zeebrugge were an invaluable advanced position from which Allied shipping could be harassed and minefields laid, although it never had the decisive value in the submarine war which had been attributed to it by Jellicoe.

The attack which Schröder had feared started at 02.30 on 28 September. Covered by a short but intense bombardment from 1,800 guns, nine Belgian and four British divisions attacked between Ypres and the sea. It was pouring with rain, and the ground, torn by four years of shelling and the consequent destruction of all the drainage in the area, seemed a bottomless swamp. Nevertheless, the Allies advanced five miles that day, the Belgian *Carabiniers* retaking Passchendaele Ridge. On this same day Scheer, back at Imperial Headquarters at Spa, realized that the war was lost and, as if to confirm that realization, Ludendorff told him that it would be impossible to release a single man for the U-boat building programme. Later that day Ludendorff himself collapsed, giving way first to fearful anger against everyone and everything – the Kaiser, the navy, the home front, the politicians. Then, purged of his rage, he walked downstairs from his office in the Hotel Britannique at Spa to the office of Hindenburg on the floor below and told him that the time had come for Germany to seek peace. The two men found themselves in agreement.

That evening Ludendorff sent to Berlin Major Erich Freiherr von den Bussche-Ypenburg, of the General Staff, to explain to a secret meeting of members of the Reichstag why peace was necessary. He took with him a description of the army's morale based on a briefing by Ludendorff; this is famous, but it is worth requoting in view of what was to happen in the High Seas Fleet four weeks later. Ludendorff wrote:

> The report of the Staff Officer I had sent to the battlefield as to the condition of those divisions which had met the first shock of the attack on 8 August perturbed me deeply. I summoned divisional commanders and officers from the line to Avesnes to discuss events with them in detail. I was told of deeds of glorious valour but also of behaviour which, I openly confess, I should not have thought

possible in the German army; whole bodies of men had surrendered to single troopers or isolated squadrons. Returning troops meeting a fresh division going bravely into action had shouted things like: 'blackleg' and 'you're prolonging the war', expressions that were to be heard again later. The officers in many places had lost their influence and allowed themselves to be swept away with the rest . . . A battalion commander from the Front, who came out with a draft from home shortly before 8 August, attributed this to the spirit of insubordination and the atmosphere which the men brought back with them from home. Everything I had feared, and of which I had so often given warning, had here, in one place, become a reality. Our war machine was no longer efficient. Our fighting power had suffered, even though the great majority of divisions still fought heroically.

Ludendorff's colossal mind had broken up. On the one hand he was urging the immediate conclusion of an armistice to save Germany from ruin, while on the other hand, it soon became clear to those around him he believed that Germany, after a short armistice, would be able to resume the war refreshed and re-invigorated. Hindenburg had the same misconception and, moreover, well into October continued to believe that the French would give up the Lorraine iron-ore fields at Briey and Longwy as part of the settlement.

In any case, an armistice was immediately necessary, and to secure it the first move by the Kaiser, Hindenburg and Ludendorff was to get rid of Hertling and replace him, as Chancellor, by Prince Max of Baden, whose known liberal beliefs might serve to show that Germany really had had a change of heart and sincerely desired a peace based upon understanding.

The new Chancellor had been appointed on 3 October to make peace, but he began by urging a delay of some four weeks to give the troops on the Western Front a chance to disengage and regroup after their disastrous defeats. But this breathing space was denied him by the Kaiser, who told him that the High Command required an armistice at once and that he had not been appointed to give trouble to the High Command.

Meanwhile, Schröder had begun the evacuation of the Belgian bases. All ships ready to sail were to leave at nightfall on 29 September. Accordingly, five destroyers and two torpedo-boats, then lying with steam up alongside the Mole at Zeebrugge, received orders, without any warning, to cast off and make for home.

On the next day, the order was given to prepare the whole coast for evacuation. All the destroyers, torpedo-boats and U-boats able to leave were brought down the canal from Bruges to Zeebrugge, passed through the locks and made ready for sea. This had to be done without delay as, at any moment, it might be necessary to blow up the locks and the dockyard at Bruges with its huge concrete U-boat pens.

Ships under repair in the dockyard, and those with too small a radius of action to steam back to Germany, were prepared for demolition and all movable stores were sent eastward by rail, road or canal to what was hoped would be safety behind the line of the Scheldt, where it was intended to make a stand in defence of Antwerp. In the end five destroyers, thirteen torpedo-boats, three U-boats and twelve motor launches had to be left behind and were scuttled.

On 30 September, the first official day of the evacuation, the Flanders U-boats began to leave for home. The RAF had seen clear signs of what was going on, and the British 20th Destroyer Flotilla had started to lay mines across the escape route which led from the Flanders coast to the Heligoland Bight, principally off Ameland, where a field of 356 mines was laid between 25 September and 2 October. At first this was avoided by the Germans who, by by keeping within Dutch territorial waters, were able to bring home safely seventeen destroyers and torpedo-boats. But, on the night of 2/3 October, about seventy-five miles north-west of Heligoland, a game of blind man's buff took place, played of course without radar, which brought losses to both sides. It was a very dark night, south-west wind Force 5, with a heavy swell and some mist. First on the scene were the nine British destroyers of the 20th Flotilla which laid a minefield and left, without seeing or being seen by three

German destroyers also on the spot. To this day, no one knows how the two groups of ships missed each other, as examination of their track charts shows them to have been almost exactly in the same place at the same time.

The German destroyers had come to meet four U-boats from Zeebrugge and a group of *Sperrbrechers* (in World War One a name given to trawlers filled with wood, cork and concrete which acted as mine-bumpers, preceding the ships that they were escorting and exploding any mines in their path by striking them), and take them safely home through the labyrinth of British minefields in the Bight.

While waiting for the *Sperrbrechers* one of the German destroyers, the half-flotilla leader *S-34*, struck two mines and sank almost immediately, with a loss of seventy-one men out of a complement of ninety. The nineteen survivors were found next morning, hanging on to a raft, by *S-33* which had been sent to look for them. Immediately afterwards *S-33* was torpedoed by the British submarine *L-10*. A little later *L-10* surfaced near *S-33* which was still afloat and which immediately opened fire, supported by three more destroyers and two trawlers which had come to her aid. *L-10* was sunk with all hands, and an attempt was made to take *S-33* in tow, but an engine-room bulkhead collapsed and, with her engine-room flooded, *S-33* was dead in the water. Further attempts to take her in tow failed and the crippled destroyer was torpedoed again, this time by the Germans to prevent her drifting away and falling into British hands.

Two nights later a German torpedo-boat and a trawler also struck mines and, on the morning of 5 October, another trawler was mined and sank within twenty seconds. The weather was now becoming very bad, not only making the rescue of the crew of sinking ships difficult but also forcing the suspension of the minesweeping which was needed to bring the rest of the ships from Zeebrugge safely home. Further to interfere with the German evacuation, a division of four British destroyers was sent into the Bight and, on 5 October, they found and attacked the trawler *Bremerhaven*. The first British salvo blew the trawler's only gun overboard and the little ship was soon sunk.

By now the Germans had decided that it was impossible to re-open Route 300, the principal swept channel through the minefields to the German North Sea ports from the westward, which had been closed by British minelaying on 2/3 October, and the remaining U-boats from Flanders were ordered to make for Baltic ports, passing round the north of Denmark. The last fugitives to get away reached safety on 11 October and eventually all these Flanders U-boats were regrouped and based on Bremerhaven, although it was not clear what their value there would be, for they were all small boats with a short radius of action. This had hardly been a disadvantage when they had only to sortie from Zeebrugge to find themselves on top of the Allied cross-Channel shipping, but from Bremerhaven to an area in which operations might be rewarding was a much greater distance.

The news of the withdrawal of the destroyers and U-boats from the Belgian coast and their return to home ports could not be kept secret from the crews of the Fleet nor from the dockyard workers at Wilhelmshaven and Kiel, to which ports the men of the Marine Corps and the dockyard hands from Belgium were evacuated.

This evacuation made things in the home ports even worse than they had been before. The morale of base elements is never notoriously high; the men from Belgium had themselves been witnesses of the consequences of a big German defeat and taken part in the great retreat which followed. Worse was the fact that the Marine Corps had been used as a kind of penal colony, not only for the most troublesome elements of the Navy itself but also for a number of men, agitators of one sort or another, who had been arrested after the strikes which had taken place during the winter of 1917-18. They were called up, put into uniform and sent off to the rear areas in Belgium where, in fact, they were able to do the greatest possible damage to the already low morale of everyone else. In addition, in Kiel itself the effects of the big strikes of the previous January were still felt. They had begun on the 25th in the torpedo factory. The authorities retaliated by calling up the shop stewards for the armed forces, but by the 29th between 23,000 and 24,000 men were out, including many from the U-boat building yards at Kiel, Hamburg, Bremen and Danzig. However, by the use of the call up and a number of sentences of imprisonment, the strikes ended suddenly on 1 February amidst great bitterness.

In the Navy it was realized that possession of the Flanders coast had made possible German resistance on the Western Front for four years, and all understood that its evacuation would never have been ordered except as the result of a terrible defeat, so terrible that a naval officer, recalling the event in very simple terms years afterwards, said, 'We knew that we had lost the war.'

Almost simultaneously on 30 September came the news of the Bulgarian surrender.

On 4 October Prince Max von Baden was appointed Chancellor, and on the same day sent off the appeal for an armistice to President Wilson.

Commenting on this, Professor H. W. V. Temperley, who edited the massive six volume history of the Peace Conference, points out that:

> It had been the hope of the German authorities that they would be able to arrange terms of armistice of such a nature that it would enable them to begin hostilities again, supposing the negotiations broke down, on conditions which would be at least as favourable as when hostilities ceased. They would indeed, unless special guarantees were required, be more favourable because the German army, which was exhausted, would have an opportunity for recovery. But on 14 October President Wilson made clear that such hopes were in vain. There was to be no prospect that the terms would be such as to enable Germany to take up arms again. 'It must not be a temporary cessation of hostilities, but complete surrender.'

Wilson went on to say that before armistice terms could be

discussed, violations of the laws of war then being committed would have to stop. The first of these current violations was the looting of the occupied towns in France and Belgium as the German army withdrew, and the deportation of members of the civilian population to forced labour in Germany. The second was the continuation of the unrestricted U-boat warfare campaign. The President wrote:

> At the very time that the German government approaches the government of the United States with proposals of peace, its submarines are engaged in sinking passenger ships at sea, and not ships alone, but the very boats in which their passengers and crews seek to make their way to safety. The President feels that it is also his duty to add that neither the government of the United States, nor, he is quite sure, the governments with which the United States is associated as a belligerent will consent to consider an armistice so long as the armed forces of Germany continue the illegal and inhuman practices which they persist in.

Wilson's feeling, and that of the Allied public as a whole, had been driven to a pitch of exasperated anger unmatched by anything since the sinking of the *Lusitania* in 1915, when, on 10 October, SS *Leinster*, a mail steamer running between Ireland and Great Britain, was sunk by two torpedoes. Of the 720 people on board, including women and children, 176 were drowned.

The idea that the unrestricted submarine warfare campaign should be suspended in the interests of the armistice negotiations was violently opposed by Scheer, who had put all his hopes for the future into U-boats and who still believed that the campaign should be kept going, as a means of keeping pressure on the enemy for milder terms. He repeated that the U-boat was now Germany's only offensive weapon and urged that the authorities proclaim a *levée en masse* (calling up all adult males, including workers not yet in the armed forces) and continue to wage submarine warfare in the most energetic manner.

It was pointed out to Prince Max by various people, including Crown Prince Rupprecht of Bavaria, the Army Group commander facing the British armies, that in the fifth year of the war a *levée en masse* would yield very little and would take from their jobs the very men whose task it would be to build the U-boats upon which the campaign depended. In addition, critics said openly that the U-boat campaign was regarded by the German people as their greatest misfortune and something for which men would see no reason at all to die.

Scheer had to give way and, on 20 October, Wilson was told: 'In order to avoid anything that might hamper the work of peace, the German Government has caused orders to be despatched to all submarine commanders precluding the torpedoing of passenger ships.' This entailed calling off the entire unrestricted U-boat campaign, since it was judged impossible for submerged submarines to distinguish between merchant ships carrying passengers and those carrying cargo only. Accordingly the U-boats were ordered to return to their bases. The return of the U-boats meant that the Fleet was no longer restricted by its duties in their support. According to Scheer, 'the Fleet had now regained its liberty of action', and the next question was how that 'liberty of action' could best be used.

Earlier, on 16 October, Scheer had stated that the Navy had no need of an armistice, which showed a somewhat peculiar view of warfare, envisaging a situation in which the Army would be observing a truce and the Navy continuing to wage war. He observed that the restrictions which had been imposed on the Fleet by the demands of the U-boat war no longer existed: 'The Fleet gets back its operational freedom,' he wrote, adding:

> It is impossible that the Fleet should remain idle during the final struggle which will precede an armistice to be concluded sooner or later. It must be committed. Even though it is not to be expected that a decisive turn will be given to events from the point of view of morale, it is a matter of the honour and the existence of the navy that it should have done its utmost in the final struggle.

Scheer and Levetzow agreed that the navy might be able to take some of the burden off the German army by an attack on

Allied shipping in the southern part of the North Sea, and Levetzow was sent to Hipper at Wilhelmshaven on 22 October with the following verbal message: 'Your Excellency, I have the following order to transmit from Admiral Scheer. The High Seas Fleet is directed to attack the English fleet as soon as possible. For that purpose all available forces of the Imperial navy should be employed.' Later, Hipper was to stress the fact that he himself had not the authority to commit the Fleet. Only Scheer could do that.

In London, and in the Grand Fleet, ever since Scheer had replaced Holtzendorff in August and the war was clearly entering its last phase, the expectation that the Grand Fleet would soon be involved in a decisive battle had been quietly, almost tacitly accepted, for it was believed that Scheer would adopt a policy more daring than that of his predecessor. In addition, it was remembered that the last two important naval wars, those between Russia and Japan, and the United States and Spain, had both ended with a naval battle in which the weaker fleet had challenged its opponent to a fight to a finish, although it was too late for the outcome of the battle to affect the result of the war and the challenger had no hope of success.

There was now the possibility that the Germans might act in the same way, and the Admiralty and Beatty took their precautions. The first move was made as soon as the sinking of merchant ships by U-boats was seen to have ended. Destroyers, hitherto engaged on anti-submarine work, were sent to join the Grand Fleet at Rosyth from Buncrana in the North of Ireland, Portsmouth and Devonport, so that for the first time in months the Grand Fleet had sufficient destroyers to give it adequate anti-submarine protection.

For the sake of security, Levetzow had brought the order from Scheer to Hipper verbally and nothing was committed to writing. The suspicion has survived that this was done not only to keep the plan secret from the enemy but also from the highest authorities in Berlin, for neither the Kaiser nor the Chancellor was told. However, on the other hand, Ludendorff was informed. Scheer, Levetzow and others afterwards explained that when Scheer said that the German fleet had resumed its freedom of action he meant that it was now at liberty to challenge the Grand Fleet and would, in fact, do so. It does not appear to have occurred to the Kaiser or the Chancellor that Scheer's words had this meaning, and that an operation of the greatest importance to the conduct of the war and the armistice negotiations was intended.

How much was really expected by the Germans from their planned attack is unclear. Levetzow, when the war was over, said, 'After a victory by the German fleet, surrender and revolution would have been a spiritual impossibility.' However, he did not explain then or afterwards how he thought the German fleet was going to be successful in the face of the heavy odds against it.

The plan for the operation which Trotha now drew up called for raids by light cruisers and destroyers, with the battle-cruisers in close support, on the coast of Flanders and on shipping in the Thames estuary; the Grand Fleet would be drawn south in order to cut off the raiders on their way home and would encounter the High Seas Fleet off Terschelling. The time-table of the operation laid down that the High Seas Fleet should sail from Schillig Roads early on 30 October, to be off Terschelling steaming south at dawn and to be back again off Terschelling for the decisive battle on the evening of 31 October.

German preparations began with the laying of mines and the stationing of U-boats off the principal British bases in the North Sea to catch the Grand Fleet which, it was anticipated, would be sent south to intercept the Germans. Hitherto, raids in the southern part of the North Sea had not been carried out by any ships bigger than destroyers. Now the German battle-cruisers, under Reuter, were to enter the estuary of the Thames itself and to wait, in support of the light cruisers and destroyers, at Black Deep, near the Sunk lightship, eighteen miles north of Margate and twenty miles east of Foulness Point. At the same time, the battleships of the High Seas Fleet would come down as far south as 51° 40′, that is, a line running between Clacton-on-Sea and the Oester Scheldt. After the light cruisers and destroyers had carried out their raids, the whole German fleet would concentrate and steam northward, expecting that on the evening of 31 October they would meet the Grand Fleet steaming south. The final battle of the war would then be fought.

If, however, this meeting of the two fleets did not take place, all available German destroyers would steer north-westwards, during the night of 31 October – 1 November towards the Firth of Forth, searching for the enemy. Should they find him, they were warned not to economize with their torpedoes. Salvos of three were recommended. The weather which, in a pre-radar age, might have caused the two fleets to miss each other was in fact good for the time of year in the southern North Sea although outside that area there were continual gales.

On their way south the German ships were strictly ordered to keep out of sight of land. Great stress was laid upon this because the British were believed to have established chains of coast watchers on Scandinavian and Dutch territory. In no other way could the Germans account for the excellent information which the British possessed as to their movements. Only long after the war was it revealed that the British had, in fact, relied largely on the code-breaking activities of 40 O.B.

When the High Seas Fleet sailed to carry out its great operation it was to be led by the First Scouting Group of five battle-cruisers, four of them veterans of Jutland, while the fifth was the newest of them all, the *Hindenburg*, flying Reuter's flag. Astern of the battle-cruisers were to follow the seven new light cruisers of the Second Scouting Group, of which the *Königsberg, Köln, Dresden* and *Pillau*, with five destroyers of the Second Torpedo-Boat Half-Flotilla, were to attack shipping in the Thames Estuary, while the *Graudenz, Karlsrühe* and *Nürnberg* were to bombard targets on the coast of Flanders.

Astern of the two scouting groups would follow the main body of the High Seas Fleet, eighteen battleships of the First, Third and Fourth Squadrons, escorted by forty-three destroyers and led by the battleship *König*, which had also led the German battle line at Jutland. Hipper's own flagship, the *Baden*, largest and most modern of the German battleships, would be the sixth ship in the line. Behind the battleships and their destroyers were to come the six minelayers of the Fourth Scouting Group, which were to lay their mines in the path of the approaching enemy.

Before the High Seas Fleet had finished assembling in Schillig Roads some mines had already been laid by the Germans as part of the scheme outside British bases, but these had been swept up almost at once in the course of routine British minesweeping operations without special significance having been attached to them.

The Germans did not know that Scapa had been abandoned by the Grand Fleet as its principal base as far back as 12 April, when it had moved to Rosyth. Thus it was about two-hundred miles nearer Hipper than he realized, which meant that the meeting of the British and German fleets would, in all probability, have taken place correspondingly earlier.

FIVE

Beginning on 22 October, six U-boats were recalled by the *Seekriegsleitung* from their patrol areas to take up new positions outside British bases in the North Sea, while a further twenty-four boats were despatched from Germany to similar waiting areas. Of these thirty boats, seven returned to port prematurely owing to various defects, and two were sunk on 28 October, *U-78* by the British submarine *G-2*, and *UB-116* on a controlled minefield while trying to enter Scapa Flow in search of the Grand Fleet, which was no longer there. For some time after the war it was believed in Britain that *UB-116*, commanded by Lieutenant Emsmann, had, for this operation, a volunteer crew composed of officers only; but this was not the case, and Admiral Spindler, the official historian of the U-boat war between 1914 and 1918, stresses in the last volume of his *History* that *UB-116*'s crew on this occasion was quite typical, although, Spindler adds, there was in fact one volunteer on board, an officer who had persuaded his friend Emsmann to let him join.

Three days after the U-boat concentration had begun, the first rumours of the impending operation spread around Wilhelmshaven, started by a young officer at a party. On 27 October came the first moves by the surface vessels of the High Seas Fleet, in execution of Hipper's plan. Almost at once there were premonitory rumblings of the disaster which was to put the Fleet out of action. The light cruisers of the Fourth Scouting Group were ordered to Cuxhaven to load mines, something which was never done unless a real operation was planned, so that this Group, at least, knew that something big was impending and accordingly disbelieved the reports carefully circulated that the Fleet was only preparing for exercises.

As the *Strassburg* of this Group was leaving Wilhelmshaven about forty-five members of the engine-room complement vanished over the side into the confusion of the dockyard, and had to be laboriously rounded up and brought back on board. Two days later all six ships of the Group were at Cuxhaven, lying alongside the Imperator Quay loading mines. The *Regensburg*, flying the broad pennant of Commodore von Karpf, commanding the Group, was ordered to coal and oil, whereupon one division of seamen refused to clear away the mess tables and benches, and one watch of the engine-room complement came on deck in their shore-going clothes and refused to work. The First Lieutenant intervened and arrested the ringleader, whereupon work was begun. Karpf reported that this demonstration and the one in the *Strassburg* was in support of Prince Max's armistice bid and was promoted by pacifist propaganda.

Meanwhile the rest of the High Seas Fleet was gathering in Schillig Roads. The Fourth Squadron from Kiel passed through the canal and arrived without incident. But when the battle-cruisers of the First Scouting Group left Wilhelmshaven for the open roadstead and passed through the locks, some 200-300 men from the *Derfflinger* and *Von der Tann* clambered ashore and they too disappeared into the dockyard, having to be brought back by the shore patrols, again quite peaceably.

The arrival in the roadstead of the three battleship squadrons and the battle-cruisers made absolutely clear to all those present what was in prospect. Usually the three battleship squadrons (First, Third and Fourth) operated separately on a rota system, one squadron at a time spending a week at sea anchored in support of the minesweepers, always engaged in the Sisyphean task of keeping the swept channels clear for the entry and exit of the U-boats, while a second squadron lay in reserve in the Schillig Roads and the third was in port at Wilhelmshaven. Further cause for rumour was given by the sight of the *Moltke* painting her second funnel red, for red or yellow funnels were recognition symbols of the big German ships in a night action.

Units of the fleet continued to arrive during the afternoon and evening of 29 October, including the Second Torpedo-Boat Flotilla, and in the falling darkness its crews, hearing cheers coming from the Third Squadron, believed them caused by the prospect of battle.

But that was not what was happening. Earlicr in the afternoon men of the watch below had begun to gather on the forecastle of the *Markgraf*, flagship of Rear-Admiral Feldt, second-in-command of the Third Squadron, to discuss events. It seemed clear to the men that the whole fleet was about to engage in battle against an enemy known to be overwhelmingly strong. Not only were the crews faced with defeat and death but they believed that, if the Germans did attack, the Allies would break off the armistice negotiations.

The mood of the men on the *Markgraf*'s forecastle became quite clear when somebody jumped up on a bitt and called for three cheers for President Wilson, which were raggedly but enthusiastically given. As one commentator remarked afterwards: 'At this time the Germans believed that they had more to hope for from Wilson than from their own leadership.' Cheers followed for peace. These were the cheers which the crews of the Second Torpedo-Boat Flotilla had interpreted as being cheers for the prospect of battle.

Then someone shouted that the *Markgraf* should not sail and that they should draw the fires in the boilers. At this stage the officer of the watch intervened. He was jostled and surrounded by angry men, someone waved a revolver, and the officer of the watch had to be rescued by petty officers and a warrant officer. The master-at-arms arrived with the ship's police and made a selection of apparent ringleaders, who were taken below to the cells.

Cheering and disorder also broke out, about this time, in the *König* and *Kronprinz Wilhelm*, two other ships of the Third Squadron.

The sun set, reflected brilliantly in the calm waters of the roadstead, while the silhouettes of the big ships and the tall straight plumes of smoke from their funnels stood out against the last light. The first stars appeared and the ships were soon glittering with lights from their scuttles. Scraps of mist drifted across the surface of the water and then, at about 19.00, the wind got up and it began to rain in a series of brief squalls.

Hipper summoned all his admirals and captains on board the *Baden* for a final briefing at 20.00, and the lights of the boats were soon seen making their way across the water to the fleet flagship. On board the battleship *Thüringen* of the First Squadron there was trouble in getting the captain's boat away; in answer to boatswains' pipes and orders nothing happened. The men who should have lowered the boat hid themselves in various parts of the ship and it was necessary to get together a scratch party to do the job. When the captain of the *Thüringen* finally reached the *Baden* he found reports coming in of the events in the ships of the Third Squadron.

Hipper's first reaction was to disregard news of these disturbances, which he attributed to too much talk of peace at a time when the war was still in progress and when it might still be necessary to fight on. But at about 22.00 that night he came to the conclusion, on the basis of the advice given by Vice-Admiral Kraft commanding the Third Squadron, that it would be impossible for the fleet to sail. The fact that there was once more a good deal of fog to seaward provided a small degree of face-saving, and the operation was postponed ostensibly on the ground of bad weather.

To a large part of the fleet, used to the changeable North Sea weather, there was nothing strange in this cancellation. No one outside the ships involved seems to have learned what had been going on. It was not until the next morning after a meeting of captains on board the flotilla leader, for example, that the Second Flotilla learnt what had happened in the battleships. The reaction of the destroyer men was that they should continue with the planned operation, whether or not the battleships sailed with them.

Hipper himself came to the same conclusion and decided

that, instead of employing the whole of the Fleet for the raid, he would use only the light cruisers and the destroyers, while the battleships of the First Squadron would cover the necessary minesweeping operations in home waters. This, of course, meant that there could be no fleet action. A little later it became clear that the First Squadron was also quite unreliable, and the *Baden* was informed that there had been disturbances in both the *Thüringen* and *Helgoland* which soon developed into full-scale mutinies.

Because of the fog the squadron had not been ordered to weigh until 08.00 on the morning of 30 October. When preparations for leaving harbour began it was seen that in both ships a number of men were not at their stations. When orders to weigh were finally given some men barricaded themselves in the forecastle and sang songs, not revolutionary ones, but sentimental ones about the *Heimat*. They stayed there all day, moving only to occupy the compartments through which passed the anchor cables and, when the order to weigh was repeated, they jammed the capstan so that the anchor could not be raised. Other men barred access to the machinery spaces, and as no one tended the fires, pressure dropped in the boilers.

The mutineers in the forecastle then put out the lights in their part of the ship and settled down to a noisy night. Earlier, during the afternoon, someone had flashed a message from the *Thüringen* to the *Ostfriesland*, flagship of Vice-Admiral Boedicker commanding the squadron, saying that the captain of the *Thüringen* was no longer master of the situation.

Boedicker took this news to Hipper at another meeting held on board the *Baden* during the afternoon and was sent back to his squadron to get definite information. It was soon clear that the First Squadron would not be available for the substitute operation which had been proposed, and the question then arose as to what was to be done.

Two fire-eating commodores, who had both distinguished themselves during the war, Michelsen, commanding the High Seas Fleet submarines, and Heinrich, commanding the destroyers, urged that the whole fleet be once more ordered to sea, with the warning that if any ship refused to sail she would be sunk at once. At sea each battleship was to be shadowed by torpedo craft with orders to sink any ship who failed to keep her proper station.

This plan was opposed by Boedicker and Reuter, who argued that the only way in which the efficiency and discipline of the Fleet could be restored was by careful handling and a gradual nursing back to a sense of duty. Hipper agreed, although immediately afterwards he wrote to Scheer urging that both Boedicker and Reuter should be replaced. As a substitute for Reuter he proposed Karpf, whose fitness for what was the second most important place in the Fleet was soon to be disproved.

Hipper next decided that the squadrons of big ships should be separated to avoid the spread of mutinous infection. The First Squadron was to go to Brunsbüttel at the western entrance to the Kiel Canal, while the Fourth Squadron was to remain based on Wilhelmshaven to support the minesweepers who, mutiny or no mutiny, still had to see that the channels were swept. The battle-cruisers were to go to Cuxhaven and the Third Squadron to Altenbruch Roads, nearby.

When Hipper announced this, Kraft disagreed strongly. He believed that it was now necessary to appease the men and persuade them that their chiefs were sympathetic, and accordingly he urged that the squadron should go to Kiel. Its home port was Kiel, he said, and it had not been there for a year. If the crews were permitted to return to their families now, it would be a clear indication that henceforward men would receive more consideration than hitherto.

Hipper agreed, and sent a signal to the Commander-in-Chief, Kiel, telling him what was about to happen. The Commander-in-Chief, Vice-Admiral Souchon, who had only taken up command two days previously, replied with a most vigorous protest against the new move. He pointed out that in Kiel there were 100,000 dockyard workers, known for their left-wing Socialist leanings, and in addition 20,000 seamen waiting for ships, under training or just returned from Flanders. In addition, Kiel like all German industrial towns had had a miserable war from the point of view of the rationing of food and fuel. Strikes had broken out at the end of March and the beginning of April, at a time when no bread had been distributed for four days, while the city records show that for weeks the population had been without cereals and potatoes. It was at this time that crowds broke into the bakers' shops, seized what bread they could find and withdrew, carefully leaving behind money to pay for what they had taken.

Souchon was now plainly alarmed and he was a man who was entitled to have his fears respected. As Rear-Admiral commanding the German Mediterranean Division in 1914, consisting of the battle-cruiser *Goeben* and the light cruiser *Breslau*, he had been responsible for the escape of the two ships from superior British forces into Turkish waters, an event which changed the whole course of the war. Then and later, his conduct had led him to be considered one of the most able German admirals. After three years in Turkish waters he had returned to Germany to command the Fourth Squadron of the High Seas Fleet. When he was appointed to Kiel, he returned to that port for the first time in ten years.

The big ships sailed from Schillig Roads, leaving only the *Thüringen* and *Helgoland* behind. It had been decided that the mutiny in these ships should be quelled, but it was appreciated that it would be best to do it out of sight of the rest of the Fleet. Hipper ordered marines to the ships to take the mutineers into custody.

To support the marines, who were embarked on board two fleet-tenders, it was decided to send a division of destroyers and a submarine. The submarine was *U-135*, a large new boat whose captain, Lieutenant-Commander Johannes Spiess, had been in submarines for six years and had been first lieutenant to the famous Otto Weddigen when that officer had sunk three British armoured cruisers in one morning. Since then he had had an excellent record as captain in his own boats.

He was not a man easily astonished, but he has put on record his feeling of shock when Commodore Michelsen, his senior officer, sent for him and asked, 'Are you completely sure of your crew?' It had never occurred to Spiess not to be, and he replied at once, 'Yes.' He knew that there had been some trouble in the High Seas Fleet during the summer of 1917, complaints over food and discipline, but as far as he was concerned it had blown over and apparently had been almost forgotten by those not directly involved. Michelsen now told Spiess that something had happened in the *Thüringen*. Marines were being sent to restore order. Destroyers were to cover them and he was to take his boat as well.

Spiess then asked for written orders to cover him if he had to open fire. Michelsen declined to issue any and, telling Spiess to do his best for the sake of Germany, sent him to see Hipper who was, he said, still on board the *Baden* in the Roads.

Starting out, Spiess met one of the staff, who told him that Hipper had shifted his flag from the *Baden* to the ancient and disarmed battleship *Kaiser Wilhelm II*, which served as his headquarters in port. Spiess commented briefly to himself on a state of affairs in which, at the height of a great crisis, the Commodore (Submarines) did not know the whereabouts of the Commander-in-Chief. However, Spiess soon found Hipper, who also refused to give a written order. This was another shock to Spiess. Hipper had earned great renown in the Fleet and in Germany for the part which he had played at Jutland, but it was now clear that he was completely overwhelmed by recent events.

Spiess left the *Kaiser Wilhelm II* and took his submarine out into the Roads, together with the two steamers carrying the marines and the five destroyers of the Fourth Half-Flotilla. *U-135* and the leader of the destroyers, *B-109*, were followed by *B-97* and *B-112* and, further astern, *B-110* and *B-111*.

U-135 went to action stations with her 5.9-inch gun manned. On board both battleships the men could be seen lolling about the upper-deck and even on the quarter-deck, where men off duty were not permitted. According to Spiess, officers and others appeared to be clearing away these idlers as *U-135* arrived, and driving them below. Mutineers were leaning out of the forecastle scuttles, waving white rags and bits of white paper with Red Crosses on them, looted from the sick-bay. The two steamers, with, in all, 250 marines on board, approached the *Thüringen* from the side where the *Helgoland* was lying, and the *Helgoland* trained the 5.9-inch guns of her port battery upon them. Officers and petty officers of the *Thüringen* manned her after 12-inch turret which was then trained on the *Helgoland*. The steamers altered course to come alongside the *Thüringen* on her port side, so that her bulk was between them and the *Helgoland*. The *Helgoland* then trained her 5.9s on *U-135*. Spiess signalled 'Train all guns fore and after'. The battleship obeyed.

There was a pause and at 14.00 the destroyer *B-97*, long, low and dark grey, began steaming slowly past the *Thüringen* from bow to stern. Her gun and torpedo crews could be seen standing by their weapons, and from her foremast the red Z pennant blew out, signifying 'I am about to open fire'. Then, as the destroyer reached abeam of the *Thüringen*'s middle funnel, the pennant fluttered down to the dip and the destroyer turned away.

The order to open fire had been countermanded at the last moment. On board the *Thüringen* the captain and officers, with members of the bridge personnel, had gone to their action stations in the open, completely exposed to the destroyer's fire. When the *B-97* had first been seen approaching, the captain's messenger had begged to be allowed to make a last attempt to persuade the mutineers to surrender. Permission was granted and the messenger slipped down a ladder on to the dark and deserted mess decks. Banging on a closed water-tight door, he managed to persuade the men inside the compartment to open up and then to surrender. The destroyer's orders were cancelled, the red Z pennant hauled down, and the marines from the two steamers clambered aboard the *Thüringen*, wearing steel helmets and carrying rifles with fixed bayonets. The cover was taken off a hatch on the forecastle, so narrow that only one man could emerge at a time. Blinking in the daylight as their heads came above the level of the deck, the mutineers found themselves faced by the commander with a drawn revolver and two marines with rifles and fixed bayonets at the ready. Across the deck, in front of the fore turret, the rest of the marines in long black leather-belted greatcoats were drawn up. One by one the surrendered men came up on deck, in various bits and pieces of uniforms, overalls, blue jumpers and the wooden clogs worn while working in harbour. Between a double row of marines, the mutineers made their way over the side into the waiting tenders. The *Helgoland* was then similarly dealt with.

Afterwards Spiess wrote: 'If we had fired into the forward battery of the *Thüringen*, where the mutineers were, discipline would at once have been re-established in the Fleet.'

All the mutineers from the *Thüringen* and *Helgoland* were lodged in the naval detention barracks at Oslebshausen, where they were joined by others from the *Markgraf*, *König*, *Oldenburg* and *Friedrich der Grosse*. The *Oldenburg*'s contingent was a party of some twenty stokers who had been ordered to replace some of the arrested men in the *Thüringen* and who had refused to go. The officer in the *Oldenburg* charged with seeing that the relief stokers in fact went to the *Thüringen* said that he quite understood that men from the *Oldenburg* would not want to take off their cap-ribbons with the proud name of *Oldenburg* upon it and substitute the name of *Thüringen*, a ship which had just proved to be a disgrace to the Imperial Navy, but that they should go all the same. They refused, and joined the others in Oslebshausen.

It is not clear whether he made this remark because he really failed to understand the men's unwillingness to leave the ship or whether he was offering a verbal olive branch, which would give them an excuse for changing their minds. These men were all young, and some of the old men intervened, haranguing them and persuading them to continue to refuse to obey orders.

The boats of the Fourth Half-Flotilla returned to Wilhelmshaven but their crews, when going ashore, were barracked and mobbed because of the part they had played in putting down the mutiny; and it was decided that, for their crews' safety, the boats should be moved to Brunsbüttel, much to the annoyance of their crews, who considered that port a dreary place.

Now the *Thüringen* and *Helgoland* were ordered back to Wilhelmshaven. They made a mournful picture, with no ensigns or pennants, no ceremonial guards and bands, watched by some with contempt and by others with trepidation as they wondered what was to follow in this extraordinary sequence of happenings.

Immediately after this mutiny had been quelled, an investigation of events leading to it was made, which appears to give a typical cross-section of opinion on the lower deck of the *Thüringen* and probably of the other battleships. The night of 29/30 October in the ship had been an uneasy one, troubled by many rumours. Officers' stewards had reported to their shipmates on the lower deck that the wardroom was talking loudly about a forthcoming battle from which they did not expect to return, and were drinking toasts to the last two thousand rounds of ammunition. In fact there does not seem to have been any appreciable amount of drunkenness, but there does seem to have been a good deal of gallows humour which served to heighten the tension in the ship. Several men said they had heard that the Kaiser was on board the *Baden*, intending to lead the Fleet in a glorious final battle.

The navigating officer was said to have got out his charts of the east coast of England, and the idea grew that the planned attack on the English coast was intended to bring about the failure of the Armistice negotiations. It was repeatedly said that Reichstag and the civil government knew nothing of these plans, so that some men claimed it their duty to stop this illegal action. Argument went on far into the night.

Several men said later that, although they would not take part in an attack on the English coast, everyone would have done their duty if the English had attacked them.

The captain of the *Thüringen* agreed to receive a deputation, who told him of the rumours that were going round the ship.

The captain said that he now had permission from the admiral to tell them about the planned operation.

According to a member of the deputation, the captain said that the German troops on the right flank of the Western Front were being shelled by English battleships, and these were to be attacked by the German torpedo-boats in the Scheldt. The battleships of the High Seas Fleet were to protect the torpedo-boats against an attack from the rear and hold open the swept channels through the minefields.

The deputation replied that it would have been better if the crew had been told earlier what was going on. Nobody in this exchange seems to have made the point that, for reasons of security, such information could not possibly be revealed while the ship was still in touch with the shore.

Another member of the deputation was asked by the captain what he thought of things, and whether he could guarantee order on board. He summed matters up by saying he could do so but that he was of the opinion they were going to sea against the wishes of the government and, if that were so, it would be his duty to stop the planned move. Afterwards the same rating added that he thought he had then given the captain a full guarantee of his personal safety, adding that he would defend him with his life.

The deputation then went into the forward battery where one of them, standing on a locker, gave an account of the talks in a loud voice. There was a good deal of shouting and some claimed that they had been lied to and still did not want to sail. In talk with another rating, the commander was said to have criticized the new government. This was widely reported through the ship and made people even more excited.

During the night, patrols of warrant officers went through the ship in pairs; they were said always to have one hand in their pockets, where they were believed to carry a weapon. This did not improve morale; men complained that, although they had done their duty for years past, they were now threatened with firearms. But the warrant officers were not the only ones preparing to use firearms: a group of men tried to arm themselves by breaking open a locked rifle-rack, but they do not seem to have been successful.

For years afterwards some German authorities agreed with Spiess, believing that it had been a mistake not to fire into the *Thüringen*, and that from this mistake sprang the revolution and the consequences which followed down to World War Two. During the twenties and thirties they drew an analogy between the mutinies at Wilhelmshaven and Kiel and those in the British fleet in 1797 at Spithead and the Nore and later elsewhere. They cited in particular the handling in 1798 by Sir John Jervis, Lord St Vincent, of the situation on board HMS *Marlborough*, whose crew he forced to hang two of their own mutinous shipmates after he had made obvious preparations to sink their ship if they did not obey. If the *Thüringen* had been ordered to sail with the rest of the fleet, had refused and then been fired on, nothing more, it was claimed, would have been heard of the mutiny.

Levetzow, when he received a report on these proceedings, scribbled in the margin in spiky German script, 'Where was Lord (sic) Jervis?' and later, 'Hipper and Trotha completely failed.'

Hipper, who had left Wilhelmshaven for Schillig Roads intending to fight a decisive battle, had now returned there and had written in his diary for 31 October:

'What a terrible day I have behind me. I never really believed that I would come back again, and now under what circumstances do I do so! Our people went on strike, I would not have been able to carry out the operation even if the weather had been possible.'

After the big ship squadrons had dispersed, Hipper at once planned changes among his flag officers and attacked the shortage of competent officers of the rank of lieutenant and lieutenant-commander, which had already made itself felt in the troubles of the summer of 1917. Now, however, the end of the unrestricted U-boat warfare would make officers available for the High Seas Fleet from the submarines, while training establishments were to be shut down to provide still more.

In addition to the lack of competent junior officers in the big ships, further trouble was caused by the manner in which captains and commanders had been changed during the weeks prior to the mutiny. Between August and October nearly half these officers in the three battleship squadrons and the three scouting groups of the Fleet had been replaced; in some cases both the captain and the commander of the same ship had been changed within this period. The primary cause for this had been the reorganization of the *Seekriegsleitung* which followed Scheer's appointment as Chief of the Naval Staff. Although in theory it had been a wise measure, giving a more intelligent system of command, its consequences had been disastrous for it had involved a great deal of disorganization at the most critical period of the war.

While considering further changes, Hipper was extraordinarily complacent over the state of affairs. On 1 November, the day after the mutinies in the *Thüringen* and *Helgoland* had been quelled, he wrote: 'There is no reason to judge too severely the internal situation in the big ships.' To which the *Seekriegsleitung* replied: 'We cannot agree with this point of view. It is a fact that a military operation has been brought to nought by the behaviour of certain members of the crews.'

Nevertheless, it was the new Secretary of State for the Navy, Vice-Admiral Ritter von Mann und Teichler, who urged that punishment of the mutineers should be concentrated on the ringleaders and that the rest should be treated leniently.

This advice seems to have been sound, because the prisoners at Oslebshausen were already an embarrassment, for the Flag Officer commanding the Wilhelmshaven base, Admiral von Krosigk, did not believe he had sufficient loyal men under his command to secure the prisoners properly. Altogether, he said, he had only two hundred trustworthy men and fifteen machine-guns at his disposal. For this reason he asked the Army for assistance, an unpopular request at a time when every available man was required on the Western Front.

For a moment there was a lull at Wilhelmshaven, as the Fourth Squadron assumed the support of the minesweepers.

It has become a part of left-wing legend that the engine-room complements of the big ships of the High Seas Fleet extinguished the fires in their boilers during these mutinies so that they could not put to sea. This story was given worldwide publicity by a highly inaccurate play called *Draw the Fires*, by Ernst Toller, but in fact only once were fires drawn in a ship and this was on 1 November, when the engine-room complement of the *Friedrich der Grosse*, protecting the minesweepers off Borkum, did do so. However, Meurer, commanding the squadron, intervened and within a short time persuaded the men to relight the fires, in exchange for a promise that there should be no punishments.

Other incidents occasioned reports that fires had been drawn and stemmed from the fact that bad will, confusion and sabotage sometimes led to boiler pressures being allowed to drop, so that the ships concerned were unable to make their full speed. Sachse, one of the leaders of the 1917 mutiny, was questioned on this point after the war and replied that concerted action of the kind needed to secure the drawing of all the fires in a big ship, with anything between twelve and twenty-seven boilers in a series of water-tight compartments, was very hard to organize.

The happenings at Wilhelmshaven had been kept out of the papers by the censor, but it was not possible to keep it secret within the navy itself, and the news began to spread, first of all to Cuxhaven thanks to the Third Squadron which steamed past the port on 31 October in full view of the light cruisers of the Fourth Scouting Group.

On the way from Wilhelmshaven Kraft had been carrying out high-speed exercises with his ships in an endeavour to get them in hand, and by the time Cuxhaven was reached he believed that he had been successful; they would soon be in

Kiel and Souchon's urgent warning would prove to have been a false alarm.

On the previous day, 30 October, the Fourth Scouting Group had been loading mines. The next day, however, came the order to unload the mines, from which officers and men concluded that the planned operation had been postponed or cancelled. Unloading was in progress when the Third Squadron appeared, steaming for Brunsbüttel at the south-west end of the Kiel Canal, obviously headed for the Baltic. It was now clear that the operation was finally cancelled. Hipper would never have sailed leaving one of his three squadrons behind.

Regensburg, as flagship of the light cruisers, had saluted Kraft's flag in the *König*, which returned the salute. *Regensburg* then saluted the second flagship of the squadron, *Markgraf*, flying the flag of Rear-Admiral Feldt. To the complete surprise of everyone on board the light cruisers the *Markgraf* went straight by, without acknowledging the salute. No one had ever seen anything like that before, and the ship had a strange air. There were large numbers of men on deck, not doing anything. It was clear that something was wrong with the ship and the squadron; the suspicion began to develop that there was something wrong with the Fleet too, and that the cancellation of the operation was not simply due to bad weather which, nine times out of ten, was the cause of last-minute changes of plan in the North Sea.

The Third Squadron passed through the Canal, stopping only to land some 150 mutineers at Holtenau, who were sent to Fort Herwath, the naval detention barracks at Wik, outside Kiel. On the morning of 1 November the squadron anchored in Kiel harbour itself.

It will be remembered that after the mutinies during the summer of 1917 Capelle had sent the head of the General Department, Rear-Admiral Hebbinghaus, to Wilhelmshaven to enquire into what had happened and that he had produced a report whitewashing Scheer and the Fleet Command. Similarly, after the first troubles at Wilhelmshaven at the end of October 1918, Mann, the new Navy Minister, sent Captain Wilhelm

Michaelis, Hebbinghaus's successor, to Wilhelmshaven; but this time the head of the General Department produced no whitewashing report. He wrote on 2 November:

> The Fleet Command had no idea of what things were like in the ships. Disobedience, insubordination (disregard of orders), especially those of junior officers, had been for a long time a matter of course. The commanding officers hushed things up, in order not to get a reputation for bad discipline. I went to Trotha. He did not agree and said that things could be calmed down by tactful handling. I went back (to Berlin) with the feeling that things in the Fleet were in a bad way.

SIX

On the morning of 2 November in the muffled luxury of the Reich Chancellor's palace, a *Geheimsanitätsrat*, Dr Wilhelm Zinn, was shouting at a patient and shaking him energetically by the shoulders in an effort to bring him back to consciousness; the patient was the Chancellor of the Reich. He had been unconscious for more than than twenty-four hours following a sleeping-draught given him by Zinn, who had not realized the extent to which his patient's conditon had been weakened by an attack of influenza, which had kept him in bed from 22 to 30 October.

The next day Prince Max finally awoke to a nightmare, having been unconscious for thirty-six hours. Walter Simons, a Foreign Office official on his staff, at once came to see him and reported that, on the preceding day, the first news of the mutiny at Wilhelmshaven had reached Berlin, four days after it had taken place. On 2 November Vice-Admiral Ritter von Mann had appeared at a Cabinet meeting presided over by the Vice-Chancellor, Friedrich von Payer, and had reported with a grave face that the crews of several big ships had refused to sail on 29 and 30 October. He said that they had openly mutinied and barricaded themselves on their mess decks. Hipper had surrounded them by torpedo-boats and had had torpedoes trained on them. They had then surrendered and those who had refused to obey orders had been arrested. The mutineers explained their action by saying that the officers and the Fleet Command did not want peace and wished to sacrifice the Fleet in a great battle. Mann asked that the government issue an appeal to the men to return to discipline, but that they should be given no promises of an amnesty. On hearing Simons' report the Prince commented that it was not clear whether discipline had been restored nor whether the disturbances had been caused by Bolshevik agitation or merely by local discontent.

To gauge the effect in Berlin of the news of the mutiny, it is to be noted that the minutes of the Cabinet meeting on 2 November devoted seven lines to Mann at the end of the document, after sixty lines dealing with other problems. These included:

1. The terms of the Armistice.
2. Internal security and censorship.
3. Relations with Bavaria. (Threat of a separate peace by Bavaria and reports that the Bavarian army was no longer willing to fight on the Western Front, since the collapse of Austria had left Bavaria open to invasion by the Allies from the south.)
4. Threat of a Bolshevik *Putsch* in Berlin organized by the Russian Embassy.
5. The future of Alsace-Lorraine.
6. Decision as to which politician should lead the Armistice delegation.
7. The return of German troops from Turkey, Romania and Hungary, and the position of those in the Ukraine and Poland.
8. Speeches which might be considered treasonable made by the extreme Left-wing leader, Karl Liebknecht.
9. Constitutional Reform.
10. Food supplies, said to be 'hanging by a thread'.

Mann returned to the Cabinet the next morning, after the meeting had begun, obviously much distressed. He reported that the Third Squadron had arrived in Kiel and conducted itself in a very rebellious manner. He then read a telegram which described events in detail. The crews had made demands of a revolutionary nature, threatening officers with death. Mann begged that a Social Democrat member of the Reichstag should be sent to Kiel at once to try to calm the situation. He produced a later teleprinter message which had reached the

Admiralty. From this it seemed that bloodshed had resulted from a collision between crews of the Third Squadron and troops, in which the officer commanding the troops had been seriously wounded and four or five men killed.

Graf Roedern, Secretary of State for the Treasury, urged that the Third Squadron be ordered away from Kiel, even if this were to imperil the defence of home waters.

Philip Scheidemann, the senior Social Democrat member of the Cabinet and Vice-President of the Reichstag, had been hourly expecting the outbreak of revolution, and he now believed that this was imminent. He recommended that conciliatory leaflets be distributed in Kiel. Things in the Navy were very bad, he said, adding that since many men had been mobilized continuously for the past seven years, shipboard life was a kind of Hell. He returned to the need for a leaflet campaign.

Mann remarked that the crews of the fleet were highly intelligent and politically conscious and the principal troubles were the unpleasant conditions of life on board, with few opportunities for recreation, and the fact that it was impossible to exercise complete supervision of discontent. He added that most damage had been caused to morale on the lower deck by discussion in the Press of the abdication of the Kaiser. Men took the line, he said, that if the Kaiser abdicated, then they were released from their oath of allegiance. Thus they need no longer obey their officers and could do what they liked. The Cabinet then went on to discuss the threat of invasion of South Germany. Should German troops be sent to the Tyrol to forestall the advancing Allies from the Italian front and should the Brenner tunnel be blown up?

Mann brought the discussion back once more to events in Kiel. The situation was very serious; help had been asked from the troops at Lübeck and Ratzeburg. It was essential to convince the ratings that the officers were not planning to destroy the Fleet rather than surrender it. This conviction could not be dissipated by public speaking, he said, but only by leaflets. One had been prepared by the editorial staff of

Vorwärts (the Berlin Social-Democrat daily) and should be jointly signed by the government and the military authorities. He begged that it be distributed at once. The question of who should be blamed for opening fire during the disturbances was one that would have to be settled on the basis of evidence. There must be agreement with the military authorities as to whether proceedings should be taken against the leaders only, or against all the rioters, and he asked whether massive deportations were advisable.

Erzberger interrupted to ask whether the military force available was sufficient to suppress the rising.

The Prussian Minister of War, General Scheüch, said that he had not heard from the General commanding in Altona that his troops were insufficient but he would enquire at once for, according to a new telegram, the situation was very grave.

Scheidemann, who had left the Cabinet room some time before, now returned and said that he had been in touch with Kiel; the leaders of the Social Democrats there were anxious that Conrad Haussmann, a Secretary of State without portfolio, should go there to calm the people, and that Gustav Noske, a member of the Reichstag and the naval expert of the Social Democrats, should go with him.

Gustav Noske, one of the most remarkable figures of the era between the wars, was born in Brandenburg in 1868, son of a weaver. Successively basket-maker and woodworker, he became a journalist on Socialist provincial newspapers and entered the Reichstag as a Socialist in 1906. He remained in Kiel as Governor after the 1918 mutiny until 11 February 1919, when he became Minister of Defence, with Scheidemann as Chancellor. When Kapp's Right-Wing *Putsch* came in March 1920 he was responsible for putting it down, but ever since the Kiel mutiny and the subsequent troubles in Berlin, the Socialists of the Left had been seeking an opportunity to secure his dismissal, and the stern measures which he had employed against the Left in 1918-19 were judged to make necessary his retirement for the sake of political peace in 1920. He was appointed *Oberpräsident* of Hanover in that year, serving until 1933, when he was removed by Hitler. Suspected of participating in the bomb plot of 20 July 1944, he was arrested and held in prison until the end of the war. He died on 30 November 1946, vainly seeking an American visa.

The appeal now taking Noske and Conrad Haussmann to Kiel had been reinforced by the arrival in Berlin of Otto Kürbis, the Social Democrat party secretary in Schleswig-Holstein. Kürbis was shown the leaflet which had been prepared and said he thought it would have a calming influence on the situation. After a brief discussion it was decided that Haussmann, Noske and Kürbis should go at once to Kiel with the leaflet, the text of which read:

Seamen! Workers!

Deplorable events have occurred in the last few days. There have been collisions between crews engaged in attempting a forcible violation of good order and discipline, and troops who had received orders to maintain it; *there have been dead and wounded.*

An inquiry has been opened,
in the course of which all circumstances which have led to these deplorable events will be carefully investigated.

According to the news which has reached us up to now, *senseless rumours* have been the occasion of the prevailing state of excitement. It has been *alleged* that the officers of the Navy were dissatisfied with the Peace policy of the Government, and had planned a stroke that involved a useless sacrifice of the lives of the crews. *The officers of the Navy receive their orders from the Government*, and *the charge* made against them of having disobeyed or of having intended to disobey these orders *is without foundation.* No one dreams of hazarding the lives of their fellow-countrymen, fathers of families many of them, to no purpose. The Government's proposal of an Armistice on 5 October was made in order to avoid purposeless bloodshed.

The fact that the Armistice is not yet concluded is due to the enemy not having yet named their terms. So long as the other side wills the war to go on, the German Command on land and by sea intends to be as sparing of human life as is compatible with the inevitable requirements of defence.

But the task of avoiding *useless bloodshed* is one that concerns the whole people and not only the Government. *We are not putting an end to war between the nations in order to start on a Civil War.* It is the height of unscrupulousness to spread fantastic rumours with the object of causing unrest and kindling the flames of Civil War.

Grievances are to be investigated, all justifiable demands will be met.

Max von Baden
Ritter von Mann
Philip Scheidemann

Haussmann and Noske found Kürbis at the Lehrter Station and he told them what he knew. During the journey to Kiel the ticket collector came into the compartment and was angry that Kürbis, who had only a third-class ticket, was sitting in a first-class compartment. They could not pacify him and he threatened Kürbis with arrest on arrival at his destination. On the way they saw soldiers in goods wagons, also on their way to Kiel. From this they concluded that the situation had become considerably worse. As they got out of the carriage at Kiel, a railway official came up to them. Noske thought that he was worried about Kürbis's ticket but he only wished to say that things were not too bad.

In the station hall there was a swarm of sailors and also some armed soldiers. Noske was soon recognized, for he was a familiar figure in his frock coat and broad-brimmed hat, the mark of the Central European intellectual, with steel-rimmed glasses and a thick drooping moustache. Somebody called his name and they all started cheering. The square in front of the station was even fuller of sailors; Noske was pushed into a horse-drawn carriage in which five or six men sat, as well as one who was standing up and waving a big red flag, shouting hoarsely, 'Hurrah for Freedom!'

A sailor named Karl Artelt put himself next to Noske and began to explain what had been happening, leaving out the fact that he had just been released from prison after serving a seven months sentence for subversive agitation among the workers of the Krupp Germania yard. Now, he had been conscripted into the Navy and was waiting for a draft chit. Considered insane by the naval doctors, it is possible that he was shamming, but his general behaviour strengthens the belief that he was, in fact, mentally unbalanced. For Noske and for everybody else in Kiel a night of excitement followed.

Artelt began by announcing that thousands of sailors had armed themselves and that the officers were completely powerless. 'There can be no going back,' he announced with evident satisfaction. He said that a meeting had been called at the Wilhelmplatz at eight o'clock, at which Noske was expected to speak, after which Noske was to go to the Trades Union headquarters and then to the Governor's office, where Souchon and his staff would meet him. Noske wrote afterwards:

> The main streets of Kiel were even more crowded than they generally were at this time of day, but there was no impression that a great revolution had broken out. Men and women laughed when my flag-waving companion shouted about freedom. Unarmed sailors strolled about with their girls in the usual way and there were a lot of red badges and ribbons around.
>
> The Wilhelmplatz was badly lit; there was an enormous crowd of sailors, girls and workmen. On the big street-lamps in the middle of the square there was a number of sailors, including a giant, blackhaired man with a red sash who was waving a looted officer's sword. Later I found out that he was a very sensible man who was most anxious to restore order. As the car stopped somebody pushed a naked sword into my hand. I refused it with thanks and somebody else gratefully took it. It had been impossible for me, so far, to get a clear picture of the situation. In my short speech I ended with an appeal that order should be maintained and this was much applauded.

Then, as he drove slowly through the crowd, a shot was fired. Noske commented: 'Despite the seriousness of the situation, it was very funny to see how quickly the crowd broke up and the people ran away. Although there was no one in sight to be fired at, firing became general and went on for some time without anyone being hurt.'

Noske carried out his round of planned visits and late that night, as he returned to the headquarters which he had set up in the railway station, he had a reasonable idea of what had been happening.

On Thursday evening, 31 October, the second staff officer of the Third Squadron, Commander Meusel, had arrived in Kiel at about eight-thirty and had gone to headquarters, where he had given Souchon his first full account of what happened at Wilhelmshaven. At about the same time that Meusel was making his report, the squadron itself was at Holtenau, landing some of the arrested men. A number of liberty men also came ashore and hurried into Kiel, thus preceding the arrival of their ships.

Stories of the doings at Wilhelmshaven spread rapidly round Kiel amongst the dockyard workers and sailors, so that when the squadron entered the harbour and moored off the town next morning (1 November), shouting and cheering crowds had already begun to gather and were able to see 180 men brought ashore, under arrest from the *Markgraf*.

It would seem that at this stage Artelt realized the opportunity he had for political activity, and hastily proposed a meeting of sailors and workers which took place that evening in one of the smaller conference rooms of the Trades Union headquarters. There were about 250 men present from the *Bayern, König* and *Markgraf*. Various speakers called on the men to refuse to obey orders and to sabotage the ships so that they could not put to sea. According to a plain-clothes policeman apparently present, the meeting ended with cries of '*Nieder mit den Lumpen*' (Down with the scoundrels). The policeman added primly: 'According to reliable information, this phrase referred to officers.'

Possessed by their success, Artelt and his immediate supporters, who included Lothar Popp, the local USPD leader, organized another meeting for the next day, while the liberty men returned to their ships amid scenes and sounds of brawling and arguments.

Early on the next day (2 November) in an attempt to

forestall the next round of troubles, Souchon closed the Trades Union headquarters, where a meeting had again been planned. Disappointed sailors then tried to hold a meeting in the Harmonie Café in the Faulstrasse but, no doubt fearing that his establishment might not long be able to live up to its name, the proprietor refused to let them in, and they went off quietly to the Waldwiese, an open space on the edge of the town.

By this time two groups of agents of the authorities seem to have infiltrated into the crowd: the police sent their own men disguised as naval ratings, while naval headquarters sent a number of warrant officers and petty officers in plain-clothes to hear what went on. In the course of the discussion they heard speakers recommend that a blow on the head with a spanner was a more discreet method of dealing with officers than shooting them, as it attracted less attention.

Some arrests were made at the end of this meeting, but the arrested men managed to escape from their not very enthusiastic captors in the dark. Earlier in the day sixty to seventy more men had been arrested on board the *Markgraf* and taken ashore by a party of thirteen marines. Members of the *Markgraf*'s crew had protested, but had not interfered.

At midnight a report on these events was given to Souchon at the Holstein Hotel, and next morning, 3 November, he urged that the Third Squadron should be ordered to sail at once. Kraft refused on the grounds that his orders would not be obeyed. A proposal to cancel all further leave was abandoned for the same reason. Meanwhile the crew of the *Markgraf* decided to put their commander ashore.

A further meeting had been called by Popp and Artelt for the afternoon of that day. It was Sunday, and after lunch crowds of men from the ships, the barracks and the yards, with a number of women, flooded through the depressing streets of the town, which showed plainly, by the lack of paint and of things to buy in the shops, the effects of four years of war. Once again the meeting was on the Waldwiese, and as it was soon clear that it was going to be much bigger than those of the previous two days, Souchon decided to ban it. Accordingly he ordered the general recall to be sounded, and patrols went through the streets with drums and bugles, reading the Governor's orders for all to return to their ships. The procedure had hardly ever been used before, was quite unfamiliar and generally disregarded. The patrols were swallowed up in the crowd, and if the drums and bugles served any purpose at all it was to advertise the forthcoming meeting. There were more speeches, demands for the release of the men arrested at Kiel and Wilhelmshaven; and demands, too, for the release of the men who had been sentenced for their part in the 1917 mutinies.

After an hour's speech-making and an attempt by the SPD leader Garge, chairman of the Kiel Trades Union council, to postpone any action, the crowd, now about 3,000 strong, decided to put the first part of its programme into action by moving off to the naval detention barracks in the Feldstrasse. In the fading light a crowd which had now grown to about 20,000 surged back through the town, stopping to enlist support from men whom they found in the various cafés and cinemas on the route. Here and there officers were stopped, their dirks taken away and their epaulettes roughly torn off. The crowd went forward until, at a bend in the road, at the corner of the Brunswickerstrasse and the Karlstrasse, they suddenly found themselves faced by a line of forty-eight armed sailors across the road.

A screaming woman stretched everybody's nerves tighter. Lieutenant Steinhäuser, the officer in command of the sailors, who were mostly senior ratings, ordered the crowd to disperse. Nothing happened, save that the crowd became more threatening, and Steinhäuser ordered his men to fire over their heads. The crowd replied, first by throwing stones and then by returning the fire. Steinhäuser ordered his men to fire into the crowd and was obeyed but, as the fire was opened, he himself was struck down from behind, it is said, by one of his own men. The crowd broke up, and the casualties were taken into the Kaiser Café to be tended; they totalled eight dead and twenty-one wounded. Steinhäuser was so badly wounded and the subsequent confusion of events in Kiel was so great that he was, for some time, presumed dead.

Souchon had been following these events in a state of indecision, far removed from the well-thought-out daring with which he had conducted the operations of the *Goeben* and *Breslau* in 1914. Earlier in the day he had asked the Army Command in Altona to send troops to help keep order; previously he had refused to do so because, mindful of the jealousy between the Army and the Navy, he did not wish to reveal that the Navy was powerless to manage its own affairs. However, after the dispersal of the crowd in the Karlstrasse, he felt himself able to cancel his request. There is little doubt that, at this moment, Souchon thought he once more had the situation in hand, but the next day was to prove him wrong. Early in the morning a crowd of about ten thousand marched on the Wik barracks, demanding the release of all arrested men. At the head of this demonstration was Artelt who, with some supporters, was received by Captain Bartels, commanding the barracks. As they talked, groups of mutinous seamen occupied part of the premises, elected a Soviet on the Russian pattern and drew up a list of demands with which Bartels, to his surprise, found himself confronted. There were seven of them:

1. The abdication of the Hohenzollerns.
2. The abolition of the state of siege in Germany.
3. The liberation of all prisoners in the Third Squadron.
4. The liberation of all the men imprisoned for their part in the 1917 mutiny.
5. The freeing of all political prisoners.
6. The introduction of universal adult suffrage for men and women.
7. The immediate conclusion of a peace without annexations or indemnities on the basis of the right of self-determination of all peoples.

Bartels pointed out that the demands were all political and that he had no power to grant them. By now most of the naval establishments in the town were beginning to break out in red flags and it was clear that he could not rely upon discipline being maintained, so he sent Artelt to see Souchon. Artelt, accompanied by his principal supporter, a stoker named Podolski from the *Grosser Kurfürst*, went off in a commandeered car flying a huge red flag to confront Souchon at naval headquarters. Souchon at this time must have felt as one ground between the upper and nether millstones, for he had just received a signal from the *Seekriegsleitung* asking why the ships of the Third Squadron had remained in harbour on Saturday and Sunday, when disturbances had already taken place as early as Friday evening. He was also asked to report on the measures taken to keep ships with unreliable crews away from Kiel, 'which,' said the *Seekriegsleitung*, 'has shown itself again as a special centre of agitation and rebellion.' Souchon received Artelt and Podolski who had now been joined by others, and said, 'Tell me what you want.'

This confrontation between the admiral and the mutinous ratings has been the subject of some lush revolutionary prose. We are told: 'Cold sweat stood on the pale foreheads of the admirals as they faced the fresh young sailors, bubbling over with revolutionary energy, in their eyes the light of hope of a better future.'

Rear-Admiral Küsel, Souchon's Chief-of-Staff, sourly commented, 'In reality the fresh young sailors looked dirty and pale, and their eyes showed a bad conscience.'

Souchon said that he could not do anything about the political demands but he did agree to a pardon for the offences committed at Wilhelmshaven, the release of the arrested men, and a change in the style used by a rating talking to his captain. Henceforward he would be obliged to say, '*Herr Kapitän*' only once, when speaking to him.

Meanwhile groups of sailors were making the rounds of naval establishments, persuading and bullying others into joining them, with threats as to what would happen to their families if they refused. Souchon sent a renewed appeal for troops, and rejected the advice of some of his officers that he order those ships still under his orders to open fire on the crowds, for he had now received orders from Berlin: 'Under no circumstances, except for the defence of life or to secure the safety of private citizens, are firearms to be used.'

Communications with the capital had been maintained throughout these events; those with the High Seas Fleet at Wilhelmshaven had been dependent on a plucky woman telephonist who, from time to time when the mutineers occupying the telephone exchange were not looking, had put through or accepted a call.

Once communications had been restored between the two naval bases, Hipper ordered the Third Squadron away, except the *König* in dry dock, and they went quietly on the same day (4 November) to Travemünde on Lübeck Bay, leaving behind a proportion of their crews demonstrating and rioting ashore. By now the revolt had spread right through the yards, and the absence of the men who had sailed made no difference to the subsequent events.

On the morning of the same day Souchon had renewed the appeal to the military authorities which he had already cancelled, and the local army command in Altona agreed to help. There was, however, a complication resulting from inter-service rivalry. Kiel was a naval command, so the Army declined to send troops under a senior army officer as he would be obliged to come under the orders of an admiral. At the same time the Navy would not agree to subordinate itself to an army officer, however high his rank. Accordingly troops were sent to Kiel without any officer specifically in command and the men, apart from one trainload, steamed straight into Kiel station where they were met by crowds of sailors, who greeted them vociferously as comrades and relieved them of their weapons. The remaining trainload had been under the command of a more sophisticated, though subaltern, officer, who had detrained his men outside the station and marched them into the town. They were the only formed body of men in the city and were sent to protect naval headquarters.

More rumours spread through the town; before daylight on

the morning of the 5th the current one was of a conspiracy led by Souchon to regain his authority. He was accordingly arrested and taken to the second-class waiting-room at the railway station, where he was held as a hostage, facing a table covered with officers' dirks and a wastepaper-basket full of officers' epaulettes which had been stripped from their owners.

During the same night a party of a dozen sailors called on Captain Heine, the commander of the fortress, and shot him dead. One of Heine's last acts had been to complain to the director of the Kiel Fire Brigade, Freiherr von Moltke, about the unwillingness of the Fire Brigade to co-operate with the authorities in dispersing the crowds by using their hoses. Moltke replied that he did not wish to endanger the popularity which the Fire Brigade enjoyed in Kiel.

There were other indications of a desire to pursue a policy of neutrality between the two sides in the dispute. One of these came somewhat surprisingly from the warrant officers, who are described as acting, in some cases, as though the mutiny were simply a matter between the officers and the ratings which did not concern them at all.

On the morning of 5 November the Red Flag was flying all over Kiel, ashore and afloat, except on board the battleship *König*, still in drydock. From her ensign staff there continued to fly the Imperial naval ensign, guarded by the captain of the ship, Captain Weniger, and two of his officers, Commander Heinemann and Lieutenant Zenker. A rating tried to haul down the flag and was shot dead by the captain; fire was then opened from buildings overlooking the dock. The three officers replied, revolver in hand, but all three were shot down; Weniger, though hit five times, survived, but the other two died of their wounds.

These were the last shots and the last bloodshed in Kiel. Noske felt himself strong enough to intervene and said to Artelt: 'This bloody business must end. You must get this shooting stopped.' Artelt replied that he would not dream of interfering if officers, sabotaging the Socialist movement, were shot.

Noske then took action by himself. He first sent a messenger to a number of officers under arrest and told them to get out of Kiel as quickly as they could and to stay out. Within a day or two, officers in bits and pieces of borrowed civilian clothes, and without any money or possessions, began to appear in Berlin and seek help from the Admiralty. During the troubles at Kiel only three officers had been killed, but some escaped at least a rough handling from the crowds thanks to friendly workers or sailors who hid them and, when matters quietened down, smuggled them to safety in civilian clothes or in workmen's overalls.

Cheering crowds created Noske Governor of Kiel by acclamation, after having offered him the Presidency of an independent Schleswig-Holstein which they wished to create by secession from the Reich. Souchon and his staff agreed to serve under Noske as his technical advisers, and he was able to work out an agreement with the mutineers, whose Council had elaborated a 14-point plan of their own during the night of 4/5 November. Their demands were:

1. The liberation of all men under arrest and of all political prisoners.
2. Complete freedom of speech and of the press.
3. Abolition of postal censorship.
4. Fair treatment of crews by their officers.
5. The return of all men to their ships and barracks without punishment.
6. Under no circumstances is the Fleet to sail against the enemy.
7. Any steps that may lead to bloodshed are to be avoided.
8. Withdrawal of all troops not belonging to the garrison.
9. The Sailors' Council shall at once establish all measures to protect private property.
10. Superior officers to have no authority off duty.
11. Men are to enjoy unrestricted freedom from coming off watch until they go on watch again.
12. We welcome all officers who declare themselves in agreement with the Sailors' Council. All others are to leave their posts without rations.

13. All members of the Sailors' Council are to be relieved of other duties.
14. All future measures are to be carried out only with the consent of the Sailors' Council.

These demands represent the orders of the Sailors' Council to all military personnel.

When this document was presented to Noske he agreed to forward the political demands to Berlin. On 5 November he set off, in streaming rain, to address meetings, watch processions, visit ships and establishments all over the Kiel area, not unreasonably proud that, as a man who had never been a soldier, he was now in command of some 40,000 men.

Afterwards, when describing his experiences with the crowds at Kiel, he used words which have been frequently quoted during student disturbances in many parts of the world: 'The most turbulent and disobedient element in Kiel were the very young who had had, so far, little or no military training.' These very young men had generally come straight from their homes, where they had received a clear impression of the hardships of war which were afflicting the civilian population.

News came to Noske, on the same day, that Prince Heinrich who, throughout the war, had remained naval Commander-in-Chief in the Baltic, had fled from his residence in Kiel Castle and had shot a sailor on the way. There was enormous excitement with loud shouts of 'Treason, treason,' and demands that the Prince be arrested. Noske gathered such evidence as he could as to what had happened, in a fashion leisurely enough to make any question of hot pursuit impossible. In the end it appeared that the Prince, together with his wife and son, had left Kiel in a car flying a red flag on the radiator, heading for the Prince's country seat near Eckernförde. On the way they had been stopped by a group of armed sailors, two of whom asked for a lift without recognizing the occupants of the car. As the car drove off with the two men on the running board, one of the sailors left behind fired at it, killing one of the men, whereat the other jumped off.

What passed for calm in Kiel returned, and Noske was able

to ask Berlin for a pardon for the mutinous seamen; he also warned the government against sending any troops, for they would stand no chance against the mutineers. On 7 November Noske announced that no more troops would be brought into the town and those already there would be withdrawn. No mutineers, he added, would be punished unless they had committed crimes. Those imprisoned for their part in the mutinies of 1917 would be pardoned and released.

One of the political demands transmitted to Berlin was for a speedy end to the war. This proved an important card in Noske's hand, since he could threaten that if the men did not return to order, the end of the war might be delayed. He further decreed that red flags were to be hauled down, that any left flying would be treated as hostile, and that officers were to be saluted on duty. He also announced that he was sending an aeroplane to Berlin to bring back money so that everybody would be paid. During the talks in Kiel and the exchanges with Berlin Noske further succeeded in strengthening his own political position and that of the SPD. Haussmann had returned to Berlin, and when Hugo Haase of the USPD – still the great rivals of the SPD – finally reached Kiel on 8 November, Noske took him into his office, explained to him that there was nothing for him to do and put him on the next train back to Berlin.

SEVEN

Noske had had an extraordinary success but it had been confined to Kiel and he could not prevent the disorders from spreading all over north and west Germany. In this way the mutinies became a revolution.

Early on 5 November the first party of mutinous sailors from Kiel, mixed with a group of men on leave, arrived at the Lehrter station in Berlin and were at once arrested. It was clear, however, that there were many more to come, and Mann proposed to the Cabinet that a blockade of Kiel be set up with a cordon across the Schleswig-Holstein peninsula to seal off the province from the rest of the Reich, a proposal which was supported in a modified fashion by Erzberger. Mann added that if necessary Kiel should be bombarded. These suggestions were immediately rejected by the rest of the Cabinet, led by Haussmann, who pointed out that their effect would be starvation for all, innocent as well as guilty, while the workers and their trades unions would be driven into the arms of the mutineers.

Later that night, Noske telephoned from Kiel to report progress and asked what the Cabinet thought about the problems of an amnesty for the mutineers and of the abdication of the Kaiser. He added that he himself was very near collapse. He wrote later that it was impossible for Germans to make even a revolution without speeches and meetings and that he had had an exhausting number of them. Meanwhile, his next problem was constituted by the hundreds of children in Kiel whose milk supply had been disrupted by the troubles. Noske turned his attention to this, and arranged for the milk to be forthcoming.

In the Cabinet there was general agreement in favour of an amnesty, General von Scheüch alone being opposed, and the Cabinet turned to the problem of how to get rid of the Kaiser, and thus satisfy President Wilson and a growing proportion of the Social Democrats, who were pressing for his abdication.

On the same day Hipper had decided that the First Squadron should be got away from Brunsbüttel and gave orders that they should leave. But that morning the *Hamburger Zeitung* brought the first news that the squadron had received from the outside world since it had been ordered away from Schillig Roads on 30 October, and the men learned what had been going on in Kiel. There was, of course, enormous excitement. A meeting of the 'activists' among the crews was called for that evening at the Café Zum Guten Eck in Westerbüttel. There were speeches, shouts, songs in the smoke-filled room, with a good deal of drinking of the watery wartime beer. In the ships the officers and men whose duty kept them on board waited for more news. Finally Boedicker ordered the squadron to be ready to sail at 21.00 that night. To do this it was necessary that the ships should be passed at once through the locks of the Kiel Canal into the Elbe, and preparations for this were begun.

The news reached the demonstrators in the café, and with yells and shouts they tore out into the pouring rain of the November night, some determined to stop the ships sailing, some worried that they might be left ashore and punished for having overstayed their leave, and the rest anxious not to miss any excitement.

As they hurried through the streets they met the shore patrols which had been sent out to recall them. One of the patrols was stopped, a fight started and, after a few shots had been fired, hardly audible over the general din, the patrol was disarmed. Somebody realized that there might be more serious work ahead and a party raided one of the forts, smashing down the door of the magazine with the butts of their rifles and helping themselves to rifles, machine-guns, ammunition and hand-grenades. Another party made for the prison and released men detained there for their part in the events of Wilhelmshaven, as well as other inmates. The signal station and the telephone exchange were also occupied and then, suddenly, it seemed as though all this might have been done too late.

As the men swarmed down to the side of the lock the great black shape of the *Oldenburg* came out of the darkness, only a few feet away. Shouting to the battleship's crew to draw their fires and return to the berth which she had just left, they opened rifle fire at a range of only a few yards, with bullets rattling against the ship's upperworks and striking sparks. With loud cries a party of men ran down on to the lock gates, overwhelmed the lock personnel and thus prevented the gates from being opened. The *Oldenburg* and the remainder of the squadron were trapped, except for the *Posen* which had passed through the locks before the rioting began. The *Oldenburg* slowly went astern; the big ship with her heavy guns and hundreds of men seemed powerless.

It was now 21.20 and the *Nassau*'s turn to move down to the locks. Appreciating the need for haste at this late moment she sailed without waiting for her libertymen, and overtook the *Oldenburg*, while from the *Ostfriesland* there was a tremendous noise of shouts, cheering, singing. A searchlight from the *Oldenburg* passed and repassed across the scene. Suddenly one sweep of the searchlight's beam showed armed men on the upper deck of the *Ostfriesland*. Gangways had been rigged to the shore, rebels had swarmed aboard and the battle ship was firmly in their hands. Pleased with themselves and giving shouts of victory, another part of the crowd bore down on the *Oldenburg*. She was alongside now, with the livid glare of the searchlights lighting up the massive shapes of the turrets, bridges, masts and funnels and throwing great angular shadows, while the low, rolling clouds of smoke from the boilers formed a vast umbrella over the whole scene. It was an easy matter for the crowd to board her and mingle their celebrations with those of the *Ostfriesland*. The two ships lay together, so that the *Nassau* was trapped. There remained the *Posen*, the only ship that had gained the open river. The mutinous ships signalled that if she did not return they would open fire. The *Posen* returned. It seemed impossible to do anything more and, at 04.00 when the middle watch ended, the men went below, some taking their rifles into their hammocks with them. No one bothered to relieve the men who had come off watch. Fog patches drifted across the port.

After breakfast the crews of the *Ostfriesland* and *Oldenburg* organized for themselves a victory march through the streets of Brunsbüttel, complete with Red Flags and brass bands. Four planes from Wilhelmshaven, sent by Hipper, reported that Brunsbüttel, like Kiel on the previous day, was full of Red Flags. The crews' triumphal round finished alongside the *Nassau*, whose officers, in a torment of indecision, had hauled in the gangways so that no contact was possible between ship and shore except by shouting. There seemed nothing else that could be done. The order not to open fire over-rode everything else, and the crowd on the quayside settled down to a noisy morning's barracking, until someone brought a gangway to the dockside and put it in place. Within a few minutes the *Nassau* also was overrun, except for the afterpart of the ship, which was defended by the officers and a handful of loyal seamen. The rest of the *Nassau*'s company and the uninvited visitors from the *Ostfriesland* and *Oldenburg* then surged ashore to yet another meeting, which was too much like the earlier ones to arouse much enthusiasm. Besides, it was dinner time, and the crowd had begun to thin out, when someone arrived to announce that a trainload of troops was approaching.

A party was sent to intercept the train, which was fired on until it stopped, and amidst the scream of escaping steam there was more fraternization between the mutineers and the soldiers who had been sent to quell the mutiny.

That afternoon there was another meeting in Brunsbüttel, at which the officers were ordered by the men to appear. Some of them did so, inspired in part by curiosity, for when the mutineers had been asked what they wanted, many had replied that they did not know, adding that they would decide at the meeting. This was held in the Kanalmündung Restaurant, where officers present and absent were denounced, but nothing decided. That night there was a sudden panic in the *Ostfriesland*. The rumour flashed round the ship that the officers were going to blow her up. Men rushed ashore in bits and pieces of their night clothing and then, finding that nothing was happening, collected themselves and returned sheepish and shivering to the ship. As a precaution they decided to arrest the officers who, in the *Oldenburg* and *Ostfriesland* had barricaded themselves into their quarters, where they were told by a message from Boedicker, still nominally in command of the squadron, that all officers should go ashore. Lines of officers carrying a few personal possessions filed over the sides of the ships, and an officer in *Nassau* shot himself dead.

Next morning the *Nassau*'s ensign hung at half mast, alone amongst the Red Flags of the town and of the other ships. Later, after the funeral service was over, the ensign was removed by a petty officer who hid it from the mutineers.

The Third Squadron, the immediate cause of all the uproar at Kiel, had missed the culminating excitement there by going to Travemünde and only learned what had happened on the next day, 5 November. The idea of spreading Socialism by 'liberating' Lübeck appealed to the crews, and groups of men commandeered trams and other transport to take them into the city. By all accounts it was a cheerful outing, with no resistance offered, but when the men returned to their ships, things seemed dull. It was clear from the papers that Kiel was where the action was, and they decided that the squadron should return there. Representatives of the men then informed the officers of their wishes, adding that they proposed to enter Kiel flying the Red Flag. The officers then organized a strike of their own and refused to sail under the Red Flag. There was deadlock, the ship remaining at Travemünde flying the old Imperial ensign. This was the only occasion on which the officers of the big ships succeeded in resisting the demands of their men. On 6 November the *Seekriegsleitung* had announced that the Red Flag was henceforward outlawed.

On the previous day troubles had quickly spread from Brunsbüttel to Cuxhaven, where the admiral, Engelhard, capitulated to a leading stoker. Afterwards, like most senior officers concerned, Engelhard excused himself by referring to the order from Berlin that fire should only be opened to protect life, and he ordered his officers to co-operate with the Workers' and Soldiers' Council which was set up adding that if they did not do so, they would receive no rations.

At this stage Scheer tried to regain control of the situation. He saw the Kaiser at Spa and urged that Souchon should be dismissed and replaced by Admiral Ludwig Schröder, from Flanders, with orders to restore order 'with an iron hand', and to treat ships flying the Red Flag as hostile. The idea appealed immensely to Schröder, lavishly publicized as the 'Lion of Flanders', and when he received his orders at 02.00 on 6 November he set about assembling a special train, a battalion of naval shock troops, with artillery, a machine-gun company and twenty 'excellent naval policemen'.

Schröder had been appointed without Mann or Captain von Restorff, the acting chief of the Kaiser's naval cabinet and responsible for the appointment of all officers, being informed. Even more important, neither Prince Max nor any members of the government had been informed either. When it was discovered what was happening there was an immediate protest in the Cabinet, for Schröder was well-known as a ferocious disciplinarian, a hot-head and an ardent proponent of the most extreme right-wing views. At once, Graf Roedern, Secretary of State for the Treasury, Erzberger and Trimborn, Secretary of State for Internal Affairs, loudly objected. The Chancellor agreed with them, and stated that he would not countersign Schröder's appointment, and it was cancelled on the following day. Roedern, at this time, produced his own scheme for dealing with the crisis, which was to abolish the Navy.

On the night of the 7th Hipper said he had not sufficient forces to suppress the mutiny, but added that he would try to maintain order in agreement with the C-in-C North Sea station, Admiral von Krosigk, and reasonable elements. A little later things suddenly seemed much worse to Hipper, for he signalled in despair: 'Cannot break resistance mutineers. Cannot assure safety German waters against enemy.'

In the meantime the revolution had started. Hamburg, on the 5th, had been the first big city to go. In the middle of the night of 4/5 November a party of twenty sailors arrived at Hamburg Central station from Kiel. With nothing to do they got into a discussion with a twenty-five-year-old sailor, Friedrich Zeller, who was on his way from Flanders to Kiel. Following some discussion, the sailors started their own revolution. They received support from the men of the light cruiser *Augsburg*, and soldiers in the town, either depot troops or recruits, who joined in the demonstrations, together with the workers of the Blohm & Voss shipyard, already in a riotous mood, having the day before wrecked their canteen as a protest against the food. On 6 November a meeting of 40,000 workers, soldiers and sailors was held on the Heiligengeistfeld in St Pauli.

Sailors were next reported heading by train from Kiel for Cologne. The Lord Mayor, Herr Konrad Adenauer, later Federal Chancellor, ordered that the train be stopped outside the town but the railway authorities refused to permit this, saying that it was essential that the train should run to time. The Lord Mayor gave way, but ordered that no sailors wearing red ribbons or rosettes should be permitted to leave the station platform. The sailors thereupon put their red ribbons in their pockets, passed the barrier and, replacing the ribbons on their jumpers and in their caps, marched on to the prison to free those inside. They then went to see Adenauer, who placed office space at their disposal in the Town Hall and had 300,000 litres of wine from Army stores poured into the Rhine as a precautionary measure.

Hamburg and Cologne were typical of all the big towns in north Germany. 'A couple of sailors, a couple of red flags and a couple of wild speeches turned everything upside down,' wrote Wolfgang Malanowski of this time. The infection at Cologne had an important effect on the whole future of the

Revolution, for it spread up the Rhine from there, and all the principal bridges fell into the hands of the rebels at the time when the Kaiser, Hindenburg and Groener, Ludendorff's successor, were discussing the possibility of the Kaiser leading his army back into Germany to put down the risings. When it was seen what had happened at the Rhine crossings the idea was abandoned.

Wilhelmshaven was fairly calm after the dispersal of the Fleet, and on 5 November at Oldenburg, thirty miles away, there took place the last State gathering of any of the German kings or princes, when Friedrich August, Grand Duke of Oldenburg, opened the autumn session of the Oldenburg parliament. It was very much a full-dress affair, with orders and decorations and the ladies in long gowns. The Grand Duke, who held a deep-sea master's certificate in sail, and of whom the Kaiser was in consequence very jealous, opened the proceedings by laying stress on the new order which was being born. As far as the Grand Duke was concerned, this new order was in fact born on 11 November, when he abdicated and his place as head of the State of Oldenburg was taken by Leading Stoker Kuhnt.

On 5 November, also, Meurer was even able to take the Fourth Squadron to sea for exercises, and on the next day they sailed again to cover the minesweepers still at work in the Bight.

The excitement from Kiel then flooded back and produced a secondary infection in Wilhelmshaven, which manifested itself on 6 November after Krosigk, realizing that the troubles of his command were by no means over, had sent an urgent message for troops to the General commanding at Oldenburg, and learned that there were none available.

Krosigk, however, believed that he still had two hundred men who would obey his orders and these, with a number of machine-guns, he posted outside the most important buildings. These precautions were judged by the ratings in barracks as a provocation, and on this pretext they organized a counter-demonstration. About 6,000 strong, they marched about the town, headed by brass bands, which had now become a regular feature of these occasions, and improvised Red Flags. At noon they arrived at naval headquarters and presented a series of demands of the usual sort to Krosigk, who accepted them, subject to their being approved by Berlin. A committee of sailors was created to deal with the naval command, saluting was abolished, rations were to be the same for all ranks, all men under arrest to be released. Reporting all this, Krosigk also asked for permission to retire from the service.

The chairman of the Wilhelmshaven Sailors' Council was Leading Stoker Kuhnt, a right-wing Socialist, although a bitter opponent of Noske. Kuhnt issued an urgent appeal for the preservation of order, and sent aircraft on reconnaissance flights to make sure that the British fleet was not in the offing, as was frequently rumoured in those days. Kuhnt afterwards became *Regierungspräsident* of Oldenburg, was arrested by the Nazis in 1933 and featured in many pictures of those days, showing him with shaven head being mocked in the streets of Oldenburg. He was then sent to a concentration camp, from which he emerged twelve years later, at the end of World War Two.

In contrast to the determination of Kuhnt at Wilhelmshaven to maintain some defensive capability, was the attitude of the mutineers' leaders at Cuxhaven, who proclaimed on 7 November: 'We reject the idea of national defence and would therefore hoist the white flag if the English were to come.' The Cuxhaven Workers' and Soldiers' Council then went on to demand:

1. The beginning of peace negotiations.
2. The abolition of the Officers' Club.
3. Officers and men to receive the same pay and the same food.
4. Recognition of the political power of the Workers' and Soldiers' Council.

Cuxhaven remained the most radical of the ports and at one stage Noske proposed sending a heavy ship from Kiel with a threat to bombard it. This proved to be unnecessary, but

Cuxhaven did not finally settle down until the following February.

At Bremen troubles started on the 6th, when a train from Wilhelmshaven stopped in the station. It contained the men from the *Thüringen* and *Helgoland* who were being sent to prison in the interior as Oslebshausen was now full. Amidst a good deal of tumult the men broke out of the train, brushed aside their guards and went out into the streets to celebrate their regained liberty.

On the next day an entirely new revolt broke out, which had nothing to do with the mutinies at Kiel and Wilhelmshaven. This began in Munich, at the other end of Germany, where alarm at the prospect of an invasion of Bavaria from the south had led to a rising in which the King was deposed and the Socialist leader, Kurt Eisner, was elected president of the Bavarian Republic. There was a naval component in the disorders here as well, for their outbreak coincided with the arrival in town of the German sailors from Pola who had provided the shore-based man-power of the German U-boat base, evacuated when it was clear that Austria-Hungary was about to conclude a separate armistice.

Back on the coast the first intense emotions of mutiny were beginning to abate, although there was a mixture of panic and paralysis which attacked some of the senior admirals. As we have seen, on 8 November Hipper himself was caught in the grip of this feeling and sent his despairing signal. He further made a bad mistake in his handling of the local situation when he ordered all the officers of the fleet at that time in Wilhelmshaven, and all the loyal ratings, to repair on board the *Baden*, and placed the ship in one of the locks between the dockyard and the sea, so that while the ship could not be seized by the mutineers, she could command the lock gates. However, the concentration of all those opposed to the mutiny in one ship meant that there was no one left ashore or aboard the other ships to dispute with the demonstrators or to rally the doubtful, who were merely following the Red Flags and the band out of curiosity. The *Baden*'s crew was then delivered over to the mutineers as a captive audience when another great procession formed and made its way to where the ship lay. Orators began a series of speeches calling on the *Baden* to rally to the Red Flag, now in plentiful evidence. The *Baden*'s captain endeavoured to reply, but he was apparently a poor speaker, and some three hundred of the *Baden*'s men drifted ashore, joining the procession which, happy and successful, then marched off with more bands to the parade ground, where about twenty different meetings began at once, groups of men gathering around anybody who felt like making a speech.

There was no coherent programme drawn up, either before or after this demonstration, and no one even suggested going to the naval prison and releasing the inmates. However, after a night's discussion, they did succeed in electing a Council of twenty-one members, which exercised a brief authority. Waves of rumour and excitement washed through the town and the report went round that the army was marching against the sailors to restore order, a rumour which proved groundless, if only because the local army command had no troops available.

In Kiel the indomitable Noske was still at work, and there were now symptoms of something of a reaction against extremist behaviour. One curious example of this reaction was provided by Rear-Admiral Feldt, second-in-command of the Third Squadron, who appeared in Berlin at the head of a deputation of about twenty sailors from his squadron, and was received by Ritter von Mann and Conrad Haussmann on 7 November.

Haussmann's notes afterwards described the sailors as being by no means overbearing, but clearly anxious to explain and excuse, even to make amends for their actions. They began by saying that they had learned from the officers' talk that the officers' corps was opposed to the new government. Then their suspicion that something exceptional was afoot had been roused by the unusually large concentration of ships at Schillig Roads, which rumour said was to prelude an attack designed to wreck the armistice negotiations. Events in Kiel, they claimed, had only had as their object the freeing of those men arrested at Wilhelmshaven; they recalled that they had previously argued that if these men were punished there would be great agitation. They added that the Red Flags in the ships had been hoisted as a safety measure, so that they should not be fired on by the forts which were in the hands of the Soldiers' Council. The delegation ended by saying: 'We wish to keep the fleet ready for action. Trust in the command is unconditional.' A man from the *Markgraf* intervened to say that they had wanted to influence the other ships. The Third Squadron, he said, had always taken the lead.

Mann and Haussmann were then asked by the sailors whether they were to take orders from the government or from the Workers' and Soldiers' Council, and whether the order issued by the squadron commander forbidding the Red Flag had emanated from Mann or been approved by him. The sailors then went on to list their demands. As reported by Haussmann to the Cabinet these were:

1. The right of assembly.
2. Lifting the ban on all newspapers.
3. No saluting off duty.
4. Same food for all and new regulations affecting punishment.

The ratings also demanded that if a man were found guilty of an offence, a representative of the accused should be heard before sentence was passed. For misconduct that was not dishonourable only fines should be imposed and not detention. For an interim period, following the introduction of new regulations, a representative of the crew should be attached to the staff of the squadron commander.

As Haussmann pointed out, very little of the foregoing was of a political nature and, speaking to the delegation, he appealed to the conscience of all seamen. It was no longer simply a question of discipline but of loyalty to Germany, he said. Any agitation against the peace policy of the government would be very wrong. 'We can still achieve a great deal at the conference table,' Haussmann went on, 'but only on condition that we have you behind us. Clemenceau wants to ruin

Germany, Wilson wishes to restore her. Clemenceau will win if the symptoms of collapse show themselves in Germany. The government has overcome the political reactionaries. Ludendorff's dismissal proves that.' (Ludendorff had resigned on 26 October when Prince Max had insisted on his withdrawing an order to the Army that it should continue to fight).

Now, in the Baltic, just as the situation at Kiel was being taken in hand, there occurred one of the most curious and complete collapses of power to be seen in the whole revolution.

Three days after the minelayers of the Fourth Scouting Group had seen the Third Squadron pass in disorder on its way to Kiel, they were ordered there as well, and arrived on the evening of Sunday, 3 November. They made fast to buoys in the harbour, and shore leave was refused to all. Next morning, there was some communication with the shore, but the only hard news was of a dispute between the light cruiser *Dresden*, commanded by the Kaiser's son, and the battleship *Markgraf*, the ship most zealous in the cause of mutiny. The *Dresden* had moored at the Castle buoy and the *Markgraf* had moored outside her, and was now refusing to move to let the light cruiser leave for Eckernförde, where she was to act as repeating ship because, communications between Kiel and the outside world were extremely uncertain. The battleship's crew then trained one of their 12-inch turrets on the *Dresden*. The Fourth Scouting Group was unable to observe the next instalment of this drama, as they were ordered to leave Kiel, but in fact nothing happened and the *Dresden* eventually sailed. The Fourth Scouting Group made its way up the coast of Schleswig towards Flensburg, and anchored in the fjord at Glücksburg. Officers and men alike were in a state of confusion, typified by affairs in the *Bremse*. This ship had had three captains during the war, the second of whom, Captain Westerkamp, was clearly one of the best officers of his rank in the German navy. The effect of his appointment to the *Bremse* had been summed up by Conrad Lotter, then serving in that ship: 'What a difference it made in three days. He gained the trust and affection of us all. He bothered about everything that affected our welfare, food, duty, sleep, leave, everything.'

Westerkamp's care for his crew and the success of the raid by the *Bremse* and *Brummer* on the Shetland convoy, together with the successful minelaying expeditions by the two ships, had given him a great reputation and when he was drafted to U-boat Headquarters there was much disappointment on the *Bremse*'s mess decks and in the wardroom alike. Now, without his leadership, as the light cruisers lay in Flensburg Fjord, officers argued amongst themselves, with perhaps an excess of simplicity, in favour of violent action, bombarding Kiel, attacking the mutinous ships and landing to seize the town, while they criticized Karpf for removing them from Kiel to a port where, for the moment, all was quiet.

But demonstrations spread to Flensburg on the 5th and the Group was ordered by Karpf to follow him to Swinemünde. As they were preparing to leave, another fugitive from Kiel appeared, the obsolete battleship *Schlesien*, which served as a cadet training ship and whose captain, Waldeyer-Hartz, had sailed her from Kiel rather than obey orders to hoist the Red Flag, after he had been told by Souchon to avoid any bloodshed and to protect the lives of his cadets. On 6 November he was warned that so-called 'Red' torpedo-boats were on their way from Kiel to sink his ship. He therefore told any of his men who wished to leave the ship that they could do so. About half went ashore, having looted the ditty boxes and possessions of the men who remained aboard. Waldeyer-Hartz then took his ship to Marstal in Sweden, which appeared to him to be the nearest safe haven offered at the time. On 9 November, upon orders from Berlin, the *Schlesien* went to Swinemünde where she met the *Dresden*, half scuttled, and the *Regensburg*, both ships having been looted and abandoned by their crews.

These light cruisers, with the *Bremse*, had reached Swinemünde on the 7th. On passage, some of the crew of the latter ship had tried to prevent the ship being blacked out, because they said a ship without lights might be taken for an enemy, but their officers succeeded in discouraging them. Then, on the night of 7/8 November Karpf, alarmed at the report that rebel ships had sailed from Kiel to attack him, suddenly alerted his officers and crews and announced that the ships were to be laid up. He thereupon hauled down his broad pennant, despite the protests of the officers of the *Bremse*, who pointed out that all the libertymen had returned to the ship that evening and that it was quite quiet ashore. Nevertheless Karpf persisted in what was literally a policy of scuttle; he ordered the magazines of the ships to be flooded and destroyed all the confidential books and cyphers. When this was done, the *Dresden* forgot to close the Kingston valves used to flood the magazines and the ship partially settled on the bottom.

News of this reached Berlin, where the Admiralty promptly replaced Karpf by the former captain of the *Bayern*, Commodore Rohardt, and the work was begun getting the *Bremse*, *Dresden* and *Regensburg* back into seagoing condition. For a start the munitions were laboriously taken out of the flooded magazines and dried out on the upper deck. At the same time it was realized that the destruction of the cyphers meant that the ships could neither send nor receive signals except in plain language. An additional complication arose with the abdication of the Kaiser on 9 November, so far as Rohardt was concerned, for he considered that this meant that the ships, which by now had gone up the Oder to Stettin, should no longer fly the old naval ensign and that he was obliged to follow the example of Karpf and place the ships out of commission. This was done in the *Regensburg* and *Brummer*, but the *Bremse*'s officers refused to obey the order and announced their intention of leaving port. Unfortunately for them, the *Regensburg* and *Brummer* were moored alongside and outboard of their ship, so she could not move unless the others moved as well, which their officers refused to permit them to do.

An officer at this stage arrived and said that he was the new captain of the *Regensburg*. Unfortunately, he had few officers and no crew, since the latter had all been arrested on their arrival in Berlin on leave, and had then been sent off under guard to a camp in Silesia. On the way the train was stopped with the news that disorders had broken out at their destination; the men then left the train and disappeared.

All these movements took place in the midst of a continued flurry of contradictory signals, orders and news bulletins. *Bremse* gave leave and hoped to have news of the two ships left in the Flensburg Fjord, the *Brummer* and *Strassburg*, which in the meantime had gone to Sassnitz, where they found five U-boats also escaped from Kiel. The captain of the *Strassburg* took command of the naval forces present and invited the crews to name a council of sailors to co-operate with him. He then announced that there would be a route march next day, to keep the men from the confusion and temptations, political and alcoholic, of Sassnitz. Somewhat surprisingly, the route march took place.

The story of the Fourth Scouting Group is of particular interest because it is one of the very few incidents in the whole of the Navy's involvement in the 1918 revolution where there is a direct conflict of evidence between Left and Right sources. For the most part, both sides are in agreement as to events that happened, although disagreeing as to the interpretation to be given them. But that is not the case for what occurred at Stettin and Swinemünde. The officers of the light cruisers concerned, as well as other naval sources, have been firm in their statements that it was only the panic action of Karpf that led to the ships being put out of action. East German Communist writers, in a book of essays issued in 1957 to celebrate the fortieth anniversary of the Russian revolution, claim that the ships were laid up because their crews had deserted *en masse*, having declared themselves finished with war.

On balance, it would seem more probable that small acts of indiscipline and leave-breaking in the Fourth Scouting Group were built up by the Communists for propaganda purposes into a fullscale mutiny to give the impression that the other units of the fleet were behind the crews of the big ships.

That this was not so was proved by the conduct, during those days, of some sixty light craft, destroyers, submarines and minesweepers, commanded by Commodore Michelsen in the light cruiser *Graudenz*. Michelsen, it will be remembered, had been one of the officers who had urged that the original operation by the High Seas Fleet should not be cancelled, but that the mutinous battleships should be compelled to sail, accompanied by destroyers, with orders to torpedo them if they fell out of station.

On 6 November Michelsen had collected a force to oppose the British if they were to take advantage of the disturbances in the fleet and ashore and enter the Bight, while he may also have had in mind the possibility of establishing a base which might be used to stem the revolutionary tide. He first went to Heligoland to seize the island but, although the garrison permitted him to replenish some of his craft with fuel and food, they soon began to act in an unfriendly manner and finally, later that day, hoisted the Red Flag and shut the great steel gates leading from sea level to the upper part of the island, where the heavy guns were situated. The destroyers retired to the estuary of the Weser and then went to the island of Sylt in search of badly-needed help, for by now most of the ships had only a day's supply of provisions on board. At List, on Sylt, no supplies were found and the ships set off again for Borkum at the other end of the Frisian islands.

As they were leaving, at about noon on 9 November, a signal arrived reporting that British forces had entered the Bight and were apparently steaming for Heligoland. Captain Quaet-Faslem, in the *Königsberg*, then took all the destroyers under his command and set off in search of the enemy.

The behaviour of these destroyers and submarines turning back to face, unsupported, an overwhelming foe in defence of a Fatherland which seemed to be disintegrating must still awaken admiration, after more than a half-century has passed.

The *Königsberg* and her destroyers remained at sea until they discovered that the report of the British being in the neighbourhood was false, and then returned to Borkum where they learned from the local papers of the abdication of the Kaiser.

EIGHT

The demand for the Kaiser's abdication had grown steadily, both inside and outside Germany, ever since the first request for an armistice had been made by Prince Max. The Allies as a whole, and especially President Wilson, had pressed for it because they did not believe that a Germany still ruled by the Kaiser could be trusted to conclude and keep a peace treaty. At the same time, in Germany, even those who theoretically still approved of a monarchy felt that Germany could obtain a better peace if the Kaiser went. There was general agreement that if the Kaiser did go, the Crown Prince would have to go as well; one senior officer, discussing this, simply declared that the Crown Prince was too 'hated' to have a chance of remaining. It was therefore planned to install the Crown Prince's son, Prince Wilhelm, then a minor, as Emperor, with one of his uncles as regent. The Kaiser, however, succeeded in destroying any chances that the Hohenzollern dynasty had of being able to continue to reign by extracting from all his sons a promise that none of them would take the throne or assume the regency if it were offered.

After the defeat of the German army in France on 8 August the Kaiser had removed himself to Wilhelmshöhe near Cassel, where his wife was taken ill; he refused to return to Berlin, or even to go back to Spa, on the ground that the health of the Kaiserin came before anything else. At the same time his chief advisers who came to see him were warned not to give him any bad news and, of course, from 8 August to 9 November, the day of the revolution, there was nothing but bad news. After a last visit to Kiel the Kaiser eventually returned to

Berlin on 2 October, where he immediately became deeply interested in the design for the Victory medal to be struck to celebrate the successful conclusion of the war. On 26 October he annouced, according to Admiral von Müller, that he had found a solution for Germany's difficulties – an alliance with Japan (Germany and Japan were then at war with each other). Japanese troops would be sent to Europe via the Trans-Siberian railway to the Western Front where, in conjunction with the German and British armies, they would drive the Americans into the sea.

Three days after this brainstorm, without warning the Chancellor, he set off for Spa. Told of this move, Prince Max refused to believe the news and thought that his informant was making a bad joke, but it was true, and the Kaiser celebrated his arrival at GHQ by stating that he would share the fate of his troops. He would 'settle for a bullet and die like millions of brave German soldiers'. Then he set off on a tour of the German-occupied areas of Belgium.

It was now reported that the French Army had mutinied, that Marshal Foch had been assassinated and that the British fleet, having hoisted the Red Flag, was steaming out into the North Sea to fraternize with its former enemies. This story had originally emanated from Berne on 8 November and had enormously alarmed the government in Berlin. If the Russians and the British had both become Bolshevik there was little prospect of a democratic socialist government surviving in Germany and, as Scheidemann remarked, the Bolsheviks were a much greater danger to Germany than were the Allies. It was soon clear in Berlin that there was nothing to these rumours of Bolshevism in Britain and France, but they were believed by many in the Fleet and some were not undeceived until they encountered the British Navy off the Firth of Forth.

Meanwihle the Kaiser was again involved in a frenzy of fantasy, for he returned to Spa from his tour and announced that he would lead his army home to victory against the revolutionary masses. His generals dashed this hope by telling him that his troops would no longer follow him. He still refused to abdicate, but he was finally deposed three times on 9 November. The first deposition by Prince Max was given at noon with the aid of the teleprinters of the Wolff Bureau, the semi-official news agency, which he ordered to announce that the Kaiser had decided to abdicate. This news, incorrect of course, did not reach the crowd of workers who had decided to demonstrate on this sunny Saturday afternoon. Some of these made their way casually to the Reichstag, where Scheidemann was lunching in the canteen. About fifty workers and soldiers crowded in, made their way towards his table and began to urge him to proclaim the Republic. Unwillingly he went upstairs to a window overlooking the crowd, spoke a few sentences deposing the Kaiser by proclaiming the Republic, and went back to his soup, described by someone there as 'a watery gruel'.

Meanwhile, after Prince Max had carried out his deposition by teleprinter he handed over the Chancellorship to Friedrich Ebert, a former saddler and now leader of the SPD. Ebert then asked the Prince to assume the post of regent or administrator of the Reich. The Prince refused, saying that he knew that Ebert believed that he had to collaborate with the USPD and that he himself would have none of such a policy. Then there followed a touching farewell between the two men. The Prince said, 'I entrust you with the Reich.' Ebert replied, 'I have lost two sons for this Reich.'

The reason for the haste of both Prince Max and Scheidemann to get rid of the Kaiser at this moment was that the USPD were known also to be planning to proclaim a republic, and their republic would be very different from that of the Majority Socialists. Power would be concentrated in the hands of the Workers' and Soldiers' Councils, instead of in those of elected members of the Reichstag.

Scheidemann's action was disapproved, not only by the Left but also by the sticklers for constitutional procedure among the Majority Socialists, including Ebert, who claimed that the monarchy could only be ended by the vote of a constituent assembly, which would have to be convened. This assembly was, in fact, held later at Weimar and drew up the constitution under which Germany was governed from 1919 to 1933, but the question of the monarchy had been settled for good by Scheidemann's lunchtime initiative. He had won the race to proclaim the republic by two hours, for at four o'clock Karl Liebknecht proclaimed another republic, a 'Socialist' one this time, from the balcony of the Kaiser's palace, to another crowd, many of which had already witnessed the earlier proclamation at the Reichstag. Neither crowd was very large, and the general effect of the revolution on the population of Berlin was one of complete surprise when, during that afternoon, motor lorries suddenly appeared on the streets all over the city, full of armed workmen, mostly youths, carrying red flags.

Some of the transport for these unrehearsed demonstrations had been stolen from the Admiralty car park. Admiral von Müller and Helfferich, the former German ambassador in Moscow, had gone for a walk in the afternoon sunshine through the Tiergarten, and when Müller returned to his office he found the workers in possession, commandeering cars and lorries and looking for officers from whose shoulders they could tear the epaulettes. They found only a few for, as a precautionary measure, most of the officers were in plain clothes. The sentries on the Admiralty and other government buildings were fraternizing with the workers. Early that morning the order had gone forth that there was to be no shooting, so the day came finally to a peaceful end, after a few rounds had been fired, at a cost of three lives. The garrison of Berlin, powerful enough on paper, had crumped up like the garrison of Petrograd in March 1917.

The Kaiser learned of his deposition while still at Spa and decided that there was nothing left for him but flight into Holland. Scheer endeavoured to persuade him to stay, telling him that, if he left, the Navy would no longer have a head. 'I no longer have a Navy,' the Kaiser answered.

Groener also wished the Kaiser to stay, for he had arranged 'a small special action' in which the Kaiser would be killed or, at least, seriously wounded, in order to raise the prestige of the House of Hohenzollern. The Kaiser would have none of it. The time for such gestures was past, he said, a remark which has sometimes been quoted by critics of the last operation planned for the High Seas Fleet.

The Kaiser left Spa before daylight on the morning of 10 November, by car, on which the Imperial crest had been covered with dirt in order not to reveal the identity of its principal passenger. Early in the morning he reached the small Dutch frontier post of Eysden near Maastricht, where he spent the next six hours amidst the derisive comments of Dutch workmen and Belgian refugees on the station platform, waiting for permission from the Queen of Holland and her Government to enter the country. The Dutch Government found itself embarrassed politically, for they did not know what would be the reaction to granting this request for asylum and, in addition, once they had decided that the fugitive could cross the frontier, they had then to decide what should be done with him. Finally, Count Bentinck, owner of the handsome castle of Amerongen in the province of Utrecht, was rung up by The Hague and asked to give shelter to the fallen monarch. The request came from his Queen, so Bentinck felt that he could not refuse. The ex-Kaiser reached Amerongen in the afternoon of the next day and greeted his unwilling host with the words, 'Now for a cup of good English tea.'

That morning the German people had awakened to discover what seemed to them the frightful terms of the armistice. Occupied territories in France, Belgium and Luxembourg were to be evacuated, as well as Alsace-Lorraine, and the German Army was to withdraw to a distance of fifty kilometres behind the right bank of the Rhine. German territory up to the Rhine, with bridgeheads around Cologne, Coblenz and Mainz, were to be occupied by the Allies.

There was to be no question of the Germans being able to re-start the war if they were dissatisfied with the terms of peace. The greater part of the Navy was to be interned; ten battleships, six battle-cruisers, eight light cruisers and fifty destroyers, all the most modern ships of their type, while all surviving U-boats were to be surrendered. These totalled 138. The Army was to surrender huge quantities of weapons: 5,000 guns, 25,000 machine-guns, 3,000 mortars and 1,700 aircraft, together with 5,000 locomotives.

As far as the naval terms were concerned, there was a provision that if the stipulated number of ships were not delivered for surrender or internment within ten days, the Allies reserved the right to occupy Heligoland. In fact the British had already considered demanding the cession of Heligoland as one of the terms of the armistice or the peace treaty, but had decided against it as they could see no way of holding the place against a determined attack.

All this time the Fourth Squadron, under Meurer, had been at sea supporting the minesweepers as Hipper had ordered on 31 October, but at 04.00 on 9 November, Meurer was told of trouble on board the *Kaiserin*, where apparently the officers had been overwhelmed and shut up in their cabins. Meurer took his flag lieutenant and went in his barge to the mutinous ship, where he found most of the crew gathered on the upper deck, with the officers below and under armed guard. There were two officers, however, who had been chosen to negotiate with the crew – the torpedo officer and an engineer. Meurer then went below and addressed the crew in the battery, promising to consider their grievances on the ship's return to Wilhelmshaven. The pacified men then agreed to release and reinstate their officers.

The announcement of the Kaiser's abdication was the occasion for an immense firework display at Wilhelmshaven, with countless signal rockets fired, while guns banged away salutes and sirens roared.

On 10 November, the Fourth Squadron, now flying the Red Flag, returned to Wilhelmshaven. Two or three days later, after the squadron had reached their base, there was an indication of a partial relaxation, at least of revolutionary zeal, provided by the *Friedrich der Grosse*. One of the ringleaders of the mutiny at the end of October and a founder-member of the ship's council was amongst those who escaped from the train at Bremen on their way to prison. Returning to Wilhelmshaven and the *Friedrich der Grosse*, he half-expected something of a hero's welcome. Little attention, however, was paid to him, and more disconcerting was the fact that no one could tell him the whereabouts of the ship's council. Finally, someone said that he thought that it met in the charthouse on the bridge. He went there and found the council in session. None of the members had been amongst the activists of the mutiny and no one seemed interested in him at all.

In execution of the armistice conditions, the ships to be interned, as well as the most important of those left provisionally in German hands, had to be reduced to a disarmed condition. This involved the removal of all ammunition and torpedoes from the ships, as well as breech-blocks from the guns, the optical gear and all other fire-control installations. To do this within the time limit set by the Allies would have been a considerable task if the fleet were in an efficient operational state; but after the events of the preceding fortnight, of course, it was not. Nevertheless, the work was begun and Noske took the lead in carrying it out at Kiel. At Wilhelmshaven it was more difficult, as the dockyard workers and seamen were still in a state of great unrest, and many varied political demonstrations were taking place, accompanied by looting of stores and of anything else that possessed a market value and could be easily transported. Carelessness, haste and disgruntlement led to extremely rough-and-ready handling of the munitions as they were put ashore but, to the surprise of everyone who knew what was going on, there were no accidents. To make matters easier the Workers' and Soldiers' Council issued an appeal to the patriotism of the men, which was read with mixed feelings by the officers.

Noske's task at Kiel was then made more difficult by one of those acts of administrative tidiness so often carried out by authorities in all countries in defiance of common sense. It was decided that the battle-cruisers, whose home port was Kiel, should return there for disarming. They had spent the past few days peacefully off Cuxhaven, without any trouble, but when they reached Kiel and found out what had been going on, their crews immediately began to agitate for the setting up of ships' councils and held meetings demanding that unpopular officers should be put ashore. This not only threatened to intensify the revolutionary movement, but also endangered the punctual arrival in British waters of the ships to be interned.

To help Noske and others to re-establish order the inner cabinet in Berlin, composed of both SPD and USPD members, issued an order on 13 November to Ritter von Mann re-establishing military discipline and stressing that calm and strict obedience should be maintained. The orders of superior authorities were to be unconditionally carried out, and discharge from the naval service was to be effected only by order of the superior authorities. Officers were to retain their side arms and marks of rank. Where soldiers' councils and commissions of delegates had been formed it was their duty unreservedly to support their officers in the maintenance of order. 'Damage to ships, military establishments and war material must not occur', said the order. 'We must all work together to see that the conditions of the Armistice are speedily and effectively carried out. The Navy must realize that upon the conscientious execution of the Armistice everything depends. We will achieve peace only if we have honestly carried out the conditions of the Armistice.'

Meanwhile arrangements had to be made for the actual surrender and internment procedures, and for this the luckless Meurer was sent to meet Beatty off the Firth of Forth in the *Königsberg* on 15 November, the German ship flying a white flag at the foretop. Beatty, like other great leaders, was a showman and he organized Meurer's reception accordingly.

First, Commodore Hodges went on board the *Königsberg*, where he was met by three seamen who announced that they were delegates of the Workers' and Soldiers' Council and that the German officers were merely their technical advisers. Hodges consulted Beatty who replied that the British would deal with Meurer and officers only, and that only they might leave the ship. This ended the role of the delegates in the proceedings. Meurer and three of his officers then boarded the British destroyer *Oak* and set off for the *Queen Elizabeth*, the British flagship.

Writing to a friend afterwards, Beatty remarked that Meurer's arrival was 'dramatic and tragic to a high degree'. It was already dark when the German admiral reached the *Queen Elizabeth*. There was a thick fog which hid all the rest of the Grand Fleet.

Beatty continued, 'I arranged a most beautiful setting. My dramatic sense was highly developed at the moment.' His only regret, he wrote, was that his second-in-command, Vice-Admiral Madden, wore a beard. This, thought Beatty, spoiled the picture, and he had contemplated asking him to shave it off.

Meurer trudged heavily up the gangway and reached the quarterdeck to find a narrow, floodlit path leading between two rows of marines with fixed bayonets to the hatchway down to Beatty's quarters. At the ship's side the German admiral was met by Beatty's Flag Captain, Chatfield, and his Captain of the Fleet, Brand, and was taken below. After having asked Meurer for his credentials and been shown them, Beatty read to him his instructions for carrying out the relevant terms of the Armistice and told him to return on the following day with his observations. He repeated to Meurer that he would not receive members of the Workers' and Soldiers' Council – 'the one source of relief to the Stricken Party,' commented Beatty. The Germans then returned to the *Königsberg* in the *Oak* and, said Beatty, 'I retired and was nearly sick.'

'The Stricken Party', his duty done, returned to his ship. All night long the British motor-launch which was guarding the German light cruiser heard, as she circled round in the darkness, voices raised in argument coming from the open scuttles of the *Königsberg*'s wardroom, and not until 05.00 were the lights put out.

Meurer went back to Germany having escaped one duty even more distasteful than that which he had already carried out. He had been designated as the Flag Officer to lead the German ships into internment, but as it was not certain that he would be back from the Firth of Forth in time the task was given to Reuter.

The German ships were collected on time at Schillig Roads, largely thanks to Noske who, on the day before the ships sailed from Kiel, received a strange invitation. It read:

> In agreement with the officers and warrant officers, the Sailors' Council of the warship *König* most heartily invites Your Excellency to a Social Gathering on Saturday evening, 16 November, at 8 o'clock, prior to the ship leaving for internment. The Chairman of the Council hopes very much that you will attend. He is most anxious to assure you of the widespread effect of your last speech. The ship is ready for internment.

Noske afterwards described the 'Gathering':

> Punctually I went on board with two members of the Sailors' Council. When I met the Chairman he spoke in the most regimental tones and no one stood more fiercely to attention.
>
> We were formally greeted and taken into the officers' wardroom, seniority firmly observed. In the place of honour was the Governor (Noske himself), on the right the Chairman of the Sailors' Council, and on my left the officer who was to take charge of the ship. Then followed the Chief Engineer, other officers, warrant officers and petty officers. The crew watched from outside, and in the next room the ship's band played light music, as an accompaniment to sandwiches and beer.
>
> If the occasion had not been so grave I would have burst out laughing at the speech of the little Chairman. A more stupid mush of phrases I had hardly ever heard before. Ending up, this revolutionary said that he agreed with Bismarck: ' We Germans fear God alone, and nothing else in the world '.
>
> With a few serious words I said goodbye to these people, and wished them a happy return from their sad journey.
>
> I went home.

The next day was Sunday the 17th, a nasty dark November day. At about noon Noske stood at the lock gates of the canal to watch the ships leave.

'A considerable part of Germany's national fortune floated away to the English coast, never to be seen again,' he wrote. 'Of the crew, it was obvious that they did not realize the deep national shame, which was the reason for this voyage. They were shouting and yelling. As one of the ships – I forget her name – passed, the band was playing merrily. I spat full of contempt into the lock, called my boat and ordered her to take me out into Kiel fjord in the gathering darkness.'

On the following day the whole force formed up, and sailed at 14.00 on the 19th. There had been trouble recruiting passage crews and finally it was necessary to offer each rating 500 marks (£25) bounty if he were married and 300 marks (£15) if single. In addition all men were insured for 1,000 marks (£50). The idea of flying the Red Flag was speedily ruled out when it was explained that it was the international symbol of piracy and could be fired upon immediately and without warning by the British. The old Imperial naval ensign was then hoisted. Several ships also affected small scraps of red bunting, but once the ships were at sea these disappeared as well.

The course through the British minefields had been buoyed and lit by the British themselves, but one destroyer struck a mine and sank; two men were killed and three wounded. The survivors were rescued and the sunken destroyer later replaced by another to make up the total of fifty stipulated for internment. At this stage the tension of proceedings was alleviated when one of the British planes taking photographs crashed into the sea, her crew being picked up by a destroyer.

The German ships, led by the *Friedrich der Grosse* flying Reuter's flag, were met by the British light cruiser *Cardiff* and other light cruisers of her squadron. The Germans were to follow the *Cardiff* to the rendezvous with the Grand Fleet. To indicate that she was to lead she broke out a huge blue ensign at her foremast.

The Grand Fleet came in sight. The British and American ships, the latter being five battleships of the Sixth Battle Squadron, had crews at action stations and trained their guns on each German ship as it appeared, the turrets swinging slowly round to keep the German ship covered, until the Allied ship next astern picked up the target and the guns of the first ship then turned to train on the next astern, until all the Germans were anchored in their predetermined positions.

The German ships were untidy and so were their crews.

Reuter wrote: 'The ships kept their station as well as it was possible for the officers to achieve it, considering the unreliability of the boilers and engines; unfortunately a bunching of the line did take place which caused one or two ships to sheer out.'

Boarding parties went on board all the ships to confirm the fact that they had all been disarmed. As this was being done Reuter was informed that, as no neutral nation had agreed to intern the German ships (Spain and Norway had been asked), they would be interned at Scapa Flow.

On the afternoon of this great day Beatty signalled to Reuter: 'The German flag will be hauled down at 3.57 this afternoon and is not to be rehoisted without permission.' The strict legality of Beatty's signal has been queried. In theory, interned warships were entitled to continue to fly their national colours, but hitherto internment had only been carried out by neutrals. Here, however, the strange situation existed in which one belligerent was interning but not taking possession of the ships of the other.

Meanwhile to the southward, at Harwich, batch after batch of U-boats were being delivered to Commodore Tyrwhitt and his force. These craft were not being interned but surrendered outright. Rigorous conditions were laid down by the Allies for the ships' stay at Scapa Flow. Most of their crews were to be sent back to Germany, and officers and men remaining were not to be allowed to land or to visit between ships. Food was to be supplied from Germany; it seems to have been sufficient but monotonous, and when the German ships reached Scapa, some with their bands playing, crews lined the rails and began fishing over the side.

Capital ships were to be allowed to retain between 175 and 200 men on board, light cruisers sixty and destroyers twenty, just enough to look after the ships and enable them to steam at reduced speed for a reasonable distance. This provision was of importance to the Germans because they still clung to the hope that the ships might be allowed, on the conclusion of the Peace Treaty, to return to Germany. In the meantime Reuter took advantage of reductions ordered in the strength of the crews to get rid of some of the worst behaved men. Matters came to a head in the *Friedrich der Grosse* at the beginning of February when a group, calling itself the 'Red Guard', began demonstrations for purposes of carrying on political propaganda and obtaining an increase in the spirit ration. This, said Reuter, 'brought about a repellent state of affairs'.

It seemed possible that the extreme left-wing element might take over the ship and Reuter had to make sure of the backing of the British admiral if something of the sort were attempted. In fact there never was an attempt, but some of the more disorderly members of the crew were sent to prison in Perth, as there was no means of keeping them in cells on board either the German or British ships. Two members of the Sailors' Council were ordered to be sent back to Germany. They refused to go until two British warships arrived with their crews at action stations.

The *Friedrich der Grosse* was now quiet, metaphorically if not literally, for it became a favourite sport of the most disorderly sailors to roller-skate for hours on end, up and down the quarterdeck over the officers' cabins. The noise made throughout the ship, with its bare steel decks and bulkheads, was of course horrible and it was not surprising that Reuter decided to shift his flag to the light cruiser *Emden*, a ship with a more tranquil crew. He then began to plan the scuttling of his fleet.

As soon as the ships reached Scapa Flow various of Reuter's officers had come to him with schemes for sinking the ships. He was obliged to rebuke these over-zealous subordinates and to order them not to do anything of the sort, for he realized that preparations for scuttling could not be hidden from the crews and that there was always the likelihood that the information might be passed on to the British by some of the malcontents. It was only on 17 June, after the last purging of doubtful crews had taken place, that orders were finally given, being distributed amongst the ships by the British duty drifter as part of the routine mail distribution. In two of the big ships the crews' suspicions were aroused and Reuter decided that it would be impossible to keep the secret any longer. Accordingly he ordered the preparations needed for the scuttling, but he stressed that he did not intend to sink the ships unless the British attempted to seize them without the consent of the German Government. He added: 'Should our government agree to the Peace conditions in which the ships are to be surrendered, the ships will be handed over, to the lasting shame of those who put us in this position.'

Neither the British nor the German Governments let Reuter know what was going on. His first idea of the situation was obtained from a copy of *The Times* dated 17 June, which he saw on the twentieth, in which it was stated that unless the Germans accepted the terms by Saturday, 21 June, the Armistice would be denounced. In fact, however, the Allies had decided to give the Germans two more days in which to make up their minds, but Reuter was not told, so that he now expected that the British would try to seize his ships at any moment. It seemed to him that these suspicions were confirmed when, at about 10.00 on the 21st, the British First Battle Squadron which had been guarding the Germans in the Flow went out to sea, leaving behind no British ships except two destroyers and some small craft. Reuter believed that the First Battle Squadron had gone to sea to meet the rest of the British battleships and that the combined fleet would then re-enter the Flow, through the various entrances, quickly come alongside the German ships and board them before they could be sunk. Accordingly, soon after 10.00 Reuter sent the preparatory signal for scuttling, and the executive at 11.20. The *Friedrich der Grosse* was the first ship to sink at 12.16 and the *Hindenburg* the last at 17.00 hours.

Preliminary measures had already been taken in accordance

with Reuter's order of 17 June: all doors and scuttles in the ships were to be left open and, where necessary, preparations were to be made to open valves admitting the sea, as well as the apertures of condensers and submerged torpedo-tubes. In some cases valves and capstans were jammed to make it difficult to stop the ships flooding or slipping their cables, which would have made it possible to free the ships from their anchors and tow them into shallow water. As far as possible sea-cocks and valves were opened on one side only, so that the ships would turn over and capsize completely, as most of them did.

In a corner of the vast Flow, around Gutter Sound, were the seventy-four German warships, sixteen of them the largest size, all rusty and ill-kempt, part of the landscape for seven months. At noon there was a sudden scurry of activity on board all of them. A German destroyer officer remarked later that this was the first time the destroyers had ever seen anyone running aboard one of the big ships.

Soon the ships began heeling over at extraordinary angles, lurching and leaning on their beam ends and then turning upside down. In the middle of the excitement was a 500-ton tug, the *Flying Kestrel,* taking a party of schoolchildren on an excursion. When the big ships began to turn over, with great rumbles and crashes as machinery and equipment inside them tore loose, and then began to sink with water streaming over their sides and decks, the children were thrilled. To them this was an entertainment especially arranged for their benefit; to their teachers and the master of the *Flying Kestrel,* the young passengers, it seemed, might at any moment be in great danger and the tug steamed away to land them, returning later to the scene.

It was possible to tow a few of the ships into shallow water before they sank; one battleship (*Baden*), three light cruisers, (*Emden, Nürnberg, Frankfurt*) and eighteen destroyers. Some rifle fire was opened from the British small craft in an effort to compel crews to return to their ships and stop them from sinking. In this firing eight officers and men were killed.

The *Emden* failed to sink because the British guard trawler, observing the Germans lowering their boats, guessed what was going to happen and steamed by quickly, collecting the boats and towing them away to a distance. The *Emden* then postponed her sinking until alternative means of preserving the life of her crew could be organized, and during this time she was towed ashore.

By about 17.00 Gutter Sound and adjoining waters were covered with wreckage. Only a few ships were left, with parts of others standing out of the water; bubbles here and there marked a ship's grave, and on the forecastle of the abandoned *Baden* a solitary seaman in whites was seen dancing a hornpipe, apparently the only man in the ship. In fact two young hands from the *Flying Kestrel* had got on board and gone below, where they were making a hasty tour of the ship pursued by a couple of officers, whether British or German the young men did not stop to find out.

The British authorities were heavily criticized for having permitted the scuttling. Criticism was especially severe in France because the British, from the very beginning, had wanted to sink all the ships, while the French had wished to incorporate a number of the most important of them in their own Navy to make up for the ships which they had not been able to build during the war. Professor Marder examines the evidence and shows conclusively that there was nothing the British could have done to prevent the scuttling attempt being made, except to place guards in the ships which, under the terms of the Armistice, they had agreed not to do.

If the French had not interfered with the original British naval proposals that all the principal German surface ships be surrendered, as were the U-boats, the scuttling would never have taken place and an enormous wrangle between the Allies as to the disposal of the ships would have occurred. With the French frustrated and the British embarrassed, only what was left of the German Navy was able to feel satisfaction at the scuttling.

Scheer commented: 'I rejoice . . . the stain of surrender has been wiped from the escutcheon of the German Fleet. The sinking of these ships has proved that the spirit of the Fleet is not dead. This last act is true of the best traditions of the German Navy.'

On the other hand, even in Germany outside the Navy, approval of the events at Scapa Flow was very qualified. Commander F. O. Busch, a retired German naval officer and naval historian, wrote:

It was typical that this manly act – the first sign of light on a dark cloud-covered horizon – was enthusiastically received in Germany itself only by small minority groups, by the Free Corps and the Naval brigades of Ehrhardt and Loewenfeldt. The great mass of the people were led to condemn the act. Even the majority of the right-wing, middle-class press could only see its consequences from the point of view of foreign policy, which were painted in the darkest colours.

NINE

During the first months of 1919 the German Navy had almost ceased to exist. Its ships, except for a handful, were either surrendered, sunk or disarmed, while its officers and men were but slowly recovering from the shock of mutiny and rebellion, and their defeated country was torn by civil strife and threatened with ruin. Altogether there were thirteen efficient warships still in service, three light cruisers and ten destroyers, all due to be handed over to the Allies. Under the circumstances it is not surprising that it was seriously proposed that the Navy be abolished entirely.

The proposal was rejected and, despite the tremendous handicaps under which it suffered, twenty years later the German Navy was able to challenge for a second time its old rival the British Navy and, a little later, the United States Navy as well, and in doing so came even nearer to victory than it had done in the years 1914 to 1918.

The terms of the Armistice which had wrecked the German fleet also gave what was left of it an important task, for they provided that Germany was to be responsible for sweeping up mines laid in their home waters in the North Sea, in the Baltic and on the Norwegian coast as far north as Russian territorial waters. When the abolition of the Navy had been proposed, it was also suggested that this vast undertaking be leased to private contractors, but in the event a fleet of some 300 minesweepers was assembled to begin the work, which lasted some three years and included on one occasion an exchange of fire between the German light cruiser *Hamburg* and Russian coastal batteries near Murmansk.

In March and April 1919 short-term measures were taken to keep the Navy in being. On 10 March the Supreme Council of Workers and Soldiers was dissolved and on 26 March Trotha was appointed head of the Admiralty, to the annoyance of Scheer who, referring to the departure of Hipper, had remarked that it would have been better if everyone else connected with recent events had gone as well. To command the rump of the High Seas Fleet in Hipper's place, Meurer was appointed, but as all the ships of the Fleet were laid up, disarmed, there was little for him to do, and he was soon moved to Kiel in command of the Baltic Station.

On 16 April the National Assembly at Weimar approved legislation establishing a provisional navy. Headquarters of the minesweeping service was established in the old, disarmed battleship *Wettin*, which, with four more obsolete battleships, were fitted to carry twelve small minesweepers each on their decks. As soon as the formation of the new service was announced the *Wettin* was overrun with volunteers, former naval personnel, merchant seamen, ex-soldiers and ordinary workmen, some attracted by the prospect of a job in the midst of growing unemployment, together with earning the bounties offered. In addition, at this time the first post-war 'Crew' (the name given to the yearly intake of cadets) was enrolled and began their naval careers on board another obsolete battleship laid up at Kiel.

Ideas as to the future of the Navy were vague. There was still a faint hope that the ships at Scapa Flow would be returned. There was also the hope that even if this were not done, the eight oldest dreadnought battleships of the *Ostfriesland* and *Rheinland* classes, disarmed under the terms of the Armistice, might be re-commissioned under the German flag.

These hopes were finally destroyed when the terms of the Peace Treaty were published in May. All the ships at Scapa, together with most of those left in Germany, were to be surrendered. In future the German Navy was limited to six pre-dreadnoughts of the *Deutschland* class, which had been obsolete before the war began, six light cruisers also obsolete and twenty-four middle-aged destroyers. In addition, two more battleships, two more light cruisers and eight destroyers could be retained in reserve. There were to be no submarines and no German aircraft at all, naval, military or civil. Battleships and light cruisers were not to be replaced until they were twenty years old, and destroyers fifteen. The size of new ships was not to exceed 10,000 tons for battleships, described in the Treaty as 'armoured ships', 6,000 tons for light cruisers and 800 tons for destroyers. Almost all the ships that Germany was permitted to keep were already over-age and could, in theory, have been replaced, but the financial state of the country meant that there was almost no money for new construction. A final important restriction was that the number of officers and ratings was limited to 15,000 of which only 1,500 were to be officers, who were to serve twenty-five years, while ratings had to serve twelve. The point of this stipulation was to prevent the enlistment of men for a short period of intensive training, followed by their discharge into reserve and their replacement by new recruits, a system which would permit the building up of a large reserve of trained men.

Despite all this there were still traces of optimism, and in 1920, when Dönitz returned from a prisoner-of-war camp in England, he was told that within two or three years Germany would have U-boats again. In consequence of this assurance, Dönitz volunteered for the new navy, but in fact he was obliged to wait for fifteen years, until Hitler repudiated the disarmament clauses of the Treaty of Versailles and the building of U-boats began again in Germany.

In 1920 the German Navy had to pass through one more severe internal crisis before it could settle down to the comparative peacefulness of the next decade and a half. Puzzled and upset by the preceding years, unused to democracy and misunderstanding their duties in the armed forces of a democracy, many officers involved themselves in politics. Meurer, for example, one of the most able and intelligent of the German flag officers, was removed from his command because he engaged in public controversy with Erzberger over the conduct of the Armistice negotiations.

In March 1920 there followed something much more serious, when Wolfgang Kapp, a civil servant from East Prussia, with General von Luttwitz commanding the troops in the Berlin area and Ehrhardt's naval brigade, seized power in Berlin, in what became known as the Kapp *Putsch*. The legal government left for Dresden and later for Stuttgart and in its support a general strike was proclaimed. Trotha placed himself at the disposal of the Kapp forces and when, within a few days, the movement collapsed and the legitimate government returned to Berlin, he was dismissed. At the same time the two naval brigades, those of Ehrhardt and Lœwenfeld, which together with the other *Frei Korps* had been permanent centres of right-wing agitation, were finally dissolved. Noske, in this crisis, acted with his usual energy and decision, but it was to cost him his career, for, confronted at this time with risings both on the Right and the Left, he was judged by his old SPD colleagues to have been much more severe against the Communists than he had been against the *Frei Korps* and the supporters of Kapp.

As Minister of Defence, Noske was succeeded by Otto Gessler, a Bavarian Democrat, who was confronted with the task of re-organizing the Navy after another mutiny. In 1918 there had been a mutiny of ratings on the Left; in 1920 the mutiny was officers on the Right, sparked off by Kapp. Trotha was now arrested and proceedings were begun against 156 other officers. Only twelve of these were dismissed from the Service, but in the meantime a large proportion of the officers of the Navy had been relieved of their duties. What authority remained was in the hands of warrant officers and petty officers, and the creation of a permanent trade union of professional soldiers and sailors was discussed; while once again, for the third time in less than two years, it was proposed that the entire Navy should be abolished. At this stage Seeckt, the virtual Chief of the General Staff, recommended to Scheer that an entirely new beginning be made. As Scheer had been critical of Trotha ever since the 1918 mutinies, there is no reason to think that he disagreed with this advice, nor that he failed to pass it on to Gessler.

During these disturbances there was trouble at Kiel and two torpedo-boats scuttled themselves, while in Wilhelmshaven there was a confrontation between the crews of the minesweepers, all men who had signed on for only a short period, and the destroyer crews who already considered themselves professional naval ratings. Only after some difficulty did their senior officer, Captain Albrecht, succeed in taking the destroyers to sea in the face of the ill-will and obstruction of the minesweepers. Gessler went to Wilhelmshaven to see what could be done to set matters right. He was first met by a warrant officer at Hamburg who attempted, unsuccessfully, to dictate to him in which ship he should continue to Wilhelmshaven. Once there Gessler was met by a deputation, headed by a trade-union leader mounted on a horse, from whom he learned that Levetzow, the local admiral, had been arrested together with 400 other officers and shut up in the naval barracks.

Gessler managed to bring matters back to something like normal, and then sought a new Chief of the Naval Staff. He soon decided that none of the serving officers was suitable and recalled to the active list Paul Behncke, now a retired Vice-Admiral; as Vice-Chief of the Naval Staff under Pohl in 1914, he had been one of the first of the 'activist' admirals and had been severely wounded at Jutland while leading the German line in his flagship, the *König*. At the same time Gessler appointed another officer who had distinguished himself at Jutland, Rear-Admiral Zenker, who had been captain of the battle-cruiser *Von der Tann*, to replace Levetzow as commander-in-chief of the North Sea Station. In 1924 Zenker in turn replaced Behncke. After his retirement Levetzow became the senior naval adviser to the National Socialist party and, when Hitler came to power, was appointed Chief of Police in Berlin.

In October 1922, after four years hard work, the German share of minesweeping was at an end, and a beginning was made with the formation of two miniature fleets, one in the

North Sea and one in the Baltic. Each comprised one pre-dreadnought battleship, two obsolete light cruisers, and eleven obsolete destroyers. In addition there were a handful of very minor ships for training purposes, fishery protection and surveying work.

In the same year, after a good deal of argument, the new Navy, made up of old ships, received a new flag – red, white and black in horizontal stripes with a large iron cross in the centre, which finally replaced the old Imperial ensign.

A beginning had been made in the previous year with the construction of the first ship for the new Navy, the light cruiser *Emden*, but shortage of money delayed her completion until 1925. Originally the Germans had proposed that two light cruisers, nearly completed, should be finished, to replace two of the six light cruisers permitted by the Treaty; but the Allies had refused to allow this, and while one new cruiser was slowly being built, eight unfinished ships, almost identical with the new one, were being broken up.

Other new ships followed very slowly during the 1920s, and up to the time of Hitler's accession to power only three out of six permitted 'armoured ships' – the famous pocket battleships – had been laid down, together with six light cruisers and twelve small destroyers. It had been a hard struggle to get funds from the Reichstag even for this modest building programme. Even more important, after the events of 1918, had been the question of providing trustworthy crews. Indirectly the Peace Treaty had helped here, for under its provisions every rating had to serve at least twelve years and this long term of service meant that virtually all the ratings were trained to the standard of specialist petty officer. The recruits' quality was of the highest, every candidate was examined personally by the same officer, a man who had been the boatswain of the Kaiser's yacht and who, very exceptionally, had been commissioned. This officer was not only concerned with the potential recruits but also with their families, which he visited at home to make sure that there was no dubious element entering the service.

During the years between the wars only two administrative measures appear to have been taken to prevent the recurrence of bad feeling between officers and men. The first was that food was to be the same for officers and men alike, a regulation which despite its importance did not long survive and, second, a warning was issued by Behncke in 1922 on the subject of correct behaviour of officers to their men. It read:

Officers on duty dealing with subordinates must maintain a calm and always objective manner even when the subordinates have behaved in a coarse fashion. Not only does the offensive attitude of a superior towards a subordinate have an effect prejudicial to discipline but even an expression of contempt or lack of attention during the reports, or statements by the subordinate, or a coarse expression of disbelief, as, for example, the word 'Nonsense' (*Quatsch*) and gestures of dismissal, give rise to criticisms of the superior and weaken the needed authority of his position from both the personal and service points of view. Calm reserve is especially necessary when receiving oral or written reports or evidence of punishable acts and in the judgement of the guilt or innocence of subordinates in connection with any events.

During the winter of 1922 the first war plans were made for the fleet. They were, naturally, extremely modest, stressing the importance of closing narrow waters with mines and light torpedo-craft and the carrying out of anti-submarine exercises. The chief task of all available forces would be to prevent an enemy forcing its way into the Baltic. To do this it might be necessary to leave the North Sea to the protection of local forces. The basic idea of these plans was a war with France and Poland, in which the French fleet would try to enter the Baltic to link up with the Poles and to cut Germany's overseas communications. Exercises and war games with this in mind were carried out and everything was done to give officers and men as much sea time as possible, either in warships or merchant vessels.

The principal obstacles to the realization of these plans were still the restrictions of the Allied armistice commission, the financial situation caused by inflation and, as late as the winter of 1922-3, lack of discipline, an indication that the havoc of the mutinies had not yet been completely repaired. A grim hope was expressed at this time that it would not be necessary to respect Danish neutrality. Further plans included the despatch of auxiliary cruisers to the Mediterranean to interfere with communications between France and North Africa, while Germany's few cruisers, together with other auxiliary cruisers, would raid French commerce on the high seas. All this, of course, was conditional upon British neutrality.

As early as May 1923, during the French occupation of the Ruhr, the Navy had investigated the use of convoys to prevent the French blockading the North Sea coast but concluded that the ships required did not exist. Nevertheless by 1925 the German Admirality was considering attacks from the sea against the French Channel ports.

These plans were drawn up by the Navy in a vacuum. The Naval staff consulted neither the Government nor the Army, and its dreams were shattered by the latter, which pointed out that there could be absolutely no question of a war between France and Germany owing to the latter's weakness, which was such that the Army would be unable to guarantee the safety of the German North Sea ports, so that it was useless for the Navy to think of carrying on a war of its own when operations on land could only end in a German defeat.

By April 1926 a more rational plan had been drawn up. The Army's main effort would be to prevent a French invasion of central Germany, although it might be necessary to sacrifice the North Sea ports. It was assumed that Germany would be able to receive supplies of arms and war materials from Russia by sea. The German Navy would provide the necessary convoy escorts and prevent the Poles from using the ports of Gdynia and Danzig. The plan was far-fetched, but it did appear to contain the only hope of checking a French invasion, and it is interesting to see that no objections were made to collaboration with Russia. However, although Russian ships were visiting German ports at this time as a step to co-operation in war, the

Germans were careful that their ratings should not come into contact with the Russians.

In 1926 a German naval mission under Admiral Spindler, the official historian of the U-boat war, was sent to Russia and was asked to supply plans of the most successful types of U-boats, details of their operational experience and the service of technical experts. In addition to submarines the Russians were also greatly interested in designs for motor-torpedo-boats and aircraft-launching catapults. There was also a certain amount of discussion of possible Russo-German co-operation in the event of either country finding themselves at war with a Franco-Polish coalition in the Baltic or the Mediterranean.

A little later Russian-German relations worsened rapidly and the German Communist party took a lead in attacking the Navy in the Reichstag and in the country. There is no doubt that one of the chief reasons for this was the Russian realization, about the year 1928, that a new German Navy was now growing up which would become an important force in the Baltic, especially as, at this time, the Russians had hardly begun to repair the damage done by the war and the revolution in their own fleet.

The year 1928 was critical for the Navy under the Weimar Republic, for in that year a proposal was announced to lay down the first of the 10,000-ton 'armoured ships' permitted by the Peace Treaty. There was a passionate debate in the Reichstag, with the forces of the Left, including the Communists, opposing the ship on the grounds that it was unnecessary and that its construction would mean a new naval armaments race. The government claimed the ship was essential for Germany's defence, but its spokesmen were led into confusion when they said the ship was designed to escort convoys between East Prussia and the rest of the Reich, separated by the Polish corridor. The distance between Stettin and Elbing, the two nearest German ports on this route, being about 250 miles there was concern when the ship's radius of action was stated to be 20,000 miles, for this made it clear that she was really intended as a commerce raider in distant seas. Nevertheless, despite criticism by the opposition, the Reichstag approved the ship and, subsequently, two sister ships, the three being named *Deutschland* [later renamed *Lützow* by a superstitious Hitler who was apprehensive of the effect on morale if a ship named *Deutschland* were to be sunk], *Admiral Scheer* and *Admiral Graf Spee*. These were the famous pocket battleships.

Not since the British built the *Dreadnought* in 1905-6 had a new warship design created such a sensation. Summing up their qualities, it could be said that the new ships were able to sink any ship from which they were unable to escape, except for three British battle-cruisers; but at that time this was not thought important, as Germany was not intending a war with Britain. The critics of the building of the pocket battleships were correct in one particular for it did, in fact, start a classic arms race. The French replied by building two ships of *Dunkerque* class, which were bigger, faster and more powerful; whereupon the Italians built four of the *Vittorio Veneto*, ships even bigger and faster and more powerful than the French.

All that was trouble which lay ahead; in the meantime, still in 1928, there broke out the last of those internal political disputes which had made life difficult for the Navy in the 1920s. A conspiracy was discovered, and made much of by the Left, the aim of which was to deceive the Allies as to the execution of the terms of the Treaty of Versailles and to deceive the Reichstag concerning the use of public funds.

In the first place, money had been accumulated by the Navy through its practice of charging extravagant sums for various purposes and then collecting the unspent money for items which never appeared in the naval estimates. In addition, special funds had been allotted to deal with hardships caused by the French when they occupied the Ruhr, and some of this was used for the clandestine purchase of arms (mostly obsolete) from Italy. These were intended for the Army, but the Navy also received a share.

The funds obtained were used for a great range of purposes connected with secret rearmament by the Navy. The building of a fleet of oil tankers by private individuals was subsidized, there were dealings with banana plantations as an excuse for building banana-carrying freighters which, though small, were comparatively fast and ideally suited to serve as armed merchant-raiders in time of war, and there were similar arrangements with fishery companies so that trawlers might be built for use as minesweepers. There was a film company to make films to encourage naval recruiting; there was an air-charter firm which provided planes for anti-aircraft target practice and the illegal training of naval flyers; and there was a salvage company which planned to raise sunken ships by freezing the sea in which they lay so that the resulting block of ice would come to the surface bringing the sunken ship with it.

In charge of these operations was Captain Lohmann, chief of the Sea Transport department of the Admiralty, but when the conspiracy leaked out both Gessler and Zenker were compelled to resign. Zenker was replaced by Admiral Raeder, who had been Hipper's Chief of Staff during World War One and who was to retain his new position until January 1943. No head of any fighting service of one of the major powers has, within recent years, held his post for so long.

It is fair to say that although Lohmann handled vast quantities of money without having to account for it, he himself benefited financially not at all. When he died suddenly shortly after the scandal broke, his widow had to borrow money to pay for his funeral. Some of his contacts, however, were much less scrupulous and these caused the scandals, the most notable of which concerned the making of films, in the course of which all the extravagances for which the motion picture industry in its heyday was a by-word were perpetrated on a scale which transcended the lavish and reached the criminal.

In October 1919 a number of committees and sub-committees set up by the Reichstag had begun a long series of enquiries into the causes of the German defeat. One of these dealt with what was called 'the inner collapse' and was concerned, among much else, with the naval mutinies. Military and political matters having occupied the enquiry for six years, the Committee first met on 22 January 1926 to deal with naval affairs and sat until 1 March 1928. The report contained no conclusion which gave any comfort to either the extreme Right or Left, but its proceedings did provide an enormous amount of information of the grievances which gave rise to the troubles in 1917 and 1918, with statements and arguments from both sides.

Among the members of the Reichstag who were members of the Committee two stood out, one on each side. On the Left was Dittmann, the former USPD leader (the USPD and the main body of the SPD had made peace with each other and had reunited in September 1922), and on the Right Rear-Admiral Brüninghaus, who had retired from the Navy after the war, during which he had been flag captain to Behncke at Jutland in the *König*; another former naval officer now a member of the Reichstag was Gottfried Treviranus, who was to rise to a challenging position on the eve of Hitler's advent to power and who, consequently, was obliged to seek flight from the SS during the Röhm purge of 30 June 1934, so rapidly that, warned by his daughter, he had to escape by climbing over his garden wall wearing tennis flannels.

Holding a watching brief for the *Marineleitung* was Commander Canaris, afterwards to be chief of Hitler's Military Intelligence and to lose his life for his part in the conspiracy of 20 July 1944. His presence with the Committee started off a controversy, for he was publicly accused of having been responsible for the murder of the two Spartacists, Karl Liebknecht and Rosa Luxemburg. He denied this, and succeeded in establishing the fact that he had been out of Berlin during the relevant period. However, when asked if he had discussed the possible deaths of the two politicians before they had taken place, he told the Committee that he was not there to answer personal questions.

Two assessors, sitting with the Committee, virtually represented the officers and ratings: Trotha for the officers, and Alboldt, a former warrant officer who had been a Writer (i.e. a secretarial assistant). On leaving the navy in 1910 he had formed the Association of Warrant Officers, and whose detestation of the officers Brüninghaus described as ' verging on fanatical hate'. Alboldt was clearly a man of considerable ability, suffering personally very much from the rigid class system of the German armed forces, which prevented a man of his background from being given an opportunity to develop his talents to the full. A complex of very nearly ferocious jealousy was the result, but even so he was able to say in praise of Trotha that 'all who knew him as an officer and as a man held him to be unique'. Furthermore, it is an interesting indication of Alboldt's standing as President of the *Deckoffiziers Verein* that he was apparently consulted by the government in the early weeks of 1919 about the appointment of a new chief of the Admiralty and that he recommended the nomination of Trotha.

Now, at the beginning of the confrontation between them, the former Admiral and the former Warrant Officer sat in the committee room of the Reichstag exchanging reminiscences of Tientsin during the Boxer Rising, when they had met in the American Mission building which served as a canteen for the German naval contingent. There was in this an element of the courtesies usually taken for granted in British public life but, as the enquiry went on, it developed in a very different way from the closely-argued and documented proceedings of a British Royal Commission. Assertion after assertion was bandied about by both sides without any attempt to provide proof of the statements made, while those accused scarcely ever challenged their accusers to provide proof of what they had said.

From the beginning of the enquiry most of the evidence was provided by spokesmen for the men endeavouring to justify their actions. This justification, presented by Dittmann, began with the contention that it was the admirals who had mutinied. The government, Dittmann argued, wanted peace and was trying to obtain it. On the other hand, the admirals wished to continue the war, had set the government at naught and had acted contrary to the wishes of the people in preparing an attack, the outcome of which, he claimed, would almost certainly have been the breaking off of the armistice negotiations. Unfortunately for this argument there is the evidence of Prince Max who, in his *Memoirs*, after criticizing the Navy for keeping him, as head of the government, in ignorance of its plans, went on to say that if he had known of the plan at the time he would have approved it. He wrote:

I cannot admit the explanation given that the time and objective of the operation had to be concealed from me on grounds of secrecy. Military operations of such far-reaching political importance must not be kept secret from the Chancellor. But I am convinced that the real motive lay in a different kind of mistrust. Considerations of military secrecy could no longer be relevant when once Hipper had given up the planned offensive; and even then I was not informed. I did not hear the truth as to the nature and scope of the proposed naval offensive until long after the Revolution.

The Navy – this is my firm conviction today – was afraid the Government would not muster up the necessary understanding and faith to be capable of approving of such a tremendous undertaking. It is true I cannot say I should have entirely shared their optimism. Had their confidence had a basis in reality, why had Admiral Scheer moved heaven and earth to prevent the abandonment of the submarine warfare? He ought then to have *demanded* it; since in the first place the submarine war could not have such speedy results as to reverse the decision of the war; and secondly the fact that it kept a good part of the High Seas Fleet occupied, and that the submarines were needed for the contemplated offensive, made its abandonment a necessary preliminary to the decisive battle.

But I admit that when once the decisive battle had been determined on, it was the duty of the Naval Command to work itself up to the temper of unshakeable confidence in victory. And even had I not been carried away by these soaring hopes, the following considerations would still have led me to give my assent in principle to the naval operation.

If we should win, and this, considering our leadership, the training of the crews and the superiority of our material, was not inconceivable, the hard-pressed army and the civil population, whose impatience and suffering were daily growing, would receive a powerful impulse to hold out. After a German naval victory, the revolution and capitulation of 9 and 11 November would have been almost a psychological impossibility. But should our Navy suffer a glorious defeat, yes, and even if this last cruise were really to be a death cruise, even then its desirability from a military-political point of view must certainly be conceded. This sacrifice would have been a moral force capable of putting to shame the many disaffected and despairing folk who would not have been able to escape its influence. I have been justly reminded of Thermopylae.

It is difficult to follow the Chancellor in some of his arguments. The odds against any German success once the two main fleets had joined battle were very great. The Supreme Army Command and Scheer both believed the war would end within four to six weeks, and a result reached in so very short a time could only be a German defeat. There were neither the time nor the resources available for any other outcome and it is hard to see that any improvement in German morale in November 1918 could have altered the result of the war; Prince Max had already decided and convinced the Supreme Army Command that a peace involving surrender concluded before the Allies invaded Germany was preferable to a fight to the last man [such as was to take place in 1945]. This was a change of Prince Max's original attitude; for when he was appointed Chancellor he had first refused to issue an appeal for peace and then had only done so after the strongest pressure had been put upon the Kaiser and the Supreme Army Command. Thus a contradiction remained. On the one hand, he wished to conclude an armistice before the Allies could invade Germany, on the other he would have endorsed a naval operation which, so far as the naval and military high commands were concerned, would only have served reasons of prestige. Even after November 1918 there was never any need for the Germans to prove to themselves, or to the outside world, that they were the most formidable fighters ever seen in history.

The attempt made by the Reichstag over two years to try and

find out what had gone wrong with the Navy was, of course, a highly political exercise. Germany was suffering very severely from the Right *v*. Left confrontation which was soon to have such disastrous consequences for the whole world, and both sides were anxious to score points and to defend themselves against the attacks of their opponents.

This had been true of all the work of the Committee ever since it had started, in 1919, with a monster propaganda blast by Hindenburg in favour of the Nationalist Right. Now, as far as the Navy was concerned, the SPD was anxious to defend itself; and to show that the USPD, now re-united with it, was not fomenting treason when it received sympathetically Reichpietsch and other leaders of the mutiny and supplied them with propaganda material. On the other hand, the Nationalists wished to prove that the Navy, and by extension the country itself, had been brought to ruin by a left-wing conspiracy and that the disaster was not the fault of those who had been in power before and during the war.

The two main points of the case for the Left were the poor food and the relations between officers and ratings. There was also evidence given before the Committee as to the treatment by investigating authorities of those people suspected of fomenting the 1917 mutinies. Reading this evidence now against the background of third degree, torture and terror employed in secret police interrogations, to which we have become accustomed over the past half-century, we may conclude that the interrogating officials, though generally harsh and sometimes pressing men unduly to confess or bear witness against others accused, never adopted the means of the Gestapo or the MVD. The conclusion that this was so is strengthened by the fact that, at the time the evidence was given, there was no police state in Germany. Accordingly, extremists on both sides were perfectly able to look after their own supporters and, in fact, complained loudly and publicly if they thought an injustice was being done. When the witnesses from the Left spoke at the enquiry there was nothing that they needed to hush up; the sentences had been heavy but, apart from the two executions which had actually taken place, all had been cancelled by the revolution a little over a year after they had been imposed, which makes it seem even more regrettable that two men were actually shot. To many it did not seem necessary at the time, and today seems even less so.

M. Vidil, in *les Mutineries de la marine allemande*, has said that the mutinies of 1917 were fairly and effectively dealt with, so that the 1918 mutinies started entirely afresh, apart from the feelings of resentment left by the heavy sentences imposed the year before. However, very little was done to remove effectively the men's grievances, although it does appear that much could have been done without undermining the discipline of the Fleet. Attempts were made to improve rations, but the fundamental problem seems to have gone unrecognized and untackled, for evidence given at the enquiry shows that, though both the quantity and quality of rations were deplorable, what really annoyed the men was that officers in the big ships had food which was more plentiful and better prepared than what they themselves had. In the little ships officers and men ate alike, but in the big ships which, from the point of view of numbers of men involved, amounted to about two-thirds of the entire Fleet, this was not the case. As for separate messing, in the big ships there could be four or sometimes five different galleys, one for ratings, one for warrant officers, one for midshipmen, one for officers and, in the case of flagships, one for the admiral as well.

It was an added cause of irritation that these galleys were frequently alongside each other, so that the ratings settling down to their frugal meals could smell, and then see, the very much better food being prepared for the officers. In the course of the enquiry Admiral Brüninghaus went so far as to admit 'that it might have been more sensible to have instituted the same messing for all', but he does not appear to have grasped the fundamental nature of the men's complaints, from which so much else was to spring – the rigid lines of class drawn between officers and ratings, and the lengths to which the officers believed they had to go to maintain them. For example, when the suggestion was made that identical messing should be introduced in one of the big ships it was rejected by the officers of that ship on the ground that to make a change would be to show weakness before the men.

It would seem that almost all other officers of senior or middle rank suffered from the same blind spot as Brüninghaus, and that there was a complete inability to appreciate the need, from the points of view of either justice or common sense, for the officers to enter into any relations with the lower deck other than those laid down by regulations and the immediate working of the ship. This lack of contact did not apply to the small ships, and it did not apply in the Army.

The army officers took care as best they might of their men, and this originated from the tradition of the Junker class which had been the backbone of the Prussian army since the days of Frederick the Great. These Junkers, the Prussian landowners, were not usually rich but they owned land, and land meant farms, and farmers and farm-workers and animals, all of which, for the most selfish reasons, had to be looked after. The Junkers fought and were killed or retired, but they trained not only the people of their own class in the way they themselves had come, but they also trained the many thousands of reserve officers who came back into the Army on mobilization from the middle classes.

On the other hand, the naval officers were mostly recruited directly from the middle classes, and never met members of the working classes in peacetime. Young officers, unless they were exceptionally intelligent and considerate, often did not know how to conduct themselves when they came to be drafted to the big ships. A rating told the enquiry: 'We had all been serving for five, six or seven years. We all saw how the cadets came on board, how they became midshipmen and then sub-lieutenants, stood in front of us and said to men who had served a long time and some of whom were married, "You fools, you ape faces"; and then there was a Lieutenant-Commander who never said anything to the men but "go away, you pig, you beast, you stink".'

One of the reasons for this attitude was the lack of contact off duty between officers and ratings; when the officers and men went ashore they went their separate ways, the officers to the clubs and restaurants and very often to their homes, while the ratings went and drank beer as long as their money lasted. At a basic rate of pay of nineteen marks, less than £1 a month, there was not much beer drinking for them, with beer at twenty-eight pfenings a *Stein*. Morale was further lowered as the quality of the beer fell as well, while it was known that the officers drew a ration of twenty bottles of wine per month as well as rum, and had access to other spirits as well. Few German officers, remembering those days, now deny that in wardrooms and in clubs ashore there was too much drinking and consequent drunkenness. No attempt was made to organize amusements for the ratings. All complained, with considerable justice, of the lack of facilities at Wilhelmshaven; but anyone who knew the British base at Scapa Flow during either war remembers that natural facilities there were even more limited. In fact they were non-existent, except those which the officers and men made for themselves.

Summing up, it may be said that in dealing with relations between officers and men during World War One there was no realization that the industrial revolution had taken place. Orders were given and living conditions enforced without most of the officers in the big ships realizing that the lower deck detested the fact that they had to submit to a discipline which they considered quite unnecessarily strict. Of this discipline, the most irksome features were the arrogance of some officers, the difference in messing scales and the lack of an intelligent and sympathetic exposition of the reasons why they were obliged to endure the rigours and, above all, the boredom of war.

Those who had been serving when the war broke out might, by the end of 1918, have been doing the same job for seven years, very often in the same ship, as in order to save time and manpower there was very little done to vary monotony by teaching new jobs.

Throughout, the officers persisted in their attitude that if they did mix with their men under any circumstances off duty, they would lose their authority and their capacity to exact instant obedience. There was not only a great gap between officers and ratings and between officers and warrant officers, but there was yet another between the executive officers and the various specialist officers, so that the most junior executive lieutenant took precedence over senior engineer officers and paymasters, a line which was drawn socially ashore as well as on duty. For example, great scandal was caused when the captain of a battleship entertained, in his home, his own chief engineer, and the captain had some difficulty in persuading the authorities that he should be allowed to conduct his relations with his officers as he thought best for the good of his ship. Another incident, which was widely reported in the Fleet and which was described to the enquiry, was occasioned by a young engineer officer who proposed to call on a more senior executive officer with his bride, and was told that while, of course, the couple would be received, his visit was not considered necessary. Shortly before the war, when considering recruitment for officers of the engineering branch, it was urged that care should be taken to select engineering cadets from a lower social class than the executive officers, so that the engineers would not aspire to a social position which they could not realize. Said one engineer officer: 'If the executive naval officer had used half as much energy against England as he devoted to oppressing the naval engineer, we would have won the war.' Ashore, executive and specialist officers rarely met and when, towards the end of the war in the interests of economy of manpower and rations, specialists were allowed to eat in the executive officers' clubs it was laid down that they were expected to leave as soon as they had eaten and should not remain in the club, reading or listening to music.

The engineer officers, years later, were to have a sort of revenge, for in the '70s there was appointed as Inspector-General of the Federal navy, an admiral who had always been an engineer officer, an appointment which provoked only the comment that in a modern navy which was so much dependent on electrical and mechanical engineering, the choice of an engineering officer to hold the highest rank in the service was a very intelligent one.

The problem of improving the quality of the executive officers was tackled as soon as the war was over with thoroughness and success, made easier by the fact that with a small service in which the officer corps numbered only 1,500 men, there was a rich selection of good human material available.

Training began with the ferocious inculcation of physical toughness, with long route marches, cross-country runs and the like. Later, in the training ships, hardiness was carried to such bizarre lengths that, in mid-winter in the Baltic, wash basins of water were placed on deck overnight, and then in the morning, before beginning to wash, the cadets were required to break, with their faces, the ice which had formed.

In the training ships, both steam and sail, the cadets played their full part in carrying out the hardest and dirtiest jobs on board, side by side with the ratings in the same way as was done in the British navy.

Cadets and ratings, by 1935, ate the same food; for different messing for officers and men had been reintroduced, despite the experiences of 1917, but the reversion to the old system does not seem to have produced any unfavourable repercussions.

When the Reichstag enquiry was over the Committee issued a report in 1928 which concluded:

1. The same causes which brought about the internal collapse of Germany also operated in the German Fleet and were intensified by the conditions of life on board.

2. Unrest and serious discontent existed from the beginning of 1915 onwards in various of the big ships. Discontent was increased by the fact that the big ships were not in action, which heightened the contrasts between the conditions of officers and men.

3. Grievances and growing discontent stemmed from the conviction that justified complaints over food and treatment by officers, and over the difference in standards of living between

wardrooms and mess decks, could have been dealt with by superiors, had these shown better will.

4. The steady growth among the German people of the longing for peace and of peace propaganda was reflected among the crews of the big ships, for lack of action itself strengthened the desire for peace.

The Committee at this stage remarked: 'It was not possible to obtain agreement as to why the Fleet was employed as it was (that is, " left in idleness " DW).'

5. Political activity was fostered in various big ships by the USPD and the left radical groups, which existed in the big ships as they did in the army and on the home front. At the same time, extreme nationalist propaganda was carried on by the officers.

6. After the March Revolution in Russia there spread a general hope for peace. Peace propaganda grew among the crews of some of the big ships, and the belief was fostered by the USPD that peace must be made from the outside, as the government would not, or could not, make it. Those supporting this idea looked hopefully to the Stockholm conference.

7. In 1917 events were sparked off by orders which were considered unjustified and against which the crews demonstrated by leaving their ships *en masse* and holding meetings ashore. These demonstrations had a political connection, as numerous ratings joined the USPD in the hope that they could hasten the coming peace.

There was no proof that leading members of the USPD knew the intentions of the seamen, or had incited or approved them.

8. The sentences passed by the courts martial in 1917 and, in particular, the carrying out of the death sentences were judged by a great part of the crews as unjust and too severe, and the sentences had the effect of embittering subsequent events.

9. The organization of seamen and stokers which had existed was broken up by the authorities in 1917, and it was not possible to establish the existence of revolutionary organizations on board after that time; nor was there any proof of further incitement to insubordination.

10. The performance of the crews up to the autumn of 1918 met all demands, according to the highest authorities.

11. Insubordination in the autumn of 1918 occurred because the crews did not believe that even a victorious naval battle could

alter the result of the war, and that the Fleet was therefore being committed for reasons of prestige. In addition the men believed that the new government of Prince Max von Baden was not in agreement with the planned attack.

12. Further, it was believed that an attack would make negotiations for an armistice impossible, and they concluded that there was no point at this time in sacrificing their lives, especially as the request of the Supreme Command for an armistice was believed to mean the end of the war.

13. As far as the majority of men were concerned, the mutinies of November 1918 did not have, as their aim, change in the form of government. The Fleet Command, on the other hand, assumed from the beginning the existence of a revolutionary movement, well organized and well led, with clearly defined aims.

In fact, however, the mutineers did not take up a clearly defined political position until after the mutiny had begun and the situation had developed. There was no sign of a central direction or of an alliance with any political organization.

14. Events in Kiel provided the prologue for the general revolution in Germany as sailors and stokers spread the revolution over northwest Germany, but it is not sure that they caused the revolution all over Germany. The revolutionary outbreaks in Munich and the other towns of south Germany were not directly caused by events in Kiel, and the workers' demonstrations in Berlin on 9 November took place without being directly influenced by the mutineers.

15. In conclusion, the collapse was due to a variety of causes and to no single one.

TEN

After the Reichstag enquiry had ended, three of the original members of the Committee, Alboldt, Brüninghaus and Dittmann, published the evidence which they had given in book form, while a fourth book was the diary of a seaman named Richard Stumpf. This had been sent by its author to Joseph Joos, a Catholic member of the Reichstag, who in turn submitted it as evidence to the Committee, whose members were so impressed that Stumpf himself was called to give evidence and act as an assessor. A book based on the diary was suitably edited by Dittmann as SPD propaganda and published in the ordinary way. Long after the end of World War Two the original diary was translated by Dr Daniel Horn, an Austrian-born American scholar, and in 1967 was published in the United States under the title of *War, Mutiny and Revolution in the German Navy* and later in the United Kingdom as *The Private War of Seaman Stumpf*.

The diary is a fascinating performance. Its author was a Bavarian, born in 1892 and a tinsmith by trade. Called up in 1912, he served on the lower deck of the battleship *Helgoland* until March 1918 when he was drafted to a depot ship, in accordance with what appears to have been a practice of withdrawing to harbour service men who had served a continuous stretch of more than five years in ships of the High Seas Fleet. At the beginning of the war Stumpf's diary, which does not appear to have been tampered with, in the light of hindsight, shows that its author was thrilled by the prospect of fighting, loyal to his German emperor and his Bavarian king, and only disappointed because it seemed at first that the war would not involve hostilities against 'the false and treacherous English'. However, he and his shipmates consoled themselves with the thought of a short and victorious war like that of 1870-1. When the British declaration of war came, Stumpf commented, 'Perfidious England . . . has stabbed us in the back with premeditation.'

For a time there was a good deal more of this sort of thing in the diary, but Stumpf was not long content to echo the official propaganda line. He was clearly most intelligent, and his keenness and his skill as a tradesman clearly made him a first-class fighting man. His book illustrates brilliantly how such a man should not be treated. Reading it makes it possible to see how and when the rot began in the Fleet, although it must be remembered that Stumpf, more intelligent than most ratings, came to the various stages of his depressing conclusions probably a little before his messmates. In March 1915 Stumpf began complaining about boredom, by June of the same year he was exasperated by the gulf between officers and ratings and the swingeing punishments inflicted for comparatively minor disciplinary offences. These reflections were accompanied by violently anti-British remarks of the sort which we have associated with Dr Goebbels, but which were common enough in the Kaiser's time.

Stumpf was at Jutland and delighted with action, but he and his messmates were not taken in by official claims of a German victory. Immediately after it, he wrote, 'One could by no means describe our spirits as happy or victorious. On the contrary, we were depressed.' A little later, on 25 July 1916, he wrote, 'Gradually I have come to the conclusion that there will be no victors or vanquished in this war.' After Jutland, insufficient food and overmuch discipline were once more the principal topics in Stumpf's diary.

After this there followed the miserable 'turnip winter' of 1916-17. Hitherto, when his turn for leave came round he had gone off to the little village in Bavaria which was his home, and on his return to his ship had written an idyllic little picture of the pleasant time that he had had. In the summer of 1917 his turn for leave came round again; in principle all ratings had a fortnight's leave every year, with the senior rates, reservists called back to the colours, and married men getting three weeks. This time, when he came back to Wilhelmshaven he wrote very differently, and shows clearly how the civilian population was being worn down by privations:

> I must confess that I did not return in a happy frame of mind. It is difficult to say why. The trip itself was very tranquil. Many of the things which formerly made the trip so interesting and stimulating did not occur. There were no blood-curdling stories, no secret predictions of things to come or discussions concerning the possibilities of peace. I missed the lusty curses of the soldiers, the suspicious listening of the dock workers and the complaints of the women. Does this mean that things are now better in the land? I am afraid not. The people are so apathetic and hopeless that it hurts my heart. It was not so bad as long as people still had the strength to vent their anger by cursing. Only when they have lost all hope and are totally depressed do they appear as disconsolate and indifferent as they are nowadays.

The mutinies of July and August 1917 followed. The *Helgoland* was little affected, which is a point of interest since she was to prove one of the most troublesome ships in October and November 1918, but her crew shared in the gains won by the mutinies elsewhere. Some time in September Stumpf wrote:

> Now something about our menu! . . . I am pleased to comment favourably on it. An immeasurable improvement has occurred so that it is now even better than before the war. Our new cook is very capable and can convert even white cabbage and barley groats into a tasty meal. Even on ordinary workdays we receive plums, apples or tomatoes for dessert. This was not the case when we were still at peace. One evening, after we had had an especially good meal, the Commander came round to ask the men if they were satisfied now. They all answered in the affirmative.

Stumpf commented: '*Panem et circenses.*'

At about this time, Stumpf learned of the outcome of the courts martial of the mutineers and was extremely shocked:

'For several days now I have tried to describe a crime which, in its horror, defies description. In vain I sought to compare it with other countries and periods.'

Two men, accused of having spoken at a meeting of disgruntled seamen, stated Stumpf, were sentenced to ten years' imprisonment. In the course of the proceedings, again according to Stumpf, the president of the courts martial said, 'I shall dispense with the testimony of witnesses, since it will not reveal anything incriminating.'

During the 1920s several works of semi-fiction dealing with the mutinies were published. One of the best known was a book called *Der Kaisers Kulis (The Kaiser's Coolies)* by Theodore Plivier, who himself served on the lower deck, became a man of the extreme Left, escaped to Russia and then, after World War Two, came back to the West where he died. His book is slightly naïve, full of an innocent surprise that things go wrong in war, but there is no doubt that his impressions were those of many of his shipmates.

Plivier lays considerable emphasis on the material shortcomings of the German Navy, an emphasis reflected in the records of the Committee. According to statements made to the Committee, British superiority had a most harmful effect on German morale and fostered a feeling amongst the Germans that a fight to the finish would result in their defeat.

In the first place, British guns were bigger, with a longer range and fired a heavier shell, and the Germans never forgot their experiences of seeing enemy shells falling closer and closer until they began to hit from a range at which they knew their own guns could not reply. It was true that, until the last year of the war, the British shells were of much poorer quality than the German, but there was no way in which the ordinary German sailor could realize this.

The other great British advantage was superior speed given by the use of oil-fuel and turbine-engines. These innovations meant a higher speed for a given machinery weight and also a steadier speed, since in coal-fired ships speed fell off after a time, owing to the growing exhaustion of the stokers. Oil-fuel also spared crews the wearisome task of coaling ship. Incidentally, it is an indication of the different approach of the British and the Germans to relations between officers and men that, in the German Navy, it was rare for officers to take part in the filthy and exhausting business of coaling, whereas in the British Navy it was a routine matter for all the officers except the captain to put on their oldest clothes and wield shovels, push barrows, man winches and hoist sacks in the clouds of coal dust which rose all day long from a ship coaling and from her collier.

These advantages, built into the British ships, were reinforced after Jutland by thorough surveys of what had gone wrong materially in the battle, followed by intensive efforts to put matters right, so that by the spring of 1918 shells, fire-control gear, night-fighting equipment, protection, especially against flash, searchlights, mines, torpedoes and shell-fuses all had been vastly improved, and the advantages which the Germans had enjoyed during the first years of the war in these matters had nearly all vanished. Writing on this point, Commodore von Schoultz, the Russian naval liaison officer with the Grand Fleet, said after the war, 'Never were the prospects for the Germans worse than at the end of 1918.'

During the war, of course, the Germans could know little of this, and when asked by members of the Committee about the morale of the High Seas Fleet in October 1918, Brüninghaus replied that it was as high as it had been at Jutland. This was really a surprising answer, and the admiral did not explain how he reached his conclusion.

When Noske's turn came to give evidence it was recalled that in 1917 he, with all the party leaders in the Reichstag, except the Poles and Alsatians, had tried to persuade Capelle to grant a reprieve to Reichpietsch and Köbis. Capelle refused, and it would seem that Scheer had made up his mind that at least two executions were necessary for the sake of discipline. He felt that he must resist every suggestion of a reprieve or that he should submit their case to the Kaiser for the possible exercise of his prerogative of mercy.

Noske was asked by the Committee whether he thought that the Fleet would have sailed had the men known that the Government approved of their doing so. Noske replied that he did not think anything could have got them to sea. He was further asked if he knew of any links between the mutinies of 1917 and 1918 and replied that he saw no sign of any, except that the sentences passed in 1917 had given rise to a sense of grievance which was still strong more than a year later.

On the other hand Stumpf, talking on this point, was more definite, saying, 'If we had not had the mutiny trials of 1917, we would not have had the rising of 1918.' Asked if he thought that the Fleet would have sailed under any conceivable circumstances, he replied that they might have done so had they believed that they were going to help their comrades on the Western Front.

A statement by General von Kuhl was recalled to the effect that the operation by the Fleet planned for October 1918 was designed to prevent the British landing in Holland. This idea was generally denounced as ridiculous, and it was not known until after World War Two that the British and Dutch General Staffs did have talks on this very point during the autumn of 1918. It was feared in both London and The Hague that in the final convulsions of the war on the Western Front the Germans might violate Dutch neutrality, and plans were made to react to such a move. There was, of course, no question of the British invading Holland, if only because the neutrality of that country, a nearby source of foodstuffs, was of the greatest value to the United Kingdom.

Noske was asked whether he thought that the mutinies had been organized by elements of the extreme Left, as both the German Communists and the extreme Right in Germany claimed. Noske replied that he saw no sign of this. He was certainly not prejudiced in favour of any variety of the extreme Left, so that it is reasonable to suppose that, had he any evidence on this point, he would have produced it. As it was, he reminded the Committee that when he arrived at Kiel on

4 November there was no outstanding person among the demonstrators except Artelt, whom Noske described as being boastful and without the qualities of leadership to organize a revolt. If the troubles had been planned, Noske went on, there must have been an organization and neither then nor later had he ever found any sign of such a thing. With a good deal of common sense Noske acquitted the USPD of inspiring any mischief at this stage because, as he pointed out, if they had been doing so their leader Haase would have remained in Berlin to direct affairs, instead of wandering round north Germany, trying to reach Kiel, at the mercy of a chaotic train service.

According to Stumpf's summing up, the whole affair was apolitical in its inception:

> Of course there was indiscipline. Already in peacetime there was more of this in the Navy than there was in the Army. We were more workers than fighting men.
>
> The officers handled us very badly and unworthily, but we all knew that the Fatherland was at stake. All that the Social Democrats did to stir up agitation did not achieve one-tenth of the discontent caused by the difference in feeding between wardrooms and mess decks.
>
> Far and away the majority of us were politically indifferent and I did not know of any convinced Socialists amongst those of us who had been serving at the outbreak of war.
>
> We had no money with which to buy political papers. It was true that in the latter years the longing for peace was strong. It is hard to keep a finely tempered instrument such as the Fleet in good condition. We all believed that the indecisive behaviour of the Fleet Command only came about because the admirals wished to save their precious lives.

The contradiction between Stumpf's claim that the passive policy of the Fleet Command was due to the officers' desire to save their own lives, and the accusation during the 1918 mutinies that the officers wished to sacrifice their own lives and those of the crews in a final 'death or glory' operation, is obvious.

On the officers' side the views of two of the most distinguished officers of captain's rank at this time on the reasons for the breakdown of discipline are important. First, Raeder, the future commander-in-chief, who after a spell in command of the light cruiser *Köln* was appointed head of the General Department of the Admiralty in October 1918. Describing his reaction to the 1917 troubles, he wrote in his *Memoirs*: 'I must admit that I was completely surprised and that I held such events to be impossible.' He then gave three reasons for what had happened:

1. The conditions of life in Wilhelmshaven, which contained all the elements that went to make *Etappenleben* (life in the rear areas) harmful.
2. The action of the dockyard workers in spreading political propaganda amongst the crews.
3. The fact that the best officers of the middle ranks, the lieutenant-commanders and lieutenants, had been drafted from the big ships to the destroyers, submarines and other small craft.

Raeder added that he thought that the sailors had received a disproportionate share of the blame for their part in the events in various parts of the Reich which had followed the mutinies at Kiel and Wilhelmshaven. Naval uniforms, he pointed out, were conspicuous in crowds while soldiers were simply part of the anonymous field-grey mass, drawn from amongst the 1,500,000 men who were absent from their units with or without leave at this time.

The second captain whose opinion is of especial value is Waldeyer-Hartz, commanding officer of the cadet training ship *Schlesien*, who, it will be recalled, had managed to get his ship and his cadets away from Kiel when trouble started, without having to haul down the old Imperial flag. In his life of Hipper, he wrote: 'Contradictory though it may sound, the truth is that German discipline broke down because it was so perfect that no one considered its failure possible.'

Another witness summed up matters at this time when he said: 'The officers had trusted in the magic formula, "I order it", and when this failed they were too shaken and troubled to be able to compel the carrying out of the order.' Another spokesman for the officers gave as one of the chief reasons for the collapse of their authority the fact that they felt there was no power, either naval or political, which would back them up.

Johann Beckers, in his broadcast from Kiel on the fiftieth anniversary of the revolution, when asked his views as to the causes of the mutinies, referred like Raeder to the harmful effects of *Etappenleben*, but in a different connotation. He said: 'The ships took the *Etappen* with them. The Front was made up of seamen and stokers, and the Rear by the officers' wardroom.'

More than fifty years after all these events there are many happenings which have not lost their power to surprise. One of these is certainly the behaviour of Hipper in the crisis. Hipper's handling of the battle-cruisers in action gained for himself, from historians as well as from his own men, a great reputation which has lasted to this day. Thus Professor Marder wrote in his fifth and final volume of *From the Dreadnought to Scapa Flow*: 'Hipper was the outstanding German Sea officer.' Another American writer, Commander Holloway Frost, USN, in his book *The Battle of Jutland* says: 'Hipper's performance put him by far in the first place (among the admirals at Jutland). His expert abilities and his fearless temperament show him to have been one of the greatest leaders in naval history.' H. W. Wilson, the British naval correspondent and historian, in *Battleships in Action* also named Hipper as the best admiral on either side in World War One.

However, Scheer, as Hipper's superior officer, took a view which was one of less than complete approval. In a confidential report written on 1 December 1917 he complained that Hipper gave his staff too free a hand. It was possibly in an endeavour to make good this defect that when Scheer hauled down his flag in the Fleet he left behind Trotha, his chief-of-staff, to serve Hipper in the same capacity. If this were so, Scheer made a mistake, for when matters of discipline were in a delicate state Trotha, as we have seen, was not a good choice to be left with too free a hand. Commander von Selchow, also a member of

Hipper's staff, wrote in May 1918 of Trotha that: '. . . he thinks it is sufficient just to give an order. I am afraid that Chaplain Deipser, with whom I discussed the chief-of-staff a year ago on board the *Hannover*, was right when he said that two men were always involved when an order was given – one who gave the order, he was very important, and one who obeyed – he was also important.'

It was hard for the German officers to believe that the navy had disintegrated because of their failure to do their duty by preventing mutiny from taking place. For mutiny to have occurred, someone else, not themselves, must have been to blame. Nelson's second-in-command, Collingwood, would not have agreed. He showed that he knew very well where responsibility for any mutiny lay when he said: 'Mutiny, sir! Mutiny in my ship! If it can have arrived at that, it must be my fault and the fault of every one of my officers.'

Selchow, like Levetzow with his cry of 'Where was Lord Jervis?' believed that the mutiny could be put down by force. He said:

> Against mutiny in a regiment, when over half the regiment is on the side of the mutineers, it is very difficult to do anything. Mutiny, in a ship, if I keep my eyes open, I can prevent. I need only to form a group of loyal men, the officers, good warrant officers and petty officers and long service men, and men from the crew of whom we can be absolutely sure. I need only to keep all arms and ammunition securely locked up and to station picked men in the most important parts of the ship. In a battleship with 1,200 men there would always be 200 men available, perhaps even today many more, always granted that I knew my men – and then I would like to see how a mutiny could break out in my ship, also granted that I would have the nerve to hang the first mutineer at the yard arm.

But of all those involved in the discussion of the situation at that time, only one officer proposed drastic measures and he received no support. One of the reasons for this was undoubtedly that any action, however vigorous, would have taken time to bring back the crews to obedience, and there was no time. The war was clearly going to end in the next few days, and the officers could only look on helplessly. Levetzow's appeal to the example of Jervis and the British mutinies of 1797 overlooked the fact that after both the Fleet mutinies in that year, as distinct from troubles in individual ships, weeks were needed in which to restore to order and battleworthiness. The first big mutiny, that of the Channel Fleet at Spithead, was settled without bloodshed to the satisfaction of officers, crews and the government alike, but that settlement took four weeks to accomplish. The second big mutiny, that of the Home Fleet at the Nore, was a much more serious affair, which ended only after the ships in the hands of the mutineers had tried to blockade London River and the authorities had instituted a counter-blockade by cutting off the supplies which the mutineers were receiving from the shore. In the end twenty-nine men were hanged and the Fleet returned to its duty, but it had all taken time.

Facing events in Kiel and Wilhelmshaven, the German Government was continually looking over its shoulder towards Moscow. Any further trouble in Germany might mean not just a series of left-wing demonstrations and riots, but a full-scale Bolshevik rising, similar to the October revolution in Petrograd twelve months previously, which Prince Max and his colleagues knew the Russian Embassy in Berlin was trying to foment. In Russia, the original, moderate, left-wing February Revolution had been brought down by the extremists because its leaders had insisted upon continuing the war. To the Berlin Government it seemed that the same thing could happen to them if they did not sign an immediate armistice and yield up the Fleet.

Ten years afterwards, Raeder was busy completing the necessary preparations for the denunciation of the disarmament clauses of the Treaty of Versailles and the expansion of the German Navy. Five years later still, Hitler had come to power. Raeder, asked his reaction to the National-Socialist government, replied, 'I will get my pocket battleships where I can.'

Altogether, between 1926 and 1934 there had been laid down for the German Navy three pocket battleships, six light cruisers and twelve destroyers. In addition, German-designed U-boats were being built in Holland, Spain and Finland, the boats being subsequently sold to the Finnish and Turkish Governments. In this way the Germans were able to keep up with the latest developments of submarine design, while, by agreement with the Finnish Government, they were able to send officers and men to be trained as submariners.

Meanwhile Raeder went on with his plans for a future war. During the early twenties he had been responsible for that part of the German official history dealing with the war at sea. The three volumes of this work deal with the operations of the German cruisers and armed merchant raiders on the trade routes, including the cruises of Spee and his squadron, the light cruisers *Emden, Karlsrühe* and the rest, together with the disguised merchantmen of which *Möwe, Wolf* and the sailing ship *Seeadler* were the most famous.

Raeder was to become unique as the only naval historian who, on the completion of his literary work, was to command a navy in wartime and apply the lessons which he had learned during his studies. In the end Raeder and Dönitz were to become the most formidable pair of admirals that the British Navy has ever faced.

During his early years as commander-in-chief of the Navy Raeder did not plan for anything beyond a war with France, but after Munich it was appreciated that war with Britain might follow, and Raeder then drew up his famous 'Z-plan' by which within six years some 800 warships would be built for the Germany Navy. These were to range in size from battleships of more than 62,000 tons to motor-torpedo-boats and minesweepers.

Altogether by 1946 the German Navy would comprise 10 battleships, 15 pocket battleships or light battle-cruisers, four aircraft carriers, five heavy cruisers, 22 light cruisers, 22 scout cruisers, 68 destroyers, 90 torpedo-boats, 249 U-boats, 10 minelayers, 75 mtbs and 227 escort vessels, minesweepers and antisubmarine craft. This enormous programme was to receive absolute priority from German industry; requirements for the Army and the Luftwaffe were to take second place.

Just as the Kaiser and Tirpitz had cherished from time to time the hope that their great naval building programme would lead to Britain becoming an ally of Germany, it would seem that Hitler and Raeder also believed, or affected to believe, from time to time, that their fleet would, in the same way, purchase an alliance with Britain.

But if there were no alliance Raeder had his war plans ready, unlike the admirals of 1914. U-boats and light craft would conduct submarine and mine warfare, the four smallest of the battleships, *Scharnhorst, Gneisenau, Tirpitz* and *Bismarck* would remain in home waters to pin down a portion of the British Fleet, while six huge battleships,* larger than anything yet built, would range the Atlantic in search of British shipping. Pocket battleships and cruisers would be available for the distant seas.

The outbreak of war in 1939 ended the Z plan and Raeder found himself with only the *Scharnhorst* and *Gneisenau* of his heavy ships ready for action. The *Bismarck* and *Tirpitz* followed in 1941, but in the meantime Raeder was determined to use what ships he had in as enterprising a manner as possible in support of the U-boats in their attacks against British trade. They were not to be held back in reserve as had been the luckless High Seas Fleet, and the first two *Flottenchefs*, Admirals Boehm and Marschall, were both dismissed by Raeder for failure to show sufficient offensive spirit. After the war had begun Boehm remained in command for only six weeks. Captain Weichold, his chief-of-staff, protested against a minelaying raid which destroyers had been ordered by Raeder to make against the English coast, on the grounds that there was to

* These battleships were to displace over 62,000 tons full load, and to be armed with eight 16-inch guns. Diesel engines were to give them a speed of 30 knots and a radius of action of 19,000 miles. Two of these ships were actually laid down during the summer of 1939, but work was stopped in October, after Hitler had given up hope that Britain and France would make peace after the defeat of Poland.

be no support from the heavy ships. Raeder ordered Boehm either to dismiss Weichold or to resign himself, and Boehm resigned on 16 October. Later he was appointed to command the naval establishments in Norway and received, shortly afterwards, a warning that he was not to concern himself with the movements of ships.

Boehm was succeeded as Flottenchef by Admiral Wilhelm Marschall, who held the post until 14 June 1940, when he reported himself sick after a series of altercations with Raeder. Suspecting that the Allies were about to evacuate Narvik, Raeder ordered an attack by the German heavy ships *Scharnhorst, Gneisenau* and *Admiral Hipper* on the port of Harstad, through which Raeder believed the evacuation to be taking place.

Marschall, rightly it transpired, did not believe that there was anything left in Harstad that was worth attacking, and led his ships off in a south-westerly direction where, between them, they sank the British aircraft-carrier *Glorious*, the 20,000-ton transport *Orama* and the destroyers *Ardent* and *Acasta*. These German successes were marred, however, by the fact that the *Scharnhorst* had been damaged by a torpedo from the *Acasta*.

Raeder described the sinking of the four British ships as 'luck' and berated Marschall for not having carried out his orders. It was then that Marschall said that he was too ill to continue in command and he was replaced by Admiral Günther Lüjens, who immediately fell foul of Raeder because, while covering the return to Germany of the damaged *Scharnhorst*, the *Gneisenau* was torpedoed and put out of action by the British submarine *Clyde*. Raeder believed Lütjens to have been responsible for a delay which had permitted this to happen, and further criticized him for not sending out his one remaining undamaged big ship, the *Hipper*, on a commerce raiding expedition. Raeder was temporarily placated but, as we shall see, the effect upon Lütjens may have been of vital importance during the *Bismarck* action. In conversation at that time he remarked that he appreciated the fact that the last two Flottenchefs had been superceded because they had failed to carry out the orders of the *Seekriegsleitung*. He, however, would take care to obey orders.

During these weeks Raeder revealed the reason for his insistence on the big ships being successfully committed, in words which echoed the concern for the future of the Navy expressed by Scheer, Trotha and Levetzow in October 1918 and by Behncke four years earlier. On 23 May 1940 he had said: 'By the indecisive use of the battleships not only will nothing be won but the future of the Navy will be lost.'

Dr Michael Salewski in *Die Deutsche Seekriegsleitung 1935-45* comments: 'Raeder made it openly clear that the future of the Navy was at stake.' Raeder had gone on to say: 'A navy which is led in daring attacks against the enemy and suffers losses in consequence will arise after victory greater than ever, while if these attacks had not taken place its existence would be threatened even after a victorious war.'

Just as in 1914-18 the Navy had feared for its future at the hands of the Army, so in 1940 it feared once more, this time threatened in addition with the hostility of Goering and the Luftwaffe.

Norwegian bases had been occupied in order that the Navy might turn the flank of the British blockade line, which stretched from the Shetlands to Bergen. Raeder insisted that the newly-won bases must be used, although the fall of France at this moment placed at the disposal of Germany the French Atlantic ports which were much more valuable and it was not until the Germans invaded Russia that the north Norwegian bases became of first-class importance for attacks on the Allies' Arctic convoys.

During the twelve months from May 1940 the *Scharnhorst, Gneisenau, Scheer, Hipper* and seven converted merchantmen were committed as commerce raiders, and in May 1941 there came the most sensational operation of all, Operation Rhine Exercise, the sortie of the *Bismarck* and the *Prinz Eugen*.

Only two officers survived from the *Bismarck*: Lütjens, Lindemann, his flag captain, and the entire staff of the Fleet were all lost, so that it is not possible to know what was being said or thought by Lütjens and his officers at this time. But it has been suggested that in an earnest discussion between Lütjens and Lindemann, the latter tried to persuade his admiral that once the *Bismarck* had been spotted by the enemy, the best thing would have been to return home, since the chances of her being able to shake off the enemy in the North Atlantic were poor. Not only, this argument runs, could Lütjens have been well pleased with his success in sinking the *Hood*, but in addition there had been the possibility of finishing off the *Prince of Wales* as well, for this ship had been almost disabled by the *Bismarck*'s guns and by the various mechanical and electric faults that she had developed. These faults arose because the brand new ship had been committed in action before the completion of the vast series of trials and tests which were necessary before any newly commissioned big ship was ready for action, tests that normally took at least six months to carry out.

The arguments for such a course of action by Lütjens speak for themselves, and if they did not carry the day it must be remembered that other voices were also speaking, the most important that of Raeder, originally raised to eradicate what he believed to have been the fatal influence of the Kaiser, Pohl and Ingenohl in the previous war. No one could have foreseen that not only would the *Hood* be sunk but that there would also be a possibility of the *Prince of Wales* being sunk as well. Raeder, however, had laid it down that the primary objective of all the operations of the big ships on the high seas was the sinking of merchant tonnage, and this was regarded by Lütjens as an order that had to be obeyed. Warships, Raeder insisted, were to be avoided for fear of the damage they might do to the raider.

However, the loss of the *Bismarck*, thanks to radar, air reconnaissance, torpedo planes and, finally, the guns of the Home Fleet, had clearly made it impossible for commerce raiding to continue in the North Atlantic. The *Scharnhorst*, *Gneisenau* and *Prinz Eugen* were pinned down in the French Atlantic ports by the RAF; the *Hipper*, always a lame duck because of her faulty machinery and boilers, together with the pocket battleships, remained at home; and the *Tirpitz* was hamstrung in her Norwegian base by shortage of fuel. Moreover the German invasion of Russia had entirely changed the part to be played by the German surface ships. The sea-routes from Britain and North America, passing close by the north coast of Norway, made the latter an area of great strategic importance, as Hitler and Churchill both knew. Churchill began to plague his advisers to produce an expedition for the capture of northern Norway, while Hitler made his preparations to withstand just such an assault and also disposed his naval forces as best he could to harass the Russian convoys. The *Scharnhorst, Gneisenau* and *Prinz Eugen* made their famous Channel dash, as the result of which all three ships were put out of action, the *Gneisenau* being so badly damaged during an RAF raid on Kiel while under repair that she was never operational again.

From the beginning of 1942 the role of the big German surface ships changed from that of a raiding fleet whose task was to attack enemy merchant shipping on the high seas to that of a fleet in being whose mere existence on the edge of the Russian convoy route was a continuous threat to the supplies intended for Russia. This threat meant that, in addition to aircraft, destroyers and escort craft needed to protect the convoys against U-boats and aircraft, Allied battleships and aircraft-carriers were also required to cover the convoys, and these were ships urgently needed elsewhere in the world. During most of 1942 the German surface threat was represented by the *Tirpitz*, with occasional support by the pocket battleships and heavy cruisers. The *Tirpitz*, however, only left her base for the open sea twice; on the first occasion to no purpose, but on the second occasion the mere news that she was at sea led to the destruction of the famous convoy PQ 17, whose escorts were withdrawn to meet the threat of the *Tirpitz*.

As a result of this, the unprotected convoy was cut to pieces by the enemy, and convoys to Russia were suspended for more than two months.

To intercept a convoy which was known to be moving through the faint light of the Arctic winter, the *Lützow* and *Hipper* sailed to attack on 30 December 1942. With a return to the custom during World War One, the *Lützow*'s captain was warned against attacking forces of greater or equal strength, a type of directive against which Raeder had often protested in the past. In bad weather, in light that was never more than twilight, the German ships in a rambling series of disconnected actions were driven off by two British cruisers, smaller and less well armed; both sides lost a destroyer and some of the Germans comforted themselves with the thought that the action had been a draw. But Hitler knew better; the fundamental fact was that the convoy had got through. In great anger he sent for Raeder, and after a long monologue which he began by pointing out that the mutinies of 1918 and the scuttling at Scapa Flow had been no ' pages of glory ' for the German Navy, he forced Raeder to resign and ordered that all the big ships should be laid up.

Asked to recommend a successor, Raeder said that it depended on what kind of war was intended; if big ship operations were to be continued he proposed Ciliax, the Flag Officer commanding battleships, who had led the Channel dash. But if the war was to be almost exclusively a U-boat war, then Dönitz, he said, was the man; and it was he who received the appointment. The new commander-in-chief had been no friend of the big ships; before the war he had opposed the Z plan on the ground that, without bases outside the North Sea and the Baltic, any German raiding ships would be at the mercy of even comparatively small damage, having no bases at which they could be repaired without returning home. Nevertheless Dönitz now went to work to persuade Hitler that the big ships should be retained in commission, to continue as a threat to operations against the Norwegian coast.

Of the two surviving capital ships, the *Scharnhorst* was sunk after an attempt to attack a convoy on 26 December 1943, and the *Tirpitz* was put out of action in September 1943 by midget submarines. As soon as she had been repaired she was again disabled, this time by carrier-borne planes in April 1944, and was finally sunk by the RAF seven months later.

Disasters to the south, the west and the east befell Germany during the spring and summer of 1944, and to many of her military leaders the war was clearly lost; the conspiracy of 20 July was the result. In this the Navy was only marginally involved; four officers, one of them Count Bertold von Stauffenberg, brother of Count Claus von Stauffenberg who took the bomb into the Führer's briefing hut, agreed that if a successful attempt on Hitler's life took place they would place the Navy's communications facilities at the disposal of the conspiracy.

There has been speculation as to why the Navy was no more concerned. Its key officers were physically remote from the levers of power and there were few, if any, formed bodies of men under naval command that were so situated that they could take control of strategic points. There is also said to have been a feeling that the Navy, remembering the events of 1918, did not wish again to be accused of having precipitated the collapse of Germany.

Whatever the Navy may have thought in World War Two of the events at the end of World War One, Hitler had certainly weighed matters carefully and had made up his mind that there should be no possibility of his being toppled from power by popular discontent, even if that meant reducing demands for sacrifices on the civil population. Albert Speer, Hitler's Minister for Armament and War Production, in his book *Inside the Third Reich*, wrote:

> It remains one of the oddities of this war that Hitler demanded less from his people than Churchill and Roosevelt from their respective nations. The discrepancy between the total mobilization of labour forces in democratic England and the casual treatment of this question in authoritarian Germany is proof of the regime's anxiety not to risk any shift in the popular mood. The German

leaders were not disposed to make sacrifices themselves or to ask sacrifices of the people. They tried to keep the morale of the people in the best possible state by concessions. Hitler and the majority of his political followers belonged to the generation which, as soldiers, had witnessed the Revolution of November 1918, and had never forgotten it. In private conversations Hitler indicated that after the experience of 1918 one could not be cautious enough. In order to anticipate any discontent, more money and effort were expended on supplies of consumer goods, on military pensions or compensation to women for the loss of earnings by their men, than in countries with democratic governments.

Whereas Churchill promised his people only blood, sweat and tears, all we heard during the various phases and crises of the war was Hitler's slogan: The final victory is certain.

This was a confession of political weakness. It betrayed great concern over a loss of popularity which might develop into an insurrectionary mood.

From 25 January 1945 until VE Day on 8 May, all the available German surface warships and merchant vessels were occupied in the Baltic, evacuating a huge mass of two million refugees, men, women and children, together with remnants of the German Army. As the Germans had withdrawn, troops and civilians alike had sought temporary safety in a collection of Dunkirk-type pockets and beachheads along the coast, in Courland and East Prussia and around the ports of Danzig, Kolberg and Stettin. Once the Russian advance had swirled around them, cutting off communications by land, the only way by which they could be brought away was by sea. Russian planes and torpedo craft endeavoured to stop them but less than one per cent of all refugees lost their lives. This vast and largely successful rescue operation provided something of a consolation to those who reflected that, for the Navy, World War One had ended very differently. Nevertheless the Scapa Flow tradition remained. A few hours before the cease-fire came into effect there was a mass scuttling of U-boats at Kiel, carried out while Dönitz was asleep, against his orders, and in violation of the terms of surrender. The order for the scuttling was given by the transmission of the code-word 'Rainbow'.

In May 1945 and for months afterwards Kiel harbour had the look of Gutter Sound, Scapa Flow on 24 June 1919. Scattered about were the remnants of a German navy. The scene was dominated by the badly damaged wrecks of the *Hipper* and the *Emden*, by the *Scheer* upside down, looking like a giant whale nearly 700 feet long, while the 24,000-ton liner *New York* lay on her side close to the shore with her decks and her bottom rising vertically like the faces of a cliff. Dotting the waters were what remained above the surface of minor warships. Ancient ships of the Kaiser's Navy, which had been re-commissioned as anti-aircraft units, awaited scrapping, and around the corner of the bay in Eckernförde were the remains of 67 of the 221 U-boats which had been scuttled in accordance with the 'Rainbow' order. Some had disappeared, the conning towers of others still lay above the waters. Patiently, British and German salvage teams were raising them, towing them out to sea and, after disabling them so seriously that they could never be serviceable again, sinking them in deep water, an operation which led to a respectful protest from Germans who suggested that the boats should not be disabled, but merely sunk in positions from which it would be possible to raise them when they were required for the next war.

The German Navy was just a collection of scrap metal, and the German Reich appeared to be in much the same condition, an impression heightened by the look of Kiel, which seemed to have suffered as badly as any town in Germany. Nobody would then have believed, had anyone been mad enough to risk the prophecy, that in ten years time there would be a German Federal Republic and a new German Navy forming part of the NATO naval forces. In 1945 it was again the German minesweepers who kept alive the idea and nucleus of a future German Navy as they had in 1919. Although in 1945 there was no longer a German Navy nor, indeed, strictly speaking a Germany, there was a large number of minesweepers maintained in commission under the title of 'German Mine-

Sweeping Administration', manned by former naval officers and ratings, now classed as civilian seamen whose duty it was, as it had been that of their predecessors in 1919-22, to help sweep up the vast number of mines laid during the six years of World War Two. The head of this service was Vice-Admiral Friedrich Rüge, who had been a minesweeping and minelaying specialist between the wars and who had, in 1944, served on the staff of Rommel as his naval adviser. When the Federal German Navy was created in 1955 Rüge became its Inspector-General, as the naval commander-in-chief was then styled.

The role of the new Navy was the defence of the Straits between the Baltic into the North Sea, and the access to the latter from the Arctic. For this the Federal Navy has a force of twenty-three U-boats built and building, thirty fast patrol boats firing ship-to-ship missiles, together with minesweepers, torpedo-boats, landing-craft, escort and support vessels. The total personnel of the Navy is 38,000, which is just about half the total strength of both the Kaiser's navy and Hitler's at the outbreak of their respective wars.

East Germany – the German Democratic Republic – has a notably smaller force, without submarines. Its personnel totals 16,000.

ELEVEN

German records show clearly enough what happened in the 1917-18 mutinies, and why it happened. They do not deal, however, with the question of how the mutinies might have been avoided, or whether they could have been dealt with and discipline restored, once trouble had started.

It is reasonable to begin with Collingwood's dictum that mutiny is the fault of the officers of the ship in which it occurs. It is part of the duty of a naval officer to see that mutinies do not take place, and everything may depend upon his qualities of firmness and imagination to do this.

When we look at the quality of lieutenant-commanders and lieutenants of the big ships in the High Seas Fleet we are struck by the way in which they appear to have been lacking in both qualities, and this impression is not gained only from mutineers and socialist politicians but from such a senior officer as Michaelis of the General Department of the Admiralty, who, in his report already quoted, remarks that the captains and executive officers allowed their junior officers to lapse into the gravest slackness.

This may have been due in the past to the almost fantastic blunder of changing half the captains and executive officers of the big ships within a few weeks of Hipper taking command of the Fleet, as a part of the reorganization judged necessary for the implementation of the Scheer programme for extended submarine warfare. Unfortunately, within a few weeks of the shake-up it was decided that the unrestricted submarine warfare campaign had to be ended, in order to obtain Allied consent to an armistice.

When the submarine war was abandoned proved junior officers began to be transferred from the submarines and the training establishments to the Fleet, but this process had not had time to go very far, and in the most critical days in the history of the High Seas Fleet the very best of the junior officers were still absent from the big ships. It is not fair, of course, to say that all the big ship lieutenants were of bad quality, but quite enough of them were; the difference between them and the little ship lieutenants was very great. There seems to have been much the same differences in quality between the admirals commanding the battleship squadrons. In the 1917 troubles only one squadron, the Fourth, was seriously involved, commanded by Vice-Admiral Mauve who, after the troubles, was moved with despatch from his post by Scheer. The despatch was due to the desire to get him away from the Fleet before the Kaiser made his next inspection. Mauve was succeeded by Meurer who, as we have seen, brought the squadron peacefully through all the troubles until the very eve of the Armistice, when there was no longer any prospect of a British attack.

On the other hand, Kraft, of the Third squadron, with his insistence on taking the squadron to Kiel, was probably more responsible than anyone else for the collapse of the situation once the mutiny had started. Nevertheless, Hipper was the *Flottenchef* and was therefore to blame for allowing Kraft to have his way; but Hipper, brave and skilful though he was in battle, was quite overwhelmed by events, and so the revolution was permitted to begin in Kiel.

What would have happened to the German revolution had the troubles not started at Kiel at this particular time is, of course, uncertain. The signing of the Armistice might have been delayed for a few days, perhaps until after the big American offensive against Metz had started on 14 November, and there had been one more proof that the German Army had been fought to a state of collapse and great portions of it would have been taken prisoner. Instead it withdrew, after the conclusion of the Armistice, in a reasonably orderly manner beyond the Rhine.

In any event it seems probable that following the end of hostilities, civil disturbances would have broken out as they did in Munich on 7 November and in Berlin on 9 November, in both cases without much impetus from Kiel. All the discontent in Bavaria came to flash point on 7 November at the fear of invasion, which was added to hunger, misery and general discouragement. Two days later in Berlin the war was obviously coming to an end with the prospect of a change of system to be attained by the deposition of the Kaiser. The demonstrations for this had barely begun before Prince Max, followed by Scheidemann, determined to announce the abdication of the Kaiser quickly, before the USPD and the Spartacists could do the same, claim credit for it and use that credit to install a government by the Councils of the Workers and Soldiers, which seemed only too likely to transform themselves into Soviets on Russian lines.

At first sight all this may seem remote from the higher conduct of the war at sea, but the path is clear. The Germans built a navy less powerful than that of Britain though large enough to alarm the British; incidentally there has been a good deal of recent research carried out in Germany which goes to show that, in the long run, Tirpitz and the others were intending to outbuild Britain, but the war came too soon for them. They did not understand how a smaller navy could be used to advantage against a bigger one, as was proposed by Behncke and also, after a moment of doubt, by Tirpitz as well. This meant that it seemed to almost all the German war leaders, soldiers and sailors alike, that unrestricted submarine warfare was the only means of checking the power of Britain, whose resources brought from overseas were the mainspring of the war effort of the *Entente*.

Unrestricted submarine warfare, when once it was finally introduced in February 1917, after the uncertainties of 1915, meant two things: first the entry of the United States into the war, and second the placing of the High Seas Fleet on something like a reserve basis, taking from it its best junior officers and giving it nothing to do except cover the channels that had been swept through the minefields by which U-boats came and went to their operating areas, and maintaining command of the Baltic, which could be assured with comparatively small forces.

The German appreciation of what unrestricted submarine warfare could do to starve Britain and prevent American help reaching Europe was based on wildly faulty intelligence; this, coupled with a bad plan for the employment of the Navy or rather no plan at all but to keep it in harbour save for occasional raids by small portions of it, meant a deterioration of men's spirits which the authorities did nothing effective to check.

INDEX

Index